UNDERSTANDING
MASS MEDIA

W9-AXF-623

UNDERS MASS MEDIA

[UNDER]STANDING

JEFFREY SCHRANK

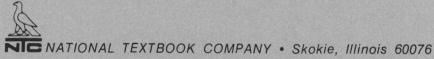

NTC NATIONAL TEXTBOOK COMPANY • Skokie, Illinois 60076

1979 Printing

Copyright © 1975 by National Textbook Co.,
8259 Niles Center Rd., Skokie, Ill. 60076
Library of Congress Catalog Number: 75-20876

PREFACE

As *Understanding Mass Media* joins National Textbook Company's ever-expanding series of texts for Language Arts elective courses, it represents an unprecedented opportunity for teachers to present a complete course or unit on one of the most important—and fascinating—aspects of modern society.

The author, Jeffrey Schrank, is winner of two Media Methods Maxi Awards. He is a veteran teacher and writer who, with this text, brings the kind of dynamism and involvement that befits this subject, just as it meets the needs of today's students in providing the kind of challenge they regard as basic to effective learning.

This is not a passive text, one that says: Read me and you will know all there is you have to know about mass media. Rather—and in all ways—this book says: Read me, and as you read me, inquire, search for yourself and with your friends, and understand how the phenomenon we call mass media is affecting—and can affect—your world.

CONTENTS

INTRODUCTION

Various communication media have always existed. Speech is the most common medium (media is the plural of medium) of communication. Music, painting, hand signals, and the printed word are also communication media. Some communication media have developed to the point where they can reach vast numbers, or masses, of people in a very short time. Because of this ability, media such as television, radio, newspapers, film, and others are commonly called mass media.

How many people a mass medium has to be able to reach to deserve the label "mass" has never been determined. A telephone, for example, is not considered a mass medium even though a battery of phones could be used in a day to reach thousands of people. Amateur shortwave radios can reach large numbers of people at one time but are not a mass medium since they are normally used to enable people to talk to each other. Mass media all share the characteristic of one-way communication. Mass media enable a few people to communicate with the masses but do not allow the masses to communicate with the few. Mass media are one-way streets.

Yet to be invented is a means of communication that would allow the president of a country, the mayor of a city, the manufacturer of a new car or the artist to communicate with a vast number of people and quickly receive their reactions. Until such a medium is invented we have to settle for our present one-way system of mass media. Because media do not allow us to talk back (with the very limited exception of letters to editors, radio phone-in shows, etc.) it is important to learn the special techniques of media persuasion. The absence of a real voice to talk back to those who speak through mass media makes the critical study of their messages essential.

In this book we will be concerned mainly with what mass media teaches and what language it uses to speak. We will consider all mass media to be educational and will examine them to determine what is being taught. The language of each medium will also be considered so that the ability of the media to deceive will be minimized.

Past ages are often known by some major force that dominated the lives of the people who lived during that time—the Ice Age, Feudal Age, Industrial Revolution, the Age of Discovery and so forth. Historians of the future may look back on us in the late 1970s and label us the Media Age. Time-use studies have shown that the average high school student has spent more time with mass media (TV, movies, radio, records, books, magazines) than with any other single activity except sleep.

We live in an environment partially shaped by the opinions, sights, sounds and values presented by mass media. To obtain some idea of the importance of media, analyze your own time and money use with the "Personal Media Inventory" on the next page. Answer the questions on a separate sheet of paper and then compare your answers with those of others. Compile all the answers to arrive at a class average: for example, "the average student in this class spends x hours a week watching televsion."

Personal Media Inventory

How much money do you spend in one year (estimate) on:

Books
    (a) for school
    (b) for other reading
Magazines and comic books
Movies
Records and/or tapes
Equipment (TV, radios, tape
   and record players, etc.)

How much time in a typical week (estimate) do you spend on these activities?

Watching television
Listening to radio
Watching movies (not on TV)
Reading comics and magazines
Reading newspapers
Reading books
Listening to records
   or tapes (not on radio)

Multiply each of the time figures above by 52 to determine the amount of time you spend with mass media each year. Realize that your answer will be very approximate. Take this approximate figure and use it to determine about how many years of your lifetime will be spent in the company of mass media.

Project Teams

Some of the projects in this book require a period of several weeks to gather information. These projects are best assigned to project teams early in the course. A project team consists of three students who are responsible for preparing a class presentation on some media-related topic. If the teams are formed now, they will have enough time to prepare the reports and present them during the course.

The presentations can be made near the end of this course or, if possible, scattered throughout the course at appropriate times. Each report should last at least 30 minutes and should include examples and demonstrations using the medium under study.

Possible Topics For Project Teams

1. Any topic about mass media that a group of three students wishes to research and present to the class. Teacher and/or class approval might be required.

2. The role of women or men as portrayed on television, both in shows and in commercials.

3. The role of women or men as presented in advertisements.

4. Find, select, and order the short films for use in the chapter on film. This team should work with the teacher and/or school media director.

5. Arrange for various guest speakers and tours during the course.

6. Do a research project on one heavily advertised product category (e.g., mouthwash, headache remedies, toothpaste). Find out the main competing brands; write down the advertising claims for those products; find out who makes the products and what they contain. Run tests where possible to see if the products satisfy their advertised claims. Write to the manufacturers and ask them to back up their claims.

7. Explain and demonstrate videotape equipment.

8. Study the image of law enforcement officers on television. Analyze how they are presented on TV and compare this with reality.

9. Study the image of any of the following as presented on television: doctors, the elderly, teenagers, or criminals.

10. Design a Personal Media Inventory Questionnaire asking the same questions as the inventory on page two. Have the parents of each student complete the inventory (it does have to be signed). Compare the totals of the student inventory for the entire class with those of the parents.

11. Arrange for two local media experts (a TV or radio announcer, station manager, filmmaker, advertiser, etc.) to appear before the class to explain their work and answer questions. Select the kinds of people the class would consider most interesting.

12. Collect as many different magazines as possible for the class to use during the study of magazines in chapter seven. Use the local library to obtain the names and addresses of a variety of magazines that students are probably not familiar with. Obtain at least one copy of fifty or more different magazines. The magazines can be acquired by requesting a sample copy from the publisher or by buying copies through the mail or from a newsstand.

13. Conduct as detailed a study as possible of all the local news outlets (radio, newspaper, TV), and present to the class a comparison pointing out their strengths and weaknesses.

14. Present a history of popular music in the United States complete with taped excerpts from records. The presentation should take an entire class period and should point out how music has changed and some of the reasons for the changing tastes of the record-buying public.

15. Present a history of the comic book. Use the local library as an information source. Perhaps a local comic book collector will provide some examples of old comic books. The presentation should attempt to explain the changes in comics over the years and relate them to changing tastes and events in American history.

Chapter 1
TELEVISION

How Does the Television System Work?

Some people say that television is the greatest invention of the twentieth century. Others claim it is a drain on valuable time, an evil influence on the nation. There are those who blame television for teaching violence and inviting young viewers to imitate criminals and gun-slinging heroes. There are those who say that TV turns people into passive vegetables able to do little more than sit and watch the tube. Still others see television as history's most effective educator, bringing the wonders and knowledge of the world into the homes of even the poorest citizens. Such education, they point out, was once available only to the very wealthy who could afford travel and the best schools. Children today seem to know much more about the world than their parents and grandparents did at the same age. Many educators give television some of the credit for this knowledge increase.

When asked for their opinion of television, some answer that TV is a harmless pastime that provides an escape from the troubles of daily life; while others argue that it presents a dangerously unreal picture of the world. The arguments rage on, and for every convincing statement about the harmfulness of TV there is an equally compelling argument about its benefits. Television is a controversial subject—but one on which everyone must take a stand. That glass-windowed box sitting in almost every household in the land demands a daily decision. To watch or not to watch, that is the decision. And each time that decision is made, a person reveals what values are important.

Drawing by Koren; ©1970 The New Yorker, Magazine, Inc.

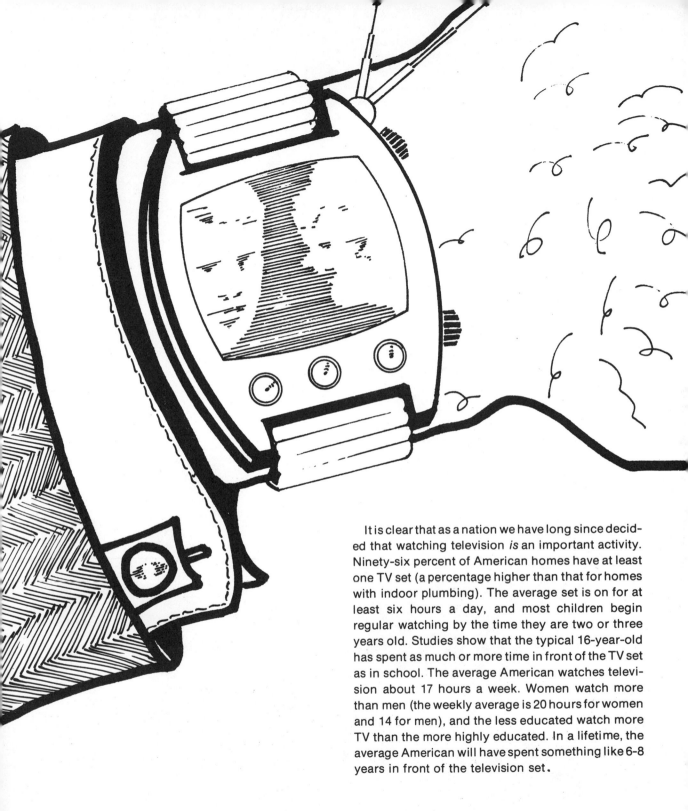

It is clear that as a nation we have long since decided that watching television *is* an important activity. Ninety-six percent of American homes have at least one TV set (a percentage higher than that for homes with indoor plumbing). The average set is on for at least six hours a day, and most children begin regular watching by the time they are two or three years old. Studies show that the typical 16-year-old has spent as much or more time in front of the TV set as in school. The average American watches television about 17 hours a week. Women watch more than men (the weekly average is 20 hours for women and 14 for men), and the less educated watch more TV than the more highly educated. In a lifetime, the average American will have spent something like 6-8 years in front of the television set.

There is no doubt that we consider television important. There is hardly an American who does not have a strong opinion about television. You probably have an opinion about television, though perhaps you haven't stopped to think about it. Take some time now and write your opinion in about 50 words: Begin with "I think television is. . . ." Do not give your opinion of any particular program on television; rather evaluate television as a mass medium. When everyone has finished the opinion statements the papers should be signed, collected, and put away until needed later in this chapter.

After the opinions are written and collected, hold a class discussion on the advantages and disadvantages of watching television. You might do this by drawing two columns on the board and listing as many "good points" and "bad points" about television as the class can suggest.

After the discussion of existing opinions, continue with this chapter. It deals with five important questions:

How does the television system work?
What kind of programs succeed?
How would life change without television?
What does television teach?
Who should have access to television time?

I think
Television is...

How the Television System Works

Here is a test you can take to see how much you already know about the workings of commercial television in the United States. The correct answers are given on the following pages. Take the test before reading past this page, note your answers on a separate piece of paper, and check them as you read on.

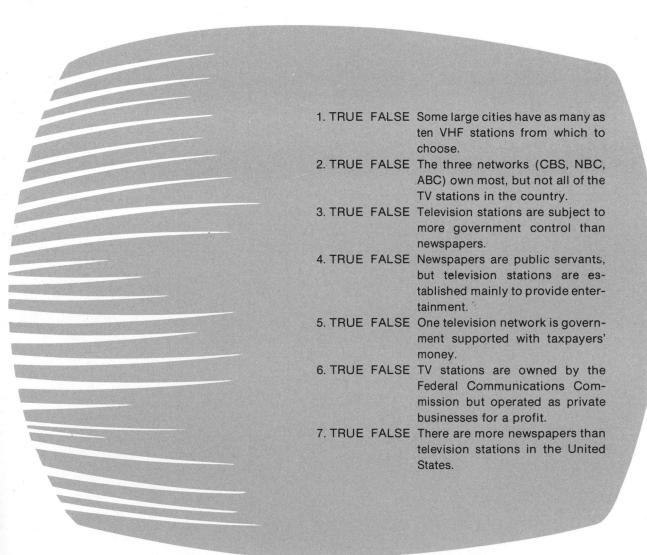

1. TRUE FALSE Some large cities have as many as ten VHF stations from which to choose.

2. TRUE FALSE The three networks (CBS, NBC, ABC) own most, but not all of the TV stations in the country.

3. TRUE FALSE Television stations are subject to more government control than newspapers.

4. TRUE FALSE Newspapers are public servants, but television stations are established mainly to provide entertainment.

5. TRUE FALSE One television network is government supported with taxpayers' money.

6. TRUE FALSE TV stations are owned by the Federal Communications Commission but operated as private businesses for a profit.

7. TRUE FALSE There are more newspapers than television stations in the United States.

There are currently about 950 television stations in the country. This is a small number in comparison with the 1,750 newspapers and more than 5,000 radio stations. Television stations operate on channels 2-13 (VHF) and channels 14-83 (UHF). Adjacent VHF channels (2 and 3 or 7 and 8, for example) in the same city could interfere with each other and so are usually separated by an unused channel. This means that even large metropolitan areas have only about five VHF stations. UHF The (*Ultrahigh Frequency*) has many more channels available but is still in the early stages of development. UHF stations have a smaller coverage area than VHF (*Very High Frequency*) stations because of the higher frequencies on which they operate. Since they reach fewer people (many old TV sets cannot even tune UHF), such stations are not as attractive to advertisers. Currently they tend to be smaller stations with smaller audiences than VHF.

VHF stations operate on frequencies similar to those of FM radio stations (in fact, TV sound is FM) and can therefore reach only an area in a 50-100 mile radius from the transmitting tower. If you had a TV set that could tune between channels 6 and 7, you could listen to local FM radio stations on the TV set; FM radio could be considered channel 6½.

Television stations are privately owned businesses just like newspapers, radio stations, or publishing companies. Unlike these other communications industries, however, television stations are licensed by the Federal Communications Commission to serve the "public interest." Every three years the station's license must be renewed, and to keep its license, the station must prove that it has served the public. In practice, the FCC has refused license renewals only a few times since the beginning of television. Still, when a station's license is up for renewal, viewers have the right to inspect its records and can challenge the station's right to continue broadcasting.

According to court-supported decisions, the channels belong to the people. TV stations are licensed to use those channels only to serve the public in their viewing area. If any person or group can prove that a station has not served the viewing public, then that station could lose its license. For instance, stations are required by the FCC to provide fair coverage of important local issues. In theory, a TV station that broadcasts only network shows and old movies could lose its license for failure to treat local issues.

Eighty-five percent of all television stations are affiliated with (but not owned by) one of the three major networks—Columbia Broadcasting System, (CBS), American Broadcasting Company (ABC), and National Broadcasting Company (NBC). The most profitable stations are generally those affiliated with the three commercial networks. A TV station that does not belong to a major network is either an independent or a member of the Public Broadcasting Service (PBS). Independent stations as a rule show mainly old movies, local sports, and reruns of TV shows from a few years ago. PBS stations, sometimes called "educational TV," carry cultural and educational programming. PBS is supported by a Congressional grant of money, by foundation donations and contributions from viewers. PBS is the only network that does not carry advertising.

Networks are not television stations; they do not broadcast programs. They supply programs to the local television affiliate by using specially rented telephone lines. Each local TV station is ultimately responsible for its own programming. A station can refuse to broadcast a network-supplied program but rarely does so. Networks supply local stations with programs for the morning (morning news, game shows), the afternoon "soap operas" (so called because they were originally sponsored by soap companies), evening news, and night-time programs. Local stations must fill in with their own programming (usually movies, local news, or reruns) when the networks do not supply programming.

The networks provide these programs to the affiliates free and are paid for the advertising time they can sell during the program. A 30-second "spot" commercial in network "prime time" (the desirable evening hours) sent to all the network affiliates in the country costs an advertiser about $1,000 per second. The exact cost depends on how popular the program is that the ad interrupts; the more viewers, the higher the cost.

A small amount of time during each program is left for the local station to sell to local advertisers. This advertising constitutes the main source of income for local stations. Local stations also receive a cut of the money their network receives for national commercials.

Networks obtain their programs either by making them on their own (news and documentaries), by covering live events (special news events, sports), or by purchasing the programs from producers. Most prime-time programs and weekly programs are supplied the networks by producers. The producers (or sponsors of an event such as the National Basketball Association or the American Football League) receive money from the networks, the networks receive money from national advertisers, local stations receive money from local advertisers.

The three networks compete with each other to attract the most viewers. The number of people who watch each program is measured by rating systems, particularly the one used by A.C. Nielsen Company. Nielsen ratings are used to determine advertising rates and can spell life or death for the continuation of certain programs or series.

1. How does the amount of television watched by people in your class compare with the national average? Determine some method to measure accurately the TV viewing of class members. (Assume that people cannot accurately answer the question "How much television do you watch?")

2. Why do you think women tend to watch more TV than men? Why do those with more schooling watch less TV than those with less schooling?

3. Which local channels in your town are affiliated with which network? Are there any "independents" in town? Who owns them?

4. Why do you think newspapers are not licensed by the government when radio and television stations are?

5. Have someone inspect the "public file for license renewal" at each local TV station and report on what that file contains.

6. Why do you think such a large percentage (85%) of stations are affiliated with one of the three commercial networks?

7. Have a person or group report on the history of television broadcasting in the United States.

8. Arrange a tour of a local television station.

9. Be able to look in your local TV listings or in *TV Guide* magazine and determine whether a program is provided by a network or by the local station.

10. Find out how much advertising time costs on local television stations. Your library should be able to help in this by supplying a copy of the *Standard Rate and Data Service* book giving spot TV information.

11. Have a person or group prepare a report on the rating systems used to determine which programs are the most watched. Write to A.C. Nielsen Company and ask for their literature on the rating system.

TV Programming:
SUCCESS and the SOAPS

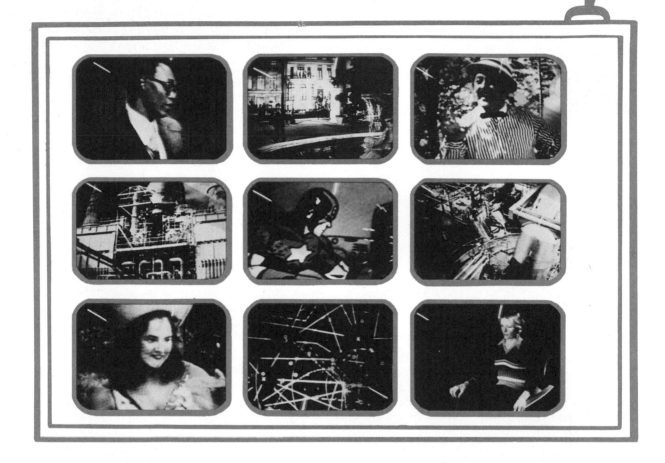

Television programs serve to gather an audience for the commercials. For this reason there has been relatively little change in programming since the beginning of television. Networks tend to stick with what has worked in the past.

When a certain type of program proves successful on one network, the other two often rush to produce a similar one. This "success copying" accounts for the waves of popularity in certain types of shows from season to season. One season medical shows may be popular; the next, ethnic humor or dramas about rural families; the next, police stories or westerns.

Most commercial TV programming can be placed in one of the following categories:

News and documentaries
Sports
Movies
Music/Variety
Westerns
Crime and spy shows
Talk shows
Quiz and game shows
Soap operas
Situation comedy
General and family drama

No one knows before a show is broadcast how many viewers it will attract. Very few series last more than three years; many are cancelled after a year or less. One of television's most profitable, long-lived, and dependable types of broadcasting is the soap opera. The functioning of soap operas reveals quite a bit about television in general. Soap operas are morality plays in miniature; they are quite important to those who watch regularly.

MAINLINING SOAPS:

The Allure of Daytime Television Drama

By Stephen West

Every weekday morning at 10:30, the first of 16 soap operas broadcast daily by the three major networks appears on between four and five million television screens across the country. By one o'clock in the afternoon, when the networks are simultaneously offering "Love Is a Many-Splendored Thing," "The Doctors," and "All My Children," all soap operas, recent Nielsen ratings show that over 13 million American homes (or about 21%) are being filled with the sights and sounds of this particular form of entertainment.

Why is this so? Why do the networks broadcast programs which almost everyone, including the viewers, seems to think are so terrible? And, more to the point, why do so many people go ahead and watch these shows anyway? The most obvious answer is that there's not much else on the air during the daytime, except for the game shows. But this can hardly be the complete answer; for in spite of the fact that it's hard to find someone who will admit to watching soap operas regularly, much less *enjoying* them, there is a good deal of evidence that we have millions of covert soap opera freaks living in our midst.

Reprinted from Popular Psychology Magazine.

The following article reveals much about television in its behind-the-scene examination of the world of soap operas. A student of television must study what is typical of television rather than what is exceptional. Some teachers will encourage or even assign students to watch educational specials, believing that this is television at its best. But in this study of TV programming it is more revealing to look at typical programming, and nothing is more typical than the soap opera.

These people may say they would rather watch something else, something "better." It is, after all, a common assumption that soap operas are trivial, silly, a waste of time. But I'm not convinced. I do not believe that anything which can command such religious devotion from so many people is a trivial phenomenon. That quality of addiction, of some need which must be satisfied, deserves a serious examination.

The networks' reason for offering these programs is quite simple: they make a lot of money at it. Along with the game shows, the other main program format for daytime broadcasting, the soap operas are the most profitable part of the television business. Although audience size—and thus, advertising income—is perhaps one-third the size of a nighttime show, the production costs of games and soaps may run only *one-tenth* as much as the expensive prime time offerings. According to one industry source, "On the average soap opera today, we make back the production expenses for the whole week on the first day, Monday. So Tuesday through Friday's advertising is pure profit for the network. Or to put it more dramatically: for every dollar of profit which CBS makes at night, they make seven dollars of profit in the daytime. If there were no daytime, there would be no network."

Thus, daytime programming supports those high-status (and license retaining) but unprofitable operations such as the news department, which runs millions of dollars in the red every year. But this need to keep production costs low has important limiting effects on daytime television. The number of hours to be filled with *something* is more than twice as great as during the evening. For the 9:00 a.m. to 6:00 p.m. period, each network must come up with 45 hours of material every week, not counting Saturday and Sunday. Every year, the number of daytime half-hour slots to be filled approaches 4,700. No wonder the networks resort to formula programming.

Soap operas are cheap because you can produce one every day with the same basic personnel and facilities. On "As the World Turns," for example, everything is shot in one studio, on four sets erected from a total pool of 29. Every day, the cast comes in early in the morning for several hours of rehearsals and technical preparations. Blocking, camera angles, cutting, sound, pacing—everything is finalized, so that when 12:30 rolls around, this four act playlet is ready to be broadcast live to an audience of almost ten million people. Unlike "As the World Turns," however, most soap operas are not, in fact, broadcast live, but are produced by a method known [as] "live on tape." In this case, the episode which is recorded on videotape today will be broadcast a few days from now. The pressure of a live performance still remains, though, because, "you don't stop that tape and waste money by starting over unless an actor literally drops dead on the set," according to one technician.

After the day's performance, the crew begins work on erecting a new group of sets, while the actors and director spend the afternoon reading through the next day's script. That evening, the cast must memorize their lines for a new half-hour episode, since the whole cycle starts again the next morning. With this kind of production schedule—compared to the week required to make an evening program, or several months for a two-hour movie—the mere fact that a coherent, reasonably polished performance can be pulled off every day is an awesome feat.

Because of these technical constraints, soap operas resemble the legitimate theater more than nighttime television or films: they are rougher, more spontaneous, more uncertain. Most are produced in New York, because Broadway has an unending supply of actors trained to memorize large sections of dialogue and to cover mistakes by improvisation in an ongoing performance, while Hollywood does not. Without background music and with relatively little cutting from scene to scene within an "act," soap operas project an intimate, almost documentary feeling, as if you're observing a few minutes of real time in some real people's lives. Somehow the clanking of forks against plates comes through much more clearly in an eating scene; the pauses, the coughs, the uncertain glances aside, all the seams in an interaction remain unclosed in these programs. They have a flatness, a looseness which resemble the tone of everyday life and which is very different from the more frenetic, tight, "flawless" productions on prime time.

Around the studio for a soap opera, everyone is concerned with only two things: maintaining a reasonable level of technical polish and keeping the Nielsen ratings high. They simply have no time to consider the broader implications of what they're doing, beyond delivering a certain number of viewers to the sponsor and thus earning a living for themselves. A question about how they think their program may be influencing its viewers will be met by a blank, puzzled stare. Hopefully, they think, the viewer will be influenced to buy the sponsors' products and to tune in the program again tomorrow; but beyond that, who cares what the viewer thinks?

The actors, director, and technical crew for a soap opera are the implementors of the script, and the pace of their job is so relentless they can hope for little more than avoiding disaster. Their chances of improving the script, of creatively enlarging its meaning through their craft, seems to be rather limited, except insofar as an actor is able to clarify the personality of his character, bit by bit, over a period of months or years. And even here the opportunities are limited. There just isn't enough time to do much more than learn your lines.

The scriptwriter himself, the creator of what seems to be the substantive core of the series, is also plagued by many of these same problems of time pressure. The language of the script is no more smooth or coherent than the acting, but the scriptwriter is responsible (along with the producer) for making choices about the plot as well as the dialogue. And it is the plot—the concrete actions which the characters make, the incredible problems which they must confront—which keeps the viewer hooked to the program.

According to Robert Shaw, a soap opera scriptwriter for over 20 years and a man who probably knows as much about the genre as anyone in the business, there are basically two parts to writing a successful series: creating major characters—especially including the heroine—for whom the viewer can feel empathy, and working out a complex, disaster-laden, but finally optimistic plot. Soap opera viewers, for obvious reasons, are overwhelmingly female; the men who watch daytime television, on the other hand, greatly prefer the game shows. (Eight of the top ten programs watched by women are soaps, while nine of the top ten watched by men are games.)

Thus, Mr. Shaw explains, "The key to daytime

serials is empathy. If we can't build empathy in a character, we haven't got a show. Empathy means, in a way, identifiability, likeability . . . and this hasn't changed since the first ones on the radio 45 years ago. There is a theory—which I believe, to a considerable extent—that women tune in soap operas to watch someone who has more misery than she does. It makes you feel good to discover that somebody else has it worse. We have found, by trial and error over the years, that one of the things that's almost impossible to do is to make a sympathetic character out of a rich woman. The average American housewife *unquestionably* believes that if you've got money, you've got *no other problems,* because money solves everything . . . Heroines almost definitely have to be poor, but honest."

The leading women, for this purpose of building empathy, are generally young, attractive, and stylish, but they still retain a good bit of that small town Protestant modesty which is so much a part of almost every soap opera series. (Consider the names of the mythical, generally Midwestern towns where the action normally takes place: Shadyside, Sunnyview, Oakville, etc.) "The ideal soap opera heroine," Shaw says, "is a woman's image of herself, which is not necessarily the truth. It's how she *thinks* of herself. A woman can be flopping around the house in a flannel bathrobe, with her hair in curlers, doing the ironing. She sees my heroine doing the ironing in a $400 tailored suit, and somehow she transfers, she thinks that's the way she looks."

In Shadyside, moreover, it is the women who are running the show, according to their own domestic set of values. It is a world of weak men and strong women, a world in which the housewife heroines know that the important things in life are *interpersonal,* not material, and certainly not political. (This is exactly the opposite of a nighttime dramatic serial, in which the men are strong and the women are weak and/or non-domestic.) If Marcus Welby suddenly found himself living in a soap opera Shadyside, he would have to get married very quickly and start demonstrating that, although he may be a fine doctor at the office, his wife is actually the one who solves all his problems at home. It's acceptable for a man to be competent at his job in the non-domestic world. After all, somebody has to be able to cure all those people who are getting sick in Shadyside—but In the truly important domestic

world, "where the heart is," the heroine is the one who is in control of the situation.

In the language of the soap operas, a connection is constantly made between the unimportant domestic chores of a housewife's work and the crucially important domestic problems which always threaten her life. "It's good writing," Robert Shaw says, "to have a woman say, 'I don't know what to have for dinner tonight. We had pot roast last night, so maybe I can make, um, a pot roast *stew* tonight.' And this is only to lead into the real problem which is much worse, that she's found out she has breast cancer, say." This linking of the trivial with the important works both ways: from the viewer's chores to identification with the heroine's serious problems, and back; from the viewer's identification with the heroine's need for a solution, to the viewer's parallel realization that she needs a solution to her *own* trivial problems, as well. And this, of course, is where the sponsor steps in, offering just the perfect item for the elimination of stubborn stains, whatever.

The implicit message of all soaps, both during the show and during the commercials as well, is that any problem can be solved. Things may be pretty messed up these days, but the system is basically sound, ladies. I hardly need to add that the sponsors of these programs have enormous vested interests in the *status quo,* in the maintenance of American housewives' optimism.

The problems which beset a soap opera heroine, and they are many and varied, basically fall into two overlapping categories: the disruption of health and the disruption of social/sexual relations. According to Robert Shaw, cancer (particularly feminine cancer, of the breast, the cervix, etc.) is probably the single best problem a writer has at his disposal for beefing up his ratings. "Of course, murder is always good, provided you murder someone the viewer cares about," Shaw says. "It has to be one of the main character's favorite brother or sister or uncle, somebody who can hold the viewer's attention for quite a while. And, of course, this is a good way to write out an actor who's leaving the show . . . Then there's infidelity, which is almost basic to *all* serials."

Disease is a common problem in the soaps because it's something everyone can identify with, an irrational threat beyond one's control. In Shadyside, if not in the rest of the world, disease is democratic: it can strike anyone, regardless of position. The doctor is held in great esteem here because, unlike most other professions, he is intimately connected to the domestic world of bedrooms, children, house calls. (Where else, except on television, do doctors still make house calls?)

Various kinds of psychological problems have recently become standard themes for these programs. Child psychology and the problems of the "disturbed child" are especially big these days, along with runaway children, amnesia, impotence, drug addiction, you name it. In the social/sexual disruption category, there are still more possible disasters: rape, incest, the beginnings of a new wave of homosexual relations, abortions and unwed mothers, and adoptions, especially those in which the biological mother returns to the home of the adoptive parents to claim her child, after years of separation. And finally, says Shaw, "If you're really stuck, you can always bring in the Bad Sister, the one nobody's heard from for years. That's tried and true, along with the in-laws as heavies, and what to do with your invalid parents. There's really no end to the possibilities."

Through all of these problems, of course, the heroine maintains her basic optimism. She lives in a totally uncertain world, but her faith in the idea that her problems will eventually be solved is never in doubt. For the viewer, this one certain feature of the program changes its entire character; it becomes like a mystery story or like pornography, in the sense that the final outcome is never in doubt. The interest in the story exists in means, not in ends, and this is why the viewer's appetite for more and more can never be satiated. A soap opera is an open-ended narrative form, like folk legends or our experience of our own lives. Were it to end, it would cease existing entirely.

By definition, there is no end to a soap opera, unless it gets taken off the air. "As the World Turns" has been churning along now for over 22 years, and it's just as superficially uncertain and basically predictable as it ever was. "I am absolutely convinced," Robert Shaw says, "that there is some relief in watching these serials . . . I think the viewer feels better after having watched, for the very reason that she's seen someone more miserable than she is. Also, our women *do* solve their problems: cancer *is* curable, husbands *do* come back . . . We're selling

hope, really, and it's not much more specific than that. We stay away from the problems of the country, we'd never mention a depression or the stock market." Then he adds, wistfully, "They live in apart from it, really."

Finally, in spite of all the personal problems which living in Shadyside inevitably entails, most viewers would probably be glad to exchange their own lives for those of the soap opera's characters. There may be a lot of problems, yes; but boredom and loneliness are not among them, and these are clearly what the viewers suffer from most. At least the characters in a soap opera have engaging, crucial problems in their lives, not an endless stream of minor frustrations and indignities, like broken washing machines, dirty dishes, and screaming kids.

The soaps open up the viewer to another world where things seem to matter. At least they provide the viewer with gossip material for times when she runs short on other subjects. I have a feeling there are millions of little networks of friendships in this country based on arguing the merits of a soap opera heroine's latest move, on filling each other in on the details of a missed episode, on trying to second-guess what the scriptwriter will do next week. And given the viewer's entrapment, this is probably better than nothing. □

1. Which category of programming listed on page 15 is currently the most popular?

2. Find some current examples of "success copying."

3. Sports programs are among the most successful and profitable television presentations. Discuss how television has influenced sports in the United States. Consider how television has helped sports;

whether television encourages or discourages adults from participating in sports, whether watching sports on TV might replace watching them in person (football games in the future played in empty stadiums and videotaped for later broadcast just like any other TV show), and which sports are most and least successful on television.

4. If your class meets while a soap opera is scheduled on any of the networks, be sure to watch and discuss at least one episode.

5. In 1971 and 1972 M.L. Ramsdell and other researchers at Rollins College watched 600 hours of soap operas and concluded that one of the messages the soaps teach is that "the good life can be achieved by anybody who is a white male professional or a white female who marries the professional and subsequently becomes a mommy." Is this message still being taught by the soaps today?

6. Why do you think soap operas are so popular?

7. Explain in your own words how the acting, camera work, and sets of soap operas are different from those in nighttime dramatic shows.

8. What kind of rules exist in your family for watching TV? Is there a difference between the rules for your parents (if any) and those for you and for your older or younger brothers and sisters? Are the rules fair? Why do they exist?

9. What would happen if the soaps were shown at nighttime instead of during the day? In answering this question consider how the daytime and nighttime audiences differ.

10. Talk with someone who watches soap operas regularly. Try to find out why that person watches them and why certain ones are favorites.

11. Why do soap operas rely so much on tragedy and disaster in their plots?

12. Do you think soap opera women are believable and real?

13. How is programming influenced by the need for the networks to make a profit?

14. Stephen West, author of the article on soap operas, says that "A soap opera is an openended narrative form, like folk legends or our experience of our own lives." Explain this in your own words.

An Experiment in Tubelessness

One way to measure how television influences the way we live would be to find a community (perhaps a town of at least 1,000) where people are *not* exposed to television. We could watch these people very closely to see how their lives are different because of their lack of television. But finding such a community is nearly impossible, for there is hardly a place in the United States that is without television. Even in the most remote and mountainous areas, at least 90% of the households have television. Since there is no city that would suit our experiment in tubelessness, perhaps we could look for 1,000 average people who don't watch television. But since these people are such a minority, they can hardly be considered average. To measure the effect of television is indeed difficult precisely because television has become so much a part of ordinary life in America.

One experiment in the absence of television was conducted in Germany, where 184 volunteer television viewers were paid to give up TV for one year. At first the volunteers reported that they spent more time with their children, went to movies more frequently, read and played more games, and visited friends and relatives more than they did before they gave up television.

But within a few weeks things began to change. Even though the people were paid not to watch, one man dropped out after only three weeks. No one lasted more than five months. Why? Tension, fighting, and quarreling increased among families without television. When the experiment was over and the sets were back on, these effects disappeared.

Television is like a drug. Habitual viewers are addicted to television and need their daily fix in order to get along. When television is not available the addicted become nervous, restless and irritable.

21

Medialab

How TV Influences the Way We Live

1. The experiment described here took place in Germany. Do you think the results would be any different if it were conducted in the United States?

2. How would your family react to such an experiment?

3. Did this experiment reveal some positive aspects of television?

4. Why did tension, fighting, and quarreling increase within the TV-less families? The psychologists who conducted the experiment made an educated guess at the answer. Stop and think of your own reasons before reading any further.

One of the psychologists who conducted the experiment believes that watching TV tends to cover up conflicts and disagreements between habitual viewers. That is, instead of working out problems, people avoid them by watching TV. TV works as sort of a buffer between people, helping them to be together without having to work out their conflicts. Take away the TV set and the rough edges begin to show.

5. Write a very short fictional story describing what happens "The Day Television Disappeared." Base your story on the unlikely happening of huge sunspots or some other unknown phenomenon that wipes out all television reception in the world. Your story should tell what might happen when people discover what has happened and then how things might change without television. You might want to include in your account some of the effects of TV on the following: family life, movie attendance, libraries, newspaper and book reading, sports, advertising, radio programming.

6. Recall the last time the family TV set broke down. How long was the set out of order? Take a survey in the class and find the average number of days or hours the set remained out of order. (If a family has more than one TV, the answer should be about the main set, the one used most often.) What does the class average say about the importance of television.

7. Find someone in the class who either does not have a TV or who lives in a family where someone almost never watches TV. Find out from that person why he or she does not watch TV. What is the extra time spent on instead?

8. One of the undeniable effects of television is that it takes up a lot of time. The "average" person watches TV for 6-8 years during a lifetime. If TV were to vanish, a lot of extra time would be available to do other things. How might people be different if they had this extra time to fill? How would you spend your time if you had no TV?

9. Talk to someone who remembers the days before television. Ask them how they think television has changed family life and the way people spend their time.

10. Television is a rather recent invention. Do you think somebody will invent something that will replace it? I imagine an invention that could capture the public's interest and time as much as television has. Would it be like television or something very different?

What Does Television Teach?

If you were to interview people selected at random and ask them, "What did you learn from television this past week?" the answers would probably fall into two categories. One common answer would be "nothing." People would say they didn't watch any TV the past week or they would think that you were asking about educational television which they didn't watch. The other common answer would be from people who would tell you something they learned from a newscast, a documentary, a special, or some program on the educational channel.

But there is another kind of *teaching* that television provides. Even the advertising and the entertainment programs on television teach—they teach what products are acceptable to use and what products promise to bring happiness. They present images of what the police are like and what kind of people are criminals. They teach how rich people live and what a happy family looks like. Television shows nice things—cars, furniture, houses, clothes—and presents them so that they appear

desirable, even necessary. Thus people want the "good life" they see on television and allow TV to shape their desires. Television teaches how people supposedly live, talk, dress, and behave. Television programming helps make the products advertised in the commercials appear necessary or desirable.

This kind of "learning" is difficult to detect. If all television is educational, we must ask what kind of education this "School of the Tube" provides. Does television present a realistic picture of the world or does it show only fantasies and fiction?

George Gerbner is a television researcher who constructed a test to measure the kind of education provided by television. Before explaining what he found, take the test yourself. The test given here is a simplified version of Gerbner's test. Write the answers on a separate sheet of paper. At the top of the paper, before you begin the test, write the estimated number of hours you watch TV in an average week.

ABCD $1800

ABCD $1200

ABCD $1100

1. What percent of the world's population lives in the U.S.? (a) 1% (b) 5% (c) 10% (d) 15% (e) 20%

2. What percent of American workers are in law enforcement jobs? (a) 1/4% (b) 1/2% (c) 1% (d) 2% (e) 5%

3. What are chances of being the victim of a serious crime this year? (a) 1 in 100 (b) 2 in 100 (c) 3 in 100 (d) 5 in 100 (e) 10 in 100

4. What percent of the victims of crime are under 30 years old? (a) 70 % (b) 55% (c) 40% (d) 25% (e) 10%

5. What percent of the victims of crime are black? (a) 70% (b) 55% (c) 40% (d) 25% (e) 10%

6. What percent of married women work at jobs outside the home? (a) 50% (b) 40% (c) 30% (d) 20% (e) 10%

7. What percent of U.S. workers are employed in managerial or professional jobs (white collar)? (a) 5% (b) 10% (c) 15% (d) 20% (e) 25%

8. What percent of workers have jobs in professional athletics or entertainment? (a) 1/4% (b) 1/2% (c) 1% (d) 2% (e) 3%

(Answers and scoring system on page 39.)

The teacher or test scorer should take the papers and arrange them into piles according to the amount of TV viewing reported. Make four piles, grouping the papers according to number of hours watched: 0-3 hours per week; 4-7 hours; 8-11 hours; and more than 11 hours a week. Then find the average test score for each group. Remember, the higher the test score, the more inaccurate a view the person has of the world and U.S. situation. The lower the test score the more accurate and realistic the view. As a class, draw some conclusions from the results.

In giving this test to adults, Gerbner found that people who watch a lot of television tend to overestimate the percentage of world population made up of Americans much more than do light TV viewers. He found that heavy viewers also overestimate the number of people employed as professionals or managers. In general he found that the more hours people watched television, the more inaccurate were their answers to the questions (the higher their test scores). Those who watch a lot of TV are much more likely to fear they will be the victims of a crime than those who watch little TV. What explanations can you offer for these findings?

1. The original TV test found that people who watch the most television have the least accurate idea of what the real world is like. Other polls have shown that the answer most people give to the question "Where do you get most of your information about the world?" is "Television." How can you explain both these findings?

2. The same experimenter who composed the test found that people who read newspapers frequently (even if they also watched a lot of TV) were much more likely to choose correct answers. What does this finding say about both newspapers and television?

3. Can you conclude from this test that "watching television makes people stupid"?

4. Are there kinds of programs that would give viewers a *more* accurate picture of the world?

The test results suggest that television viewing and a highly accurate picture of the world do not go together. Sometimes the teaching television does is very obvious and can be seen in occasional small news stories. Here is a sort of scrapbook of news stories related to the teaching done by television. Read the stories and attempt to draw some further conclusions about the educational effect of television.

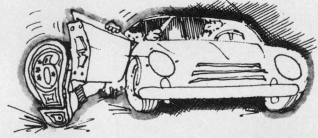

Another view of the effects of television is sometimes seen in satirical cartoons. Take a look at the cartoons on this page and discuss what statement about television they make. Do you agree or disagree with each viewpoint? Make a cartoon of your own that shows your opinion of television.

CHICAGO SUN-TIMES, Tues., Apr. 17, 1973

TV film on air pollution starts panic in Germany

Agence France-Presse

BONN — A particularly realistic television film on atmospheric pollution started a wide-scale panic among West German viewers when it was screened Sunday night.

The film, directed by Wolfgang Menges and titled ''Smog,'' showed the catastrophic situation which could be brought about by a saturation of carbon dioxide in Dortmund, a city in Germany's heavily industrialized Ruhr district. It showed children asphyxiated, people struck down on the streets and traffic brought to a complete halt.

After the film was shown, telephone switchboards at the television station were practically blocked. One man asked how to save his children, while another asked how to get gas masks.

In Dortmund, the biggest blast furnace in Europe had to slow down production two weeks ago because of the pollution hazards when it was going full blast.

RANCHO CORDOVA, Cal., May 31 [UPI]—Two teen-age gunmen surrendered to police today after a tense, seven-hour drama in which they held more than 20 persons hostage in a suburban bank, received a $1 million ransom, and appeared on television to tell their story.

The hostages—most of them women and children —all were released unharmed.

Michael D. Madigan, 18, and Brian James Young, 19, walked out of a suburban shopping center bank surrounded by more than 50 deputies, agents of the Federal Bureau of Investigation, and police after they were promised they could watch themselves on television.

Coroner's Jury Blames Alice Cooper Stunt For Boy's Self-Hang Death

Calgary, Alta, June 25.

A Calgary boy's death by hanging in March resulted from his attempt to imitate a mock-hanging performed by a rock music star during a television program, a coroner's jury has ruled.

The jury, investigating the death of 14-year-old David Andrew Coombs, ruled it accidental and called for banning of television programs which depict simulated hanging or similar violent acts. This was a reference to a program seen by the youth on the Canadian Broadcasting Corp. network in which rock star Alice Cooper performed his hanging stunt.

Dr. John Butt, a pathologist, told the jury that youthful experiments with hanging have been ''widely reported'' among adolescent boys recently, and he suggested public attention should be called to what he termed ''this dangerous practice.''

Coroner Dr. W.M. Wilson said he had called the inquest to bring the practice to public attention to ''let youngsters know how lethal this can be.''

The boy's father told the inquest his son and daughter saw the television hanging routine and afterward the boy was heard to tell his sister it was just a trick he could do himself.

After seeing the show, the jury was told, the boy attended a party where several youngsters emulated the mock hanging act.

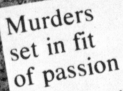

Murders set in fit of passion

REDDING, Cal., May 21 [Reuters]—Gerald Bishop was so angry because the San Francisco Giants lost a baseball game he pumped 17 rifle bullets into his television set.

The bullets went thru the walls of his mobile home and penetrated a house 300 yards away.

Lula Jorgenson, in her 70s, was sitting quietly at home knitting, but fled in panic when bullets began whizzing round her room.

After his arrest, Bishop asked Policeman John Grimes: ''Haven't you ever wanted to shoot your TV set?''

Wednesday, May 15, 1974

Kid Knieveled, Parents Sue

Philadelphia, May 14

Claiming their 10-year-old son suffered a ruptured spleen, a concussion and other injuries after trying to emulate Evel Knievel because of toy commercial, a Prospect Park, Pa., couple has instituted a $24,000,000 damage suit against WTAF-TV, the Ideal Toy Corp., manufacturer of the Evel Knievel Stunt Cycle, and Helfgott, Towne & Silverstein, Inc., a New York ad agency.

Mr. and Mrs. Aubrey R. Clark are seeking $4,000,000 apiece for themselves and for their son, Aubrey Jr., from each of the three companies named.

The Clarks contend that "goaded, inspired and urged" by a commercial for the toy, which duplicates in miniature the barrel-jumping feats of daredevil Knievel, the boy tried to jump a bike over some piles at a construction site, using makeshift plank ramps.

Gorillas going ape over television

William Hines
Times Bureau

[W]ASHINGTON—In some [qu]arters it might be consid[er]ed cruelty to animals, but [th]e keepers of the nation's [la]rgest collection of great [ap]es have started letting their [an]thropoid charges watch [tele]vision during the day.

Public-spirited citizens [an]d business firms in Atlanta [co]ntributed 19 TV sets to the [Ye]rkes Primate Research [ce]nter at nearby Emory [U]niversity after an appeal by [Ye]rkes' director, Dr. Geoff[re]y H. Bourne.

[T]he 136 gorillas, chimps [an]d orangutans were getting [bo]red, Bourne explained, [an]d TV seemed to be the [an]swer. By all indications,

Bourne said in a telephone interview, the experiment is a huge success.

One of the apes, a chimp named Dobbs, was a ready-made TV fan by virtue of two six-month stays in the home of a woman in Santa Barbara, Calif. He got hooked on Westerns—the more violent the better, Bourne said.

"Dobbs can even tell the bad guy," Bourne related. "He associates the bad guy with violence, and sometimes he starts jumping up and down even before the bad guy starts anything rough."

Lest anyone doubt the effects of TV on impressionable minds, Bourne told of one occasion when an animal show depicted two chimpan-

zees making a shambles of the inside of a house.

"Next day Dobbs tore up his room," Bourne said.

Except for the veteran tube-boob, Dobbs, the primate colony hasn't been exposed to TV long enough yet to develop tastes in entertainment. Nor are the animals allowed to sit up till all hours watching the box, as a questioner learned when he asked Bourne if they had watched President Nixon and the three commentators on Wednesday night.

"I don't think so," he said, "We usually just let them watch from 9 to 5."

TV serves a useful, humane purpose when it is necessary to isolate the animals for long periods to conduct metabolic tests, Bourne

explained. "They're locked away by themselves sometimes for months at a time and get terribly lonely," he explained. "We feel that TV is a real contribution here."

Bourne was asked whether the center uses closed-circuit TV or videotape machines to document activities or to entertain the animals by allowing them to see themselves as others see them. He said funds weren't available for such equipment but that he would be more than delighted to accept it as a gift if offered.

"We'd like to be able to run tapes and films of our own choosing," Bourne said without elaborating on the type of TV fare he would offer his charges if he were in charge of programming.

Another view of the effects of television is sometimes seen in satirical cartoons. Take a look at the cartoons on this page and discuss what statement about television they make. Do you agree or disagree with each viewpoint? Make a cartoon of your own that shows your opinion of television.

Reprinted by permission of The Toronto Sun Syndicate. Punch ©1973.

"He said his first word today — 'polyunsaturated'."

Reprinted by permission of George Dole.

Reprinted by permission of The New York News, Inc. Copyright 1974. All Rights Reserved.

Reprinted by permission of the Chicago Tribune. Copyright 1973. All Rights Reserved.

Meedalab

What TV Teaches

1. Many of the news stories describe how TV inspires people to imitate what they see. Do you think these are rare cases or rather common ones?

2. Can you recall imitating TV characters or shows when you were younger? Do you see your smaller brothers and sisters doing that today?

3. If you believe that TV does encourage certain kinds of behavior, do you think it encourages more good or bad behavior? What kind of actions does it encourage most?

4. Do you think that television is specifically to blame for the fact that some people may imitate what they see and hurt themselves or others? Might something else influence them just as strongly? Or is TV's impact unique?

5. One story is about a film on air pollution that started a near panic in Germany. Could something like that happen in the U.S.? Did it ever happen in the days before television?

6. Consider television as a kind of educational system, a sort of informal school of the airwaves. What lessons in living does regular commercial TV teach?

7. What opinion about television is expressed in each of the cartoons?

8. Why do you think there are more cartoons drawn and published that are critical of TV than cartoons that point out the advantages of television?

9. Draw your own cartoon about television. If you can't draw, use cut-outs or photographs.

BLOOD ON THE TUBE:

The Violence Question

The critics of television often point an accusing finger at television's role in teaching about violence. Perhaps you already have an opinion on the question of whether or not television encourages violent behavior. On the following pages one person presents a strong argument that "TV Violence *Is* Harmful."

STAYSKAL
1975
CHICAGO
TRIBUNE

TV VIOLENCE

" IT'S BLOOD !! "

by Jesse L. Steinfeld, M.D.

TV Violence Is Harmful

Every day some 40 million American children ages two through eleven tune into their family television sets for an average of 3½ hours of watching. By age 12, they total an estimated average viewing time of 13,500 hours apiece — far more than double the time they spend in the schoolroom. In the process, they will have watched 101,000 violent episodes, including an estimated 13,400 deaths.

What is the effect of all this television mayhem on our young people? Consider these recent findings:

• At the University of North Carolina Child Development Center, researchers recently paired ten pre-schoolers who had similar television and play habits. Then, over an 11-day period, one child was shown a violent Saturday-morning television offering, while his partner watched a non-aggressive show. The five exposed to violent programming became remarkably more aggressive, some even tripling their violent acts (kicking, choking, hitting, pushing), while their mates' scores remained largely unchanged.

• Two Penn State researchers carefully recorded the level of physical and verbal attacks among 92 kindergartners, then divided them into three groups to watch different half-hour television films over a four-week period. One group saw "Superman" and "Batman" shows, each containing several physical and verbal assaults. A second group saw "Mister Rogers' Neighborhood," whose puppet vignettes teach youngsters how to cope with anger, jealousy, fear and frustration. As a control, the third

Dr. Jesse L. Steinfeld has been a professor of medicine at the University of Southern California and an official of the National Institutes of Health. He served as Surgeon General of the United States from December 1969 to January 20, 1973.

groups saw neutral shows. Among children who had measured initially low in aggression there wasn't a significant response one way or another. Children from the lower socio-economic backgrounds who saw "Mister Rogers" improved strikingly in cooperation, obedience to rules and daily relations with others. However, among those who were above average in aggressiveness—fully half the total—exposure to the violent films caused a sharp increase in their attacks on playmates.

• In 1959, New York Department of Mental Hygiene researchers evaluated both television-violence viewing and aggressive behavior of 184 third-grade boys. In a follow-up study of the same group ten years later, they discovered an astonishing long-term effect. "Regardless of whether the individual's behavior at age eight was combative or non-aggressive, if he watched high levels of television violence he was likely to rank high in aggression ten years later," concludes Dr. Monroe Lefkowitz, the senior researcher.

• Survey teams studied 2900 junior- and senior-high-schoolers and 1,500 graduates from almost 100 schools throughout the nation. In each group the researchers found a correlation between television-violence viewing and a wide range of troublemaking behavior.

Research Proves the Point. These studies—and scores of similar ones—make it clear to me that the relationship between televised violence and antisocial behavior is sufficiently proved to warrant immediate remedial action. Indeed, the time has come to be blunt: We can no longer tolerate the present high level of televised violence that is put before children in American homes.

Many citizens and parents have long fretted over the impact of television on our youth. Therefore, in March 1969, Sen. John O. Pastore (D., R.I.), chairman of the Senate communications subcommittee, asked that the Surgeon General create a Scientific Advisory Committee on Television and Social Behavior to determine "what harmful effects, if any, these programs have on children." Three years later, the work of hundreds of scientific investigators, spelled out in 2500 pages of studies, left no doubt that televised violence adversely affects our younger generation. Dr. Robert M. Liebert, State University of New York expert in imitative learning and child development, best summarizes the researchers' findings: "We have impressive evidence that watching television violence causes a significant increase in aggressive behavior. It is not the only or even the most significant cause of antisocial behavior, but it certainly is one of the major contributors. It also happens to be one cause we *can* change."

The high level of violence is truly appalling. For six years, Dean George Gerbner, of the University of Pennsylvania's Annenberg School of Communications, studied violence levels on all three networks. The combined output contained incidents of physical force intended to hurt or kill at a rate of about eight per hour. And cartoons—the mainstay of children's programming—averaged 22 such incidents hourly.

Indifference to Harm. Gerbner's study is supported by Boston University Prof. F. Earle Barcus. In 1971, Barcus monitored all the Saturday children's programs of his city's three network stations and one UHF independent. He found 71 percent of the stories had at least one instance of human injury or killing, and about a third of the dramatic segments were "saturated" with violence.

Why? To find out, Prof. Muriel G. Cantor of American University, interviewed 24 Los Angeles producers and scriptwriters—a group responsible for nearly all the cartoons and live-action programs aimed at the Saturday-morning children's market. None had any specific academic background for preparing children's programs. Over half had been in entertainment, advertising, promotion or publicity. Most displayed an appalling indifference to possible harmful effects of their output on children. "As long as we are on the air," said one producer, "I don't care." Always, the ruling consideration seems to be audience size.

Yet the violence-equals-ratings-equals-profits formula is not infallible. A survey in England showed that children overwhelmingly prefer humor to "action" or "adventure." Could this be true also in the United States? We don't know. Our commercial broadcasters have never bothered to conduct extensive research, and thus American audiences simply have had little choice.

One thing is clear, however: by equating violence with profits, our commercial networks have often missed the boat. Consider "Sesame Street," a program designed by educational psychologists for preschoolers. Its creator, Joan Ganz Cooney of Children's Television Workshop, offered the concept to two major networks, was turned down, and had to resort to government and foundation funding. The show was a smashing success. Says Federal Communications Commission (FCC) Chairman Dean Burch, "The networks' refusal to finance 'Sesame Street' ranks with the Edsel among the worst business decisions of all time."

The sad truth is that programming for children grew up within the television industry almost accidentally, without any thought to their welfare. And so today we have put vast control over our children's minds into the hands of broadcasters, toy and food manufacturers, and other commercial interests whose dominant concern is what's good for profits and sales. "We are the only nation whose broadcasting treats children as a means of advancing corporate profits and not as a national treasure," says Mrs. Cooney.

Toward Concrete Reforms. What can be done about this scandalous situation?

First, we must refrain from using television as a baby-sitter. One Advisory Committee survey of parents of 274 first-graders shows that one third actually encouraged their children to watch TV just to keep them occupied—in some cases for five or more hours daily. Schools, churches, PTAs and other groups should ask their television stations for public-service time to present the message: "Too much TV can be hazardous to

*See " 'Sesame Street' Opens the Door," The Readers Digest, May '70.

33

your child's mental health." In addition, parents must spend more time watching with their children, and simply shutting off the violent programs. Since reading the Advisory Committee's research findings, I have adopted this rule with my own daughters.

Second, we need an independent system of television evaluations provided by child-development specialists. Under a Department of Health, Education and Welfare grant, the University of Pennsylvania is attempting to develop an objective method of monitoring trends in the level of network - television violence and correlating them with children's behavior. We also need to evaluate the beneficial programs. Studies show that programs like "Sesame Street," "Electric Company," and "Mister Rogers' Neighborhood" produce truly marvelous benefits in our children's learning. Perhaps the FCC could require stations to give advance publicity to such an objective rating guide so parents could decide for themselves the programs their children should watch.

Third, the FCC has before it a suggestion to declare the 7:30-to-9 p.m. slot "family television time" and to restrict adult content to later programming. It should act on this suggestion. An Advisory Committee researcher matched the 18 most violent prime-time network programs with audience ratings in October 1970 and found that they attracted an astonishing number of children. The National Association of Broadcasters' (NAB)

own code acknowledges that "programs broadcast during times when children may constitute a substantial part of the audience should be presented with due regard for their effect."

Finally, to have better TV fare for their children, American parents must *demand* it. Four Boston mothers who banded together in Action for Children's Television (ACT) have proved what can be done. In response to ACT's campaigning for better material, all three networks have appointed top executives to improve children's programming, and the NAB cut the commercial time permissible on weekend programming for children from 16 to 12 minutes per hour (still 50-percent greater than the average of eight minutes allowed on most prime-time evening hours) ACT, now nationwide in scope, has petitioned the FCC to ban all commercials on children's programs and to require every station, as part of its public-service commitment, to run 14 hours per week of quality programming designed for various preschool and elementary-school audiences. More than 100,000 Americans have written the FCC supporting the ACT petition and criticizing the present children's fare.

Through Congress and the FCC all of us have an obligation to let the entire television industry know that it must provide better, more varied and less exploitive programming for our children. For what is at stake is not just the quality of what our youngsters watch, but the quality of our lives now and in the future.

1. Conduct a class study to measure the amount of violence currently shown on television. Divide the class so that a group of students is assigned to each local TV channel. Each group should divide viewing time among its members so that the entire prime time schedule of its station can be monitored during one week. In addition to evening hours also assign someone to monitor the Saturday morning children's shows. Each person should keep a written record of all the televised violence that would include the following information: Date, time, channel, name of program or programs viewed. Note each act of violence committed during viewing and write down a description of each act in a few words. Also note why the violent act was committed (for example, self-defense, to escape the police, etc.). List each weapon seen and keep track of the number of people wounded and killed.

After one week of watching for TV violence each group should gather its data and compile a record of that channel's "violence report" for the entire week.
Once these are compiled compare the local stations and programs to determine which is the most and which the least violent.

Judging from your statistics, how many killings appear on television in an average year?

The article by Jesse Steinfeld quoted a study that found an average of eight incidents per hour on TV of "physical force intended to hurt or kill." How does this compare with your more recent findings?

Which programs seem to depend the most on stories in which killing is involved?

What kind of violence is most common on Satur-

day mornings? Is there more or less than on prime time?

What are among the most common reasons for the violent acts shown on television?

Reach some conclusion from your violence study.

2. Think of at least one good argument in favor of the opinion that "TV Violence is *Not* harmful." Discuss these arguments in class. If you cannot think of one reason, do some library research using the *Reader's Guide to Periodical Literature* under the heading, "Television."

3. The article tells of experiments by "two Penn State researchers." Read this section (fourth paragraph of the article) carefully and discuss their findings.

4. Is there any study mentioned in the article that concludes simply, "Watching television makes children more violent"?

5. One suggestion Jesse Steinfeld makes in the article is that violence should be eliminated from early evening programs. Did your violence study find this to be true?

6. What do you think of the ACT suggestion to ban all commercials from children's television?

7. Is there any kind of control on your television watching or on that of your younger brothers or sisters in regard to violent programs?

8. Write a short essay in which you state your own opinions about violence on television.

Who Should Have Access to Television: A Debate

Television stations are all licensed to serve the public. The station management must decide who deserves valuable air time. The following pages give information for a debate based on a situation that really happened not too long ago.

The next page shows a print version of a television commercial that Mobil Oil wished to telecast on three networks in late 1974. Two of the major networks refused to accept the ad; only NBC agreed to broadcast it.

The question under debate is this: Who deserves time on national television to express a viewpoint? That is, who should have access to television? Should access be controlled completely by the three networks? Should only advertisers who can afford the necessary tens or hundreds of thousands of dollars be allowed on the air? Should anyone with a cause be given time? Should access to television be government controlled?

One idea causing much controversy within the broadcast industry comes from a new interpretation of the right to free speech. According to this idea, the Constitutional right to free speech means little in a mass media society unless citizens have access to the mass media to express their opinions. Television (and, to a lesser extent, newspapers, magazines, and radio) is limited in the number of opinions it can present. Therefore, the question becomes: Who has access to the limited time on TV to express their opinions? So far, the answer has been "anyone with the money to buy the time; namely, corporations selling products." But what if a corporation wants to buy time to influence public opinion? Enter Mobil Oil versus the networks.

For this debate, three students should represent Mobil Oil, three ABC, three NBC, and three CBS. Three more students represent a citizens' clean-air group that has been refused air time to present a message urging people to walk and ride bikes whenever possible, instead of driving. The remainder of the class will be members of a fact-finding commission who will vote on the question according to their beliefs and the arguments presented in the debate. Decide on your own structure, time limit, and rules for the debate. Devise some kind of voting procedure to end the debate. Allow a day or two for the debaters to prepare their positions.

The following written statements of position are presented here as they appeared in writing when the ad was originally presented to the networks. These positions should be viewed only as starting points by the debate teams. The CBS and ABC teams must argue against allowing the ad on TV, the NBC team in favor of allowing it, and the Mobil team must argue in favor of the ad.

OPEN ON WIDE SHOT OF BEACH AND
OCEAN.

TURN TO WATER: CAMERA MOVES
OVER WATER AT RAPID PACE.

FRAME FREEZES

ANNCR. VO: "According to the U.S.
Geological Survey, there may be
60 billion barrels of oil or more
beneath our continental shelves."

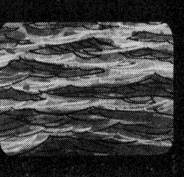

"Some people say we should be drilling
for that oil and gas. Others say we
shouldn't because of the possible
environmental risks. We'd like to
know what you think."

"Write Mobil Poll, Room 647, 150
East 42nd Street, New York 10017."

SUPER CONTINUES ON SCREEN

Why do two networks
refuse to
run this commercial?

CUT TO LOGO

ANNCR. VO: "We'd like to hear from
you."

Summary of the CBS position:

Summary of the ABC position:

Summary of the NBC position:

NBC:

"We regret that the subject matter of this commercial...deals with a controversial issue of public importance and does not fall within our 'goods and services' limitation for commercial acceptance."

"This will advise that we have reviewed the above-captioned commerial and are unable to grant an approval for use over our facilities. It is against our policy to sell time for the discussion of controversial issues of public importance. Such matters are most responsibly handled in our news and public affairs programs where both sides of an issue can be presented. We have reported on the energy crisis and have run 14 Mobil commercials which were within our accepted guidelines."

"Approved as submitted."

Summary of the Mobil Oil position:

As you can see from the storyboard we want to ask the public how it feels about offshore drilling.

But the policies of two national television networks prevent us from asking this question.

This is dangerous, it seems to us. Any restraint on free discussion is dangerous. Any policy that restricts the flow of information or ideas is potentially harmful.

The networks say that the public's need for information is best served in news programs prepared by broadcast journalists.

Behind the networks' rejection of idea advertising may be the fear that demands for equal time will be made. We have a reasonable answer to

that. We offer to pay for equal time, when the request is legitimate.

We think *more* discussion, not less, is needed of vital issues such as the issue of America's energy needs. We're willing to buy the time to say what we should be saying. We're willing to buy time so you can hear opposing views.

But two big networks aren't willing to make time available, in this case.

You know the principle at stake here. You've seen it in writing, more than once: *"Congress shall make no law . . .abridging the freedom of speech."*

You've seen it in the First Amendment to the Constitution of the United States. So have we.

We'd like to know what you think about either of these issues. Write Room 647, 150 East 42nd Street, New York, N.Y. 10017.

Projects

I. Design a TV schedule for one day of programming of your own experimental television station. The schedule should reflect the prime purpose of the station to "serve the public interest of those in the viewing area." Your schedule should run for one 24-hour day, should contain *only programming that cannot be found on other TV stations* in the area (no movies, reruns, or network shows allowed), and should reflect an active imagination. Here is part of one such "Experimental TV Schedule":

Evening

5:30 - 6:00
30 Minute Meal. Turn the TV on in the kitchen, follow the directions of the TV chef, and 30 minutes later you have dinner. Necessary ingredients are listed in the newspaper each day.

6:00 - 7:00
Newsmakers in the City. While other stations are having news reported by announcers, this station has a one-hour news program in which there is no announcer. If a robbery is in the news, the entire report will consist of the person robbed telling the story of what happened. All film presentation.

7:00 - 10:00
Citizen Access. Groups and individuals with something important to say will be given free time to speak. Videotape equipment will be provided along with instructions on how to make the presentation interesting. Detailed contents of program will be listed each day in the newspaper.

10:00 - 10:30
Consumer Guide. Guide to where to get the best prices in the city on various products. This show will name names and give prices. Also it will give warnings about shoddy merchandise or unethical salespeople working in the city.

10:30 - 11:30
Crime Beat. Portable camera will ride along with squad car or follow detectives while they work. Other weeks this show will follow people in other occupations to give an idea of what it is like to be a computer programmer, radio disk jockey, construction worker, etc.

11:30 - 1:30
Night Life. Portable cameras visit city night life (night clubs, popular hangouts, etc.) to show what happens at night.

1:30 - 3:00
Insomniac's Special. Soothing music and hypnotic visuals especially designed to induce sleep.

2. Take a survey of the class to find out which program is watched by the most class members. Discuss why that program is the most popular and what it teaches.

3. Write a critical review of a television program that you have watched. Point out both the weak and strong points of the program.

Answers to TV Test:
The most correct answer to each of the eight questions is *b*. For every answer in which you chose *a* or *c* score 2 points. For every *d* you selected, score 5 points; for every *e* score 10 points. Add up your total score.
On another piece of paper write:
1. Number of hours a week watching TV
2. Score in TV test
Do not put your name on the paper.

4. Arrange to have in class as many TV sets as there are local stations (or as many as possible). Turn all the TV sets on at once (each tuned to a different station), with the sound off. Watch the sets during the class. Be able to tell the difference between a live or videotaped program and a film program. What part of the programs has the fastest visual pace, the most changes of picture per minute? How is the effect of TV without sound different from that with sound? How is televiewing different when multiple sets are used?

5. If the school has videotape equipment available, arrange for as many people in the class as possible to produce their own TV program. Three people can work as a team to make one program. So that all the programs can be seen, limit each to one, three, or five minutes in length.

6. The project teams formed at the beginning of the course should now present their reports on the image of various groups as television portrays them. Allow plenty of time for each report and for questions from the class. Teams include those on the images of law enforcement personnel, doctors, elderly people, teenagers, women (or men), criminals or any topic chosen by a project team.

7. Explain the cartoon illustration used at the beginning of this chapter. What comment on television is the artist making?

8. Attempt to group television programs by types: situation comedies, soap operas, quiz shows, talk shows, etc. First draw up a list of as many types of programs as you think exist. Next test your list of types by attempting to classify all TV programs according to the list. Use the daily newspapers or *TV Guide* to provide program names.

9. Select one TV show to watch during prime time (evenings). On a sheet of paper make two columns: "How the Program is Realistic" and "How the Program is Unrealistic." Fill in both columns as you watch and then report or discuss your findings with the class. This project can also be done by having the entire class watch the same program (or programs) and compare and discuss their lists.

10. Those who have no television at home should write about the advantages of having no TV.

11. Watch some TV programming intended for children and make a written or oral report. Since much has been written in books and magazines about children's programs, this could be an excellent research project. Select either entertainment-type programs such as those seen on Saturday mornings or educational programs such as "Sesame Street" or "Electric Company" or watch both kinds and compare them.

12. Prepare a report on how televised sports programs affect family life.

13. Prepare a report on censorship on television. (This subject can be researched quite easily in books and magazines.)

14. Do a study to find out how much time in each television hour is given to commercials. Note how many different commercials are given in one time period. The percentage of time devoted to ads will vary according to the time of day—daytime, prime time, and late night. Keep track of these differences.

15. Studies have found that well over 50 percent of people who watch TV in the evening do not bother to change channels. They start on one channel and remain with it for hours at a time. Do you believe this? Can you explain why it might happen?

16. Watch one hour of programming on your local Public Broadcasting Service station (educational TV).

17. Read any one chapter in any one of the following books and make a report on its contents:
Television: The Business Behind the Box, by Les Brown.
About Television, by Martin Mayer.
The Age of Television, by Leo Bogart (third edition).
The Crowd Catchers: Introducing Television, by Robert Lewis Shayon.
Any other book from the public library about television.

18. Prepare an "information sheet" on all your local TV stations. List (a) the channel and call letters of all TV stations in your area; (b) the network each belongs to, if any; (c) the location of the station's studio and transmitting tower; and (d) the owner of the station.

19. Have one student find the *Standard Rate and Data Service* book that gives information about spot advertising on television (this book can be found in the reference section of many libraries). Check in the book to find out how much each local TV station charges for advertising. Report the findings to the class. (Once the book is located, the actual research for this project should not take more than 15 minutes.)

20. Have someone in the class who enjoys and understands electronics report on how television works. What makes color in a TV picture, and how does a picture travel from a TV studio to the home TV set?

21. Have a class discussion/poll and select the three worst programs on TV. Explain and defend your choices.

22. Examine the opinion about television you wrote at the beginning of this chapter, and rewrite it based on what you have learned in this chapter. You do not have to change your opinion.

STUDENT PRESENTATIONS

The following is a list of forty possible research topics or sources. The topics should be distributed among class members who will each prepare a 1-3 minute report for the class. For topics, the student should find and read one relevant magazine article or book chapter. (Research for topics should not be done in an encyclopedia.) Research sources are magazine articles that should be available in libraries. Most of the research for these student presentations will have to be done in a public library.

1. Violence on Television
2. Television Ratings
3. Televised Sports
4. Educational Television
5. Advertising on Television
6. Children's Television
7. Advertising on Children's Programs
8. Moral Aspects of Television
9. Television News
10. Censorship of Television
11. CBS
12. ABC
13. RCA
14. How Television Works
15. Television as presented in Ray Bradbury's novel *Fahrenheit 451.*
16. Television as presented in George Orwell's novel *1984.*
17. Television as presented in Aldous Huxley's *Brave New World.*
18. Television as presented in Jerry Kosinski's novel *Being There.*
19. "Should the FCC Reward Stations That Do a Good Job?" in *Saturday Review*, August 14, 1971.
20. "Talking Back to TV" in *New Republic*, January 22, 1972, p.10.
21. "What is TV Really Doing to Your Children" by Marshall McLuhan, in *Family Circle*, March 1967.
22. "Notes from the Video Underground" by Neil Hickey, in *TV Guide*, Dec. 9 and Dec. 16, 1972.
23. "The Counter Commercials" in *Newsweek*, June 5, 1972, p. 65.
24. "The Videophobes" in *Time*, November 8, 1968.
25. "NOW Says TV Commercials Insult Women" by Judith Adler Hennessee and Joan Nichols, in *New York Times Magazine*, May 28, 1972.

26. "Are TV Commercials Insulting to Women?" in *Good Housekeeping*, May 1971.
27. "TV For Kiddies. Truth, Goodness, Beauty—and a Little Bit of Brainwash," in *Psychology Today*, November 1972.
28. "Television Quiz Shows" by Stuart Werbin, in *New Times*, December 1973.
29. "Test Pattern for Living" by Nicholas Johnson, in *Saturday Review*, May 29, 1971.
30. "How to Win Friends and Influence Kids on Television" by Marilyn Elias, in *Human Behavior*, April 1974.
31. "Staked Out in Hollywood" by John Fleischman, in *Human Behavior*, December 1973.
32. "It Was Just a Joke, Folks: How a Casual Remark from Johnny Carson Emptied Supermarket Shelves All Over the Country," in *TV Guide*, May 18, 1974.
33. "We as Parents Accuse You of the Five Deadly Sins," in *The New York Times*, February 27, 1972.
34. "A Carrot for the Brute" by Norman Mark in *The New Republic*, December 25, 1971, page 24.
35. "The New Stereotypes are No Better Than the Old," by Roger Wareham and Peter Bynoe, in *The Urban Review* , November/December 1972.
36. "The Visibility and Image of Old People on Television" by Marilyn Petersen, in *Journalism Quarterly*, Autumn 1973.
37. "A Heartwarming New TV Season from the Same Folks Who Brought You Law and Order," by Dick Hobson, in *Human Behavior*, October 1974.
38. "The Technology of TV Violence" by Roger Field, in *Saturday Review*, June 10, 1972.
39. "What's Television Doing for 51% of the Population?" in *TV Guide*, February 27, 1971.
40. The short story "Added Inducement" in *The Worlds of Robert F. Young* (a story collection).

Chapter 2

ADVERTISING

Claims Analysis:

The Fine Art of Deception Detection

Advertising is the fuel that makes mass media work. Television is free for the viewing audience —while advertisers gladly pay thousands of dollars a minute to reach those who are watching. Newspapers, magazines, and radio stations would almost all cease to exist if advertisers deserted them for other media.

(The blank spaces in this paragraph are intentional. As you read, supply your best guess at the answers; later research will provide more accurate ones.) When you watch television _____ percent of the time is devoted to "messages." Your favorite radio station gives about _____ minutes in every hour to ads, and in the morning paper _____ percent of the space is advertising. A mass circulation magazine will be about _____ percent advertising.

It would be unrealistic to study mass media without taking a very careful look at the world of advertising.

Advertising has probably been around since one of our ancient ancestors let out a yell and offered to trade two deerskins for someone else's "hand-crafted never-miss arrows." Today advertising is one of the nation's largest businesses, and many consider it our most influential mass medium.

By the time a person is 60 years old, he will have seen and heard approximately 50 million advertising messages! Most will be ignored, some will prove helpful and honest, but others will mislead.

Advertising can be either constructive or harmful. It can help consumers (and everybody is a consumer at some time) discover new products they want or it can tell where to buy something at the lowest possible price. But it can also mislead people into buying things they don't want or thinking a particular brand or product is better than it is in reality. To be able to tell the difference, each person needs to become a skilled reader of ads.

To make advertising serve rather than mislead you, there are two important skills to learn. The first is the ability to determine exactly what facts are presented in an ad. The second is the ability to recognize how the ad is trying to make the product appealing. These sound like two simple skills, but advertising experts spend millions of dollars to make the job difficult.

Looking for facts in ads and commercials requires the mind of a Sherlock Holmes and the logic of a computer. Almost every advertisement makes what is called a product *claim*. The claim is simply what the ad says about the product. For example, "Jumbo pens write longer than any other ballpoint pen" *claims* very clearly that the Jumbo pen writes longer than any other pen. That sounds simple, yet claims are rarely as clear as that made for the Jumbo pen.

There are two basic kinds of claims—one that provides information useful in making a purchase decision and the other that tells little or nothing factual. Here are some advertising claims similar to ones that have been used repeatedly on radio and television and in print advertising. Look at each ad claim and then write (on a separate piece of paper) what you think the commercial "claims" about the product. Rate each claim as either (a) one that provides useful information or (b) one that gives little or no useful information. After you have done this with each of the four ads, go on and read the comments made by a skilled ad reader.

CLAIM 1

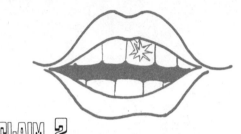

"Everbright toothpaste helps get your teeth whiter and cleaner. Its special ingredient XT-40 fights tooth decay."

CLAIM 2

"Brushing with Goodteeth toothpaste helps fight tooth decay. Nine out of ten dentists interviewed agreed that brushing with Goodteeth is effective in combating decay."

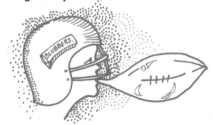

CLAIM 3

"New improved Blubbers bubble gum now has twice as many sticks of gum. New Green Blubbers is chewed by more professional football players than any other bubble gum. Look for Blubbers in the bright green package wherever good gum is sold."

CLAIM 4

"Strictly controlled scientific tests by an independent testing laboratory show that Imperial gasoline with PowerTane outperforms any gasoline made without PowerTane. Get Imperial gasoline with PowerTane to help your car run quieter, smoother, and get more miles per gallon."

Comments of a Skilled Ad Reader (Do not read this until you have made your own comments about the four fictional ads on the previous page.)

1 This ad contains no useful information. Many ads make use of comparative adjectives such as *whiter, cleaner, quieter,* etc., without saying whiter or cleaner than what. Cleaner than if you used mustard as toothpaste? Whiter than if you used licorice paste? The ad doesn't say. Perhaps the ad means only that brushing teeth is better than not brushing. The claim invites the reader to supply the missing comparison by saying "cleaner and whiter than any other toothpaste." But the ad does not say this, and to believe it does is to misunderstand it. The ad is not misleading only if it is read very carefully.

Another claim made in the ad is that Everbright contains a special ingredient—XT-40—to fight tooth decay. Who knows what XT-40 is? It could be something that has always been in the toothpaste; it could be something that all toothpastes contain.

The claim "fights tooth decay" is very carefully worded. It doesn't say "stops" tooth decay. If Everbright were able to stop tooth decay, the ad would say that. Brushing with water also "fights tooth decay"; so do toothpicks.

2 The word *helps* is used thousands of times in advertising. Remember that "helps" does not mean "does"—it means "helps." It would be perfectly accurate to say that "a bucket of water helps fight forest fires." But that is not the same as saying that a bucket of water can put out a forest fire.

"Nine out of ten dentists" (or doctors, athletes, or whomever) means simply that the company was able to find nine who agreed. Note that dentists would agree that brushing with anything would help fight decay; Brushing is more important than what is put on the brush. Dentists know that the proper brushing technique is more important than the brand of toothpaste. The statement doesn't say that Goodteeth itself stops or fights decay—it says that *brushing* with Goodteeth "helps" (remember that word) fight decay.

3 The word *new* (or *revolutionary,* or *improved,* or *all new*) is another of the advertiser's favorites. "New" does not necessarily mean better—it simply means different.

The fact that Blubbers has twice as many sticks is not the same as saying twice as much gum. They may have simply cut the same amount of gum up into smaller pieces. If the amount of gum had doubled, the ad would probably state that very clearly.

The claim that pro football players chew Blubbers means little. Perhaps each player was mailed a case at the beginning of the season. It would be a very hard claim to either prove or disprove. Also, there is no real connection between chewing gum and playing football well.

4 Be careful with this claim. Begin with the knowledge that gasolines are all pretty much the same. The claim here sounds good, but if you read carefully you can see that you never find out exactly what "PowerTane" is (remember "XT-40"). If "PowerTane" is simply a trademarked name for some common ingredient, then it would certainly be honest to say that "Imperial gasoline outperforms any gasoline made *without* PowerTane." In fact, all gas does have the same ingredient that Imperial calls PowerTane. But Imperial has registered the name "PowerTane" so that no other company can use it—this is called a registered trademark. The claim amounts only to saying that "our car with wheels rides smoother than any car made without wheels."

The ad encourages the unskilled reader to think that Imperial outperforms any other gasoline. But the ad does not actually say that. If Imperial did indeed outperform any other, you can be sure the ad would say so very clearly. Notice that the ad never uses untruth. Also notice that the final sentence again contains comparisons without an ending. Quieter, smoother, and more miles per gallon than what?

A Short Course in Advertising Claims

If your analysis of the four fictional claims was not as perceptive as that of the "advertising expert," you need at least a short course in advertising analysis.

One basic rule to remember in analyzing ads is that if any product is truly superior, the ad will say so very clearly and will offer some kind of convincing evidence of its superiority. If an ad hedges at all about a product's superiority, you can suspect that it is not really superior. You will never hear Standard Oil (or any other brand) say "Standard gasoline in your car gives you four miles per gallon more than any other brand." Standard would love to make such a claim, but it simply isn't true. Comparable types of gasoline are all pretty much the same. Although there were some clever and deceptive ads a few years ago, no one has yet made an outright claim that one brand of gasoline is better than any other brand.

To create the necessary illusion of superiority, advertisers usually resort to one or more of the following ten basic techniques. Each of them is common and easy to identify.

I. The Unfinished Claim

The unfinished claim is one in which the ad claims that the product is "better" or has "more" of something but it does not finish the comparison.

Samples:
"Magnavox gives you more." (More what?)

"Supergloss does it with more color, more shine, more sizzle, more!"

"Twice as much of the pain reliever doctors recommend most." (Twice as much as what?)

"You can be sure if it's Westinghouse."

"Scott makes it better for you."

"Ford LTD —700% quieter."

2. The Weasel Word Claim

A **weasel word** is a modifier that makes what follows nearly meaningless. The term **weasel word** comes from the habits of weasels who suck out the inside of

a raw egg through a tiny hole. An unsuspecting person picks up what looks like a whole egg only to find it is empty. Weasel word claims sound convincing at first, but upon closer examination turn out to be empty claims.

The most common weasel words include *helps* (perhaps the most used), *virtual* or *virtually*, *like* (used in a comparative sense), *acts* or *works*, *can be*, *up to*, *as much as*, *refreshes*, *comforts*, *fights*, *the feel of* (also *the look of*), *tastes*, *fortified*, *enriched*, *strengthened*.

Samples:

"Helps control dandruff symptoms with regular use"
(This claim is an accurate statement about the product. A consumer would be wrong to think that the claim is the same as "cures dandruff.")

"Leaves dishes virtually spotless"

(An unskilled ad reader will remember the claim as being "spotless" and not *almost* ("virtually") spotless. We hear so many weasel words that we tend to tune them out—which is exactly what advertisers want.)

"Only half the price of many color sets"

("Many" is the weasel here. The ad does not claim that this set is inexpensive, only that there are some that cost twice as much.)

"Fights bad breath"

(This is much like "helps control dandruff"; it does not say "stops bad breath.")

"Lots of things have changed, but Hershey's <u>goodness</u> hasn't."

(This claim does not say that Hershey's chocolate has not changed).

"Bac*os, the crispy garnish that tastes just like its name."

(This does not say that Bac*os tastes the same as bacon).

A Special Weasel—"better" and "best"

The reason so many ads need to use weasel words and the other techniques described here is that they are applied to *parity products*. A parity product is one in which all or most of the available brands are nearly identical. Since no one superior product exists, advertising is used to create the illusion of superiority. The largest advertising budgets are devoted to such parity products as beer and soft drinks, cigarettes, soaps, and various drugstore pain remedies.

In parity claims, the words *better* and *best* take on unique meanings. In such claims, "better" means "best" and "best" means "as good as." Here's how this word game works: Let's say that in a given product category there are a number of brands that are alike. Legally this means that each can claim to be best—they are all "superior." Since they are all equal, they must all be best. So "best" means that the product is as good as all the other superior products in its category. If one orange juice says "the best there is," this means only that it is as good as (not better than) any other orange juice on the market.

On the other hand, the word "better" has been legally interpreted as a comparative and therefore becomes a clear claim of superiority. That orange juice ad could not legally have claimed "better than any other brand." The only times "better" can be used are (a) if the product is indeed better than anything else; (b) if the "better" is actually used to compare the product with something else ("our orange juice is better than powdered drinks"); or (c) if the "better" is part of an unfinished claim ("the better breakfast drink").

Samples of "better" and "best" weasels:

"Hot Nestles' cocoa is the very best."

"Tests confirm one mouthwash better against mouth odor."

3. The "We're Different And Unique" Claim

This kind of claim states simply that there is nothing else quite like the product advertised. For example, if a beer manufacturer added pink food coloring, it could advertise, "There's nothing like new pink Masterbrew." The uniqueness claim is supposed to be interpreted by readers as an indication of superiority.

Samples:

"There's no other mascara like it."
"Only Doral has this unique filter system."
"Cougar is like nobody else's car."
"Either way, liquid or spray, there's nothing else like it."
"If it doesn't say Goodyear, it can't be Polyglas."

("Polyglas" is a trade name copyrighted by Goodyear. Goodrich or Firestone could make a tire identical to the Goodyear one and yet they couldn't call it "Polyglas"—a name for fiberglass belts.)

"Only Zenith has Chromacolor."

(This is the same as the "Polyglas" gambit. Admiral has "Solarcolor" and RCA has "Accucolor.")

4. The "Water Is Wet" Claim

"Water is wet" claims say something about the product that is true for any brand in that product category (e.g., "Schrank's water is really wet"). The claim is usually a statement of fact, but not a real advantage over the competition—though it is made to sound like one.

Samples:

"Mobil: the Detergent Gasoline" (true of any gas).
"Rheingold, the natural beer" (made from grains and water just like any other beer).
"Brasilia: The 100% Brazilian Coffee" (most American brands import coffee from Brazil).
"Great Lash greatly increases the diameter of every lash" (any mascara does).
" Skin smells differently on everyone" (as does all perfume).

5. The "So What" Claim

This is the kind of claim to which the careful reader will react by saying "So what?" A claim is made that is true but that gives no real advantage to the product. This technique is similar to the "water is wet" claim except that it does claim an advantage that is not shared by most of the other brands in the product category.

Samples:

"Campbell's gives you tasty pieces of chicken and not one but two chicken stocks." (What good are two stocks?)
"Geritol has more than twice the iron of ordinary supplements." (But is twice as much any better?)
"Strong enough for a man but made for a woman." (This deodorant claim says only that the product is aimed at the female market).

6. The Vague Claim

The vague claim is simply not clear; this category often overlaps others. The key to the vague claim is the use of words that are colorful but meaningless, as well as the use of subjective and emotional opinions that defy verification. Most contain weasels.

Samples of the Vague Claim:

"Lips have never looked so luscious." (Can you imagine trying to either prove or disprove such a claim?)
"Lipsavers are fun—they taste good, smell good and feel good."
"Its deep rich lather makes hair feel new again."
"For skin like peaches and cream."
"The end of meatloaf boredom."
"Take a bite and you'll think you're eating on the Champs Elysées."
"Winston tastes good like a cigarette should."
"Fleischman's makes sensible eating delicious."
"The perfect little portable for all-around viewing, with all the features of higher priced sets."

7. The Endorsement or Testimonial

A celebrity or authority appears in an ad to lend his or her stellar qualities to the product, whether they are related or not. Sometimes the people actually claim to use the product, but very often they don't. Some agencies survive by providing "names" for testimonials.

Samples:

"Freshness never tasted so good." (Ann Blyth in a commercial for Hostess cupcakes)
"Darling, have you discovered Masterpiece? The most exciting men I know are smoking it." (Eva Gabor)
"I've been a MacGregor man from the beginning. So I am delighted to introduce the new Jack Nicklaus VIP iron."
Henry Aaron for Magnavox

8. The Scientific or Statistical Claim

This kind of ad refers to some sort of scientific proof or experiments, to very specific numbers, or to an impressive-sounding mystery ingredient.

Samples:

"Wonder Bread helps build strong bodies 12 ways."
(Even the weasel "helps" did not prevent the FTC from demanding this ad be withdrawn. But note that the use of the number 12 makes the claim far more believable than if it were left out or replaced by, say, "many ways."

"Easy-Off has 33% more cleaning power than another popular brand."
("Another popular brand" translates simply as some other kind of oven cleaner sold somewhere. What the claim probably means is that Easy-Off comes in a can 1/3 larger than the can used by another brand.)
"Special Morning—33% more nutrition" (also an unfinished claim).
"Certs contains a sparkling drop of Retsyn."
"ESSO with HTA."
"Sinarest. Created by a research scientist who actually gets sinus headaches."

9. The "Compliment the Consumer" Claim

This kind of claim butters up the consumer by some form of flattery.

Samples:

"We think cigar smokers are someone special."
"You've come a long way, baby."
"You pride yourself on your good home cooking . . ."
"The lady has taste."
"If what you do is right for you, no matter what the others do, then RC Cola is right for you."

10. The Rhetorical Question

This technique demands a response from the audience. A question is asked that is worded so that the viewer or listener is supposed to answer in a way that affirms the product's goodness.

Samples:

"Plymouth—isn't that the kind of car America wants?"
"Shouldn't your family be drinking Hawaiian Punch?"
"What do you want most from coffee? That's what you get most from Hills."
"Touch of Sweden: Could your hands use a small miracle?"
"Wouldn't you really rather have a Buick?"

l. As a class, go through the list of claims below and note for each (a) what a casual or non expert reader might believe each ad says, and (b) what an expert ad analyst would say about the claim:

"Built better, not cheaper."

"You're not getting older. You're getting better."

"The taste of extra freshness."

"Five of these six top shipping pros are more than satisfied with the new Pony Express Shipping System."

"New lemony Woodwright gives you the look of hand-rubbed wood beauty instantly. "

"Hair Beauty shampoo is enriched with protein and conditioners to make hair look healthy."

"Custom Blend Coffee lets me be different."

"If you care enough to serve the very best, you serve Crystal Springs natural beer."

"Super-Clean works to eliminate unwanted odors. It works faster and smells fresh."

"Give an acne pimple something to worry about. Use Wipeout medicated soap. Fortified with AR-2."

2. Take about one week to find examples of each of the ten advertising techniques pointed out in this chapter. Tear the ads out of magazines or newspapers or quote directly from TV or radio.

3. Select one or more products and devise a way to compare the advertising claims made for that product with the product itself. Construct a test (or a series of tests) to verify or disprove the advertised claims.

V.P. COPYWRITER

4. Rewrite some ads so that they change from ads presenting little or no information to ads that are genuinely helpful to consumers.

5. Find examples of claim category #11—The Honest Claim.

6. What kinds of products do you believe have the most useful and honest advertising? Which have the least useful? Is it possible to generalize?

7. Write letters to the manufacturers of some products whose advertising you believe is deceptive. Explain your case in writing. As a class, decide on the best letters and mail them.

8. Write some advertising copy that accurately describes a product you really believe to be of high quality. Make your ad useful to consumers and completely honest—but at the same time make it one that will sell the product.

Understanding Emotional Appeal

Once you are able to evaluate ad claims so that they don't mislead you, you are ready for the second important skill necessary to deal with advertising. You need to be able to see how the ad is attempting to appeal to you, how it is trying to involve your feelings, wishes, and dreams. Ads attempt to make products look luxurious, sexy, grown-up, modern, happy, patriotic, or any one or more of dozens of other desirable qualities.

Nearly every ad (except purely factual advertising such as may be done by a grocery store listing its prices) attempts to give the impression that the product advertised will make the user one or more of the following:

Popular
POWERFUL
Happy
free
Successful
Loved
MORE GROWN UP!
Younger
A Real Woman
A REAL MAN
IMPORTANT
SAFE, SECURE
"WITH IT"
or
"IN"
CREATIVE

Of course toothpaste or shampoo or soap or deodorant will *not* make their users any of these things. But the advertiser tries to say that the user will *feel* loved or popular or whatever if he or she uses the product.

A product claim is an attempt to convince potential buyers that a certain product is better than any other and that it works. The appeal in the ad is to feelings and emotions. Many studies have shown that people's choice of a specific product and brand is more often based on feelings than on specific product claims. Most ads have both a reasonable-sounding claim and an appeal to feelings. The careful viewer or listener should be able to see in any ad not only what claim is being made, but also what emotional appeal is being used.

Here are some descriptions of ads or portions of ads. Read each and determine what feelings the ad implies the product will give its users. After you have done this, read the comments of a skilled ad reader that follow.

Appeal #I:

Picture of a cowboy riding a horse across the prairie with a sunset in the background. Cowboy is smoking a Manden cigarette.

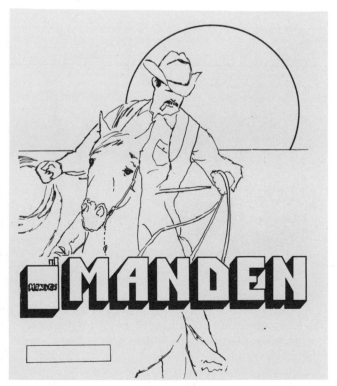

MANDEN

53

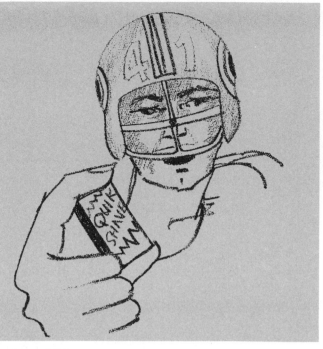

Appeal #2:
Automobile ad. The auto being advertised is parked in front of a huge mansion. A uniformed chauffeur stands nearby as a man in a tuxedo and a woman in a formal gown get into the car.

Appeal #4:
Football player in uniform holding up a package of Quik-Shave razor blades, saying "If Quik-Shave can shave me close, it can shave anybody."

Appeal #3:
Ad for any one of many possible products: Picture of a handsome man and a beautiful girl hugging each other while standing barefoot on a rock overlooking a lush green valley.

Appeal #5:
Picture of a beautiful rose with fresh morning dewdrops on its petals. The rose is growing out of a sink filled with soapsuds. Somewhere on the ad are the words "For hands soft as roses use Rosebud."

CU--Man with dandruff on his coat.

MS-- man looking at his dandruff.

man: Billy, Why don't you use. . .

CU--Man and woman.

Man: Jeanie, I don't know what I would do without you.

LS--Family in living room. Father taking pictures.

CU--Camera with chromakeyed sunset.

CU--Film and logo. Chromakey of sunset. Music over.

Appeal #6:

TV commercial. A man is unable to get a date with a girl he likes. A friend of his tells him that he has bad breath (or dandruff or body odor or acne or messy hair, or wears the wrong kind of clothes, or any one of dozens of such evils). He takes the advice of his friend, switches to the product being advertised, and in the end he and the girl are together.

Appeal #7:

TV commercial. A happy family is together in front of a fireplace. The father is taking a picture of the rest of the happy family. The ad is for a certain kind of film.

The Ad Reader's Comment

Appeal #1: The picture in this cigarette ad suggests the romantic ideal of the old West where every man was his own boss—a rugged individualist. It further suggests wide-open spaces and freedom. The ad appeals to people who wish to be considered rugged and strong, to people who feel a longing for freedom such as that suggested by the wide-open spaces of the wilderness. The ad suggests that smoking a Manden is somehow associated with these feelings. It also suggests that, since this rugged individual smokes Manden, if you consider yourself that kind of person you too should smoke this brand. The ad does not say that people will think you are a rugged masculine man if you smoke Manden, but the picture implies it.

Appeal #2: In looking for the emotional or feeling hook in an ad, always notice the setting in which the product is placed. Placing the automobile by the huge mansion with a chauffeur and people in expensive clothing says that this is a car for wealthy people: If you want to feel wealthy or be considered wealthy by others, then buy this car. The ad would never come out and say "Buy this car and people will think you're rich," but that is what the picture implies. Always look for the setting in which the product is placed for a clue to the feeling hook in each ad.

Appeal #3: This picture could be used for perhaps hundreds of different products. Probably the ad would show a bit of ad copy (written claims) at the bottom and a picture of the product somewhere. The picture suggests love, beautiful people, freedom, the beauty of nature, and even a certain "naturalness" and youth (the bare feet). The picture might be used in an ad for shampoo, deodorant, clothes, hair spray, or even cigarettes or jewelry. The emotional appeal of the ad is that by using the product advertised you will somehow be associated with the feelings the picture suggests. At the very least, the picture creates a good mood, so that the reader will experience a pleasant feeling when seeing the product's name.

Appeal #4: An ad in which a famous person appears is called an "endorsement" or "testimonial." Famous people are paid large sums of money to appear in advertisements holding, or sitting in, or wearing, eating, or drinking certain products. If you view such ads carefully, you will see that the celebrity rarely says he or she uses the product all the time. An advertiser can pay for famous people to appear to endorse his products. He will pick the person according to the feeling this person communicates—it should be a feeling the advertiser wants to be associated with the product. In the Quik-Shave ad, the maker assumes that men like to think of themselves as rough and tough, and the football player is an excellent choice to suggest such a person.

The idea behind endorsements is that some of the heroics and fame of the star becomes associated with the product and therefore with all the users of that product. The ad suggests that you, too, can be like this famous person just by using Quik-Shave.

Appeal #5: The rose suggests softness, beauty, and delicacy. By placing the rose in the soapsuds, the ad suggests that your hands will feel as soft as rose petals if you use Rosebud. The picture says this far more appealingly than words could.

Appeal #6: This is a very common kind of commercial. The suggestion is that simply by using a certain product, the user will become popular, be accepted where he was rejected before and will instantly solve his problem. The ad appeals to people who feel "left out" or unpopular. People who are popular know that their popularity has nothing to do with which brands they use.

Appeal #7: This ad creates good feelings by showing the happy family around the fireplace. The suggestion is that by using the kind of film being advertised, you too can achieve such family joy.

More Activities in Advertising Analysis

I. Make a portfolio of ads from magazines illustrating the various types of emotional appeals. Write an explanation of each ad's appeal.

AD: | APPEAL:

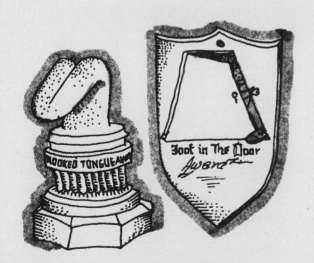

2. Have each class member pick either an ad in print (magazines, newspapers) or a TV commercial that best fits each of the following categories:

The World's Most Honest Ad.

The Crooked Tongue Award—For skill in sneaky, misleading, and deceptive use of language in ads.

The At-Least-It's-Fun Award—to the most entertaining ad.

The Foot-in-the-Door Award—to the most persuasive ad found.

The World's Worst Advertisement.

My Favorite Ad.

3. Write and/or draw an ad you consider to be honest, helpful, and important. The ad can be for some service or quality—peace, the elimination of poverty, love, better education, ecology, justice, etc. You may pick your own topic for the ad or use one of the following:

A horse is better than a car.

Garbage is valuable—save your garbage.

A toothpick

A button is better than a zipper.

No one over 21 should hold public office.

The legal age to vote should be 14 years.

Water.

A machine that dispenses a whiff of fresh air for 25¢.

An automatic watermelon deseeder.

A new invention—black and white television.

Old, warped phonograph records.

4. Find some old advertisements either in old magazines (at least ten years old, preferably older) or in books that reprint old ads. Bring some to class and examine how advertising has both changed and

remained the same in the past 50 years. You might also want to consider whether the changes in ads mirror the changes in people.

5. In some European countries that have commercial television, the ads are lumped together at the beginning of a program segment. If a one-hour program is shown, the first 8 or so minutes contain all the ads, and the program then runs uninterrupted for the next 52 minutes. What do you think of this system compared with ours? How might it affect the ads themselves?

6. In many countries the television and radio stations are run by the government. They contain no advertising at all. Do you think such a system (one in which the government provides all the money) has any advantages over a system like ours, in which advertisers provide the money? Are there disadvantages?

7. What kinds of ads are most commonly found in comic books? Why do you think advertisers choose these books?

8. One of the most important selling techniques in advertising is repetition. Repetition is used within an ad, and ads themselves are repeated frequently. A common means of repetition is to repeat the selling message several times within each ad. Ads on TV and in magazines are used dozens or even hundreds of times. Do you think this repetition irritates people or increases the likelihood of the ad's being successful? Is repetition used in a similar way in school?

9. Which of these do you think benefits most from good advertising: A truly superior product better than its competition? A product no better and no worse than its competition? A product obviously worse than its competitors?

10. Bring to class examples of what you consider the best ad and the worst ad you've ever seen. Be ready to defend your choices.

11. What would happen if all advertising were abolished?

12. Read and report on one chapter from any one of the following books:

The Permissible Lie, by Samm Sinclair Baker.
Test Pattern for Living, by Nicholas Johnson (available only as a Bantam paperback).
The Hidden Persuaders, by Vance Packard.
Down the Tube, by Terry Galanoy.
I Can Sell You Anything, by Paul Stevens.
Hot War on the Consumer, edited by David Sanford.
The Day the Pigs Refused to be Driven to Market, by Robin Wight.
Motivating Human Behavior, by Ernest Dichter.

13. Using everything you've learned in this chapter, analyze the ads on the following pages. Point out strengths and weaknesses, selling techniques, and psychological hooks.

14. If the project team on "The Image of Women/Men in Advertising" is ready, their report could be presented now.

Chapter 3
FILM

A blind man in a regular theater and a deaf mute in a movie theater should still get the essentials from the performance.

—Renḗ Clair, French filmmaker

Do you know what impressed me most about America? How photogenic everything was. The blocks and blocks of used car lots, and the endless freeways curling like gigantic snakes around the mountains. And the steel buildings shining through the clouds of pollution. The billboards—JESUS SAVES . . . DRINK PEPSI—all over. Americans are unaware of America! They eat hamburgers at a drive-in and stare out the car window but they don't see. Images are vital to me. They are strong and mysterious and they explain things to me about people.

—Michelangelo Antonioni, Italian filmmaker, giving his impressions on a tour of the U.S.

How can Alfred Hitchcock make any more motion pictures, now that things are happening in real life which once only happened in his films?

—Alfred Hitchcock, filmmaker

SO YOU THINK YOU UNDERSTAND FILM:
A Test

If you can correctly answer six out of the following nine questions before reading this chapter, you already know so much about film that you should be making films instead of reading about them. If you cannot answer at least six correctly you need to read the rest of this chapter.

The questions are not the most important ones that can be asked about film, but they do require a firm understanding of film.

I. A recent feature film produced by a major Hollywood studio left the audience sitting in front of a blank screen for 45 of its 90 minutes. The film was a box office success and played in your town. What was the film and why did the audience put up with the blank screen? (The blank screen was part of *every* showing and was not caused by equipment failure.)

2. The film *Fiddler on the Roof* was shot almost entirely with the camera lens covered by an ordinary nylon stocking purchased in a local department store. Why was this done?

3. If you watch a feature film for one hour, how many separate still pictures do you see? (Assumption: You don't fall asleep or leave for popcorn.)

4. You have a reel of film about two minutes long containing pictures of a rather expressionless face. How could you show this film in such a way that an audience would believe the face shows a variety of emotions? You may add additional film but cannot change the two-minute film you have.

5. Define (a) a scene, (b) a cut-away, (c) an establishing shot.

6. Which arts do not have "editing" as part of the creative process?

7. During which years did people go to movies and watch films without sound? (Pick any one year for your answer. If that year is one in which people watched films in silence the answer is correct.)

8. When were movies invented? (Answer must be accurate within five years of the exact date.)

9. How many pictures does a professional movie camera take in one minute of shooting?

ANSWER KEY:

Answers to the test questions can be found on the following pages of this chapter.
1 on page 68
2 on page 94
3 on page 69
4 on page 81
5 on page 72 and 74
6 on page 80
7 on page 95
8 on page 68
9 on page 69

People go to the movies for the various ways they express the experiences of our lives, and as a means of avoiding and postponing the pressures we feel. This latter function of art—generally referred to disparagingly as escapism—may also be considered as refreshment, and in terms of modern big city life and small town boredom, it may be a major factor in keeping us sane.

—PAULINE KAEL, American Film critic

Cinema, I suspect, is going to become so rarefied, so private in meaning, and so lacking in audience appeal that in a few years the foundations will be desperately and hopelessly trying to bring it back to life, as they are now doing with theater.

—PAULINE KAEL

I would say that there is no art form that has so much in common with film as music. Both affect our emotions directly, not via the intellect. And film is mainly rhythm; it is inhalation and exhalation in continuous sequence.

—INGMAR BERGMAN, Swedish filmmaker

You can't say as much as you can in writing, but you can say what you say with great conviction.

—ROBERT FLAHERTY, Documentary filmmaker

There is a simple law governing the filming of novels: if it is worth doing it can't be done, if it can be done, it isn't worth it.

—JOHN SIMON, film critic

"IT" the Film MEETS "I" the Viewer

Film critics writing about Stanley Kubrick's film *2001: A Space Odyssey:*

I think Stanley Kubrick's 2001: A Space Odyssey is some sort of great film and an unforgettable endeavor.

—PENELOPE GILLIATT in *The New Yorker*

In the first thirty seconds, this film gets off on the wrong foot and, although there are plenty of clever effects and some amusing spots, it never recovers. Because this is a major effort by an important director, it is a major disappointment.

—STANLEY KAUFFMANN in *The New Republic*

The world's most extraordinary film. Nothing like it has ever been shown in Boston before, or, for that matter anywhere.

—MARJORIE ADAMS in *The Boston Globe*

A regrettable failure, though not a total one. This long film is fascinating when it concentrates on apes or machines (though there is too much of this, too), and dreadful when dealing with the in-betweens: human beings.

—JOHN SIMON in *The New Leader*

Whenever the thunder of critical controversy rips through the air, one thing is certain: Lightning has struck. Stanley Kubrick's 2001: A Space Odyssey is just such a bolt of brilliant, high-voltage cinema.

—JOHN ALLEN in *The Christian Science Monitor*

2001 is not the worst film I've ever seen. It's simply the dullest.

—PETER DIBBLE in *Women's Wear Daily.*

You might think that six professional critics should be able to decide whether a major film is a crashing bore or an exciting masterpiece. But as the above excerpts from film reviews show, opinion on *2001: A Space Odyssey* was quite divided. Six jewelers would not disagree on whether a necklace was made of diamonds or glass; six wine tasters would never confuse a fine French wine with a homemade brew from last year's grapes. But six film critics can look at the same film and judge it anywhere between "dull" and "extraordinary."

Critical opinion of almost any film, whether by professional critics or the weekend filmgoer, will vary from those who consider it the best film they have ever seen to those who find it puts them to sleep. Often a film widely praised by critics will play only to the projectionist and empty seats, while another film generally conceded to be junk will break box office records.

One explanation for this wide range of opinions about film is that no two people "see" the same film. Each viewer enters into the world of the film and becomes part of that world. Comments made about films are often not comments about the film at all, they are comments that people make about themselves.

To help explain the special problem of talking about film, take a look at the drawing on this page and quickly (in five seconds or less) describe what you see:

Some will say the picture is an old lady, while others see a fashionable young woman. The problem is not one of disagreement about age. If you look at the picture long enough, you will see it change from young woman to old lady and back again. To see the gnarled old woman, focus on the neck band of the young woman—this is the old lady's mouth. The young woman's chin is the nose of the old woman.

The picture is no more an optical illusion than any other picture—or any movie. In looking at any object, we see selectively and are often surprised to find that others looking at the same picture or situation see something completely different.

You cannot accurately say the picture is of an old lady any more than you can say it is of a young woman. You *can* say, "I see an old woman" or "I see a young lady." Or "First I saw the young woman,

then I saw the older one." In other words, you can make a statement about yourself that is accurate. The same is true in film.

After watching a film, listen to an audience as it leaves the theater. You will overhear some say the film was terrific, good, artistic, perhaps a masterpiece. Others will call it a bore, dumb, meaningless, or simply bad. Some will leave the theater and have a long discussion, perhaps an argument, about whether the film was good or bad. But such a discussion is similar to an argument about whether the picture is of an old or a young woman.

Most likely the participants in such a discussion are not talking about the film at all; they are making statements about themselves but disguising the remarks as film criticism. In other words, most people do not distinguish between revealing personal reactions to film and criticizing the film itself. Let's say you watch a film and later tell someone, "It was a bore." What you really mean is, "I was bored." There is a big difference between the two. Your comment is about *yourself* and not the film. Probably there were some people in the audience who were not the least bit bored. There is no commonly agreed-upon standard by which to judge whether a film is boring or not. But it is easy for you to recognize your own feeling of boredom.

In talking about films, you should be able to distinguish between comments about the film and comments about your reactions to the film. When talking to friends you will probably stay on the level of speaking in terms of yourself—unless you want to impress someone with your knowledge of film. When attempting film criticism, especially in communicating with an audience who does not know you, making statements about yourself is of limited value. If someone tells you he found a certain film "sickening," that does not mean you will find it "sickening"; you might enjoy the same film. If you know the person well, you might be able to say, "If he found it sickening I wouldn't like it either." A most common error in film discussion is to confuse statements about the film with statements about oneself.

The following statements were taken from remarks overheard or from written film criticism. Each statement is presented in terms of talking about the film. Imagine you are the person who made each statement and change each comment into a statement about yourself. Do *not* do this by adding "I think" to the beginning of the statement. For example, the statement "It was good but too long" could be changed to "I enjoyed the film but was bored towards the end."

"It was a sick film."
"It was a confused movie with a stupid and complicated plot."
"A moving work of art that will drive you to tears."
"This flick is really fantastic—you just *have* to see it."
"A collection of clichés long overused in science fiction films."
"The film drives home an important message that will make you think deeply about the problem of honesty."
"A dumb, idiotic film that didn't make any sense."
"A brilliant comedy marked by a sparkling sense of humor."

66

Questions and Activities About Film Viewing

I. Explain the different feelings you have when you talk about a film in terms of yourself and when you comment in terms of the film alone. Which is most difficult?

2. What special skills or attitudes are needed for each kind of statement?

3. Reread the critical comments about the film *2001: A Space Odyssey* that began this chapter. Which are statements about the film and which about the critic? Do you think any of them are statements about the critic "disguised" to look like statements about the film?

4. Some film critics write more about their personal reactions to films, while others attempt to be more objective and judge the film on its merits as a work of art or entertainment. Examine several film reviews by any critics (such as those in a local newspaper or a magazine you read) and decide which approach they use most. Which do you prefer? Which would you use if you were a professional movie critic?

5. We could call those who write mainly in terms of their own reactions "subjective critics" and those who write about the film as "objective critics." Why is it not possible to be completely objective about a film? Is it possible to be completely subjective?

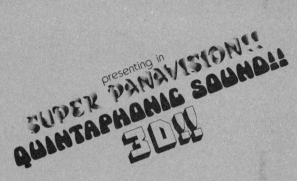

6. Earlier in this course, students selected a number of short films for classroom use. During this chapter, look at these films and talk about them as a class and in smaller groups. Talk about them in terms of yourself at first. As you gain more of the knowledge and vocabulary needed, talk about the films more objectively. Never have a discussion in which all you do is talk about "it"—the film.

7. Write two film reviews of some feature film you have seen recently or a short film shown in class. Review 1 should present you, the subjective critic, providing personal reactions to the film. Review 2 should present you, the objective critic, talking mainly about "it"—the film.

How Still Pictures Become Movies

Motion pictures are an art form, but they are also a mechanical process. The beginnings of all the other arts are lost in early history. No one knows who discovered sculpture, who made the first painting, or who wrote the first music. Film (and its cousin—photography) are the only art forms whose beginnings are known to us. The reason for film's unique position in the arts is that in order to have an art of film someone first had to invent photography and then find a way of showing photographs to create the illusion of movement. The invention of movies is often credited to Thomas Edison around 1895.

Let's take a look at the machinery of film—at what makes movies move.

Would you go to see a movie that sounded entertaining and exciting but featured a sign at the theater entrance that read:
"For One Hour Of This Two Hour Film The Audience Will Look At A Blank Screen!!"

Maybe you wouldn't, but you already have. In fact, every time you go to a film you spend half the time watching a blank screen. Perhaps an explanation is in order.

If you look at a piece of motion picture film, you see that it consists of a series of tiny pictures one on top of another, each divided by a thin black line. Home movie film is 8 millimeters wide, film used in school and on television usually is 16 millimeters wide, and film in movie houses is 35 millimeters wide, but they all work basically the same way. Looking at the piece of film, you will notice that each frame is a picture of the same thing in a slightly different location each time. The illustration on this page is 24 frames long and therefore shows movement over a one-second period of time.

One side of the film has holes, the other carries the sound track. The holes fit the sprockets and claws of a projector that moves the frames between the projection bulb and the magnifying lens 24 times each second.

The illusion of movement in movies comes more from the projector in the theater than from the camera used to make the film. A movie camera takes only still pictures, just like a snapshot camera. The main difference is that the movie camera takes 24 "snapshots" every second while a still camera, operated by hand, takes pictures only as fast as the photographer moves. A movie camera is a rapid-fire still camera; it doesn't actually take "moving pictures," it takes still photographs.

Films become moving pictures only because our process of seeing is sluggish. The retina of the eyeball (which sends images to the brain) retains images for about 1/30 to 1/10 of a second after an object is out of sight. A most extreme example of this after-image (often called "persistence of vision" because the image "persists" for a time) is the white or blue spot you see after someone has taken a picture of you with a flashbulb. This after-image persists much longer than most images because of its intensity and brightness.

When you watch a film you are "seeing" what was on the screen a fraction of a second ago. The movie projector has gears and claws that jerk the film in front of the lens in a stop-and-go-motion. Each frame stops in front of the projector light for about

1/24 of a second. Then the projector shutter (a whirring disk with holes that alternately block light and let it through) blocks the light while the next frame is pulled into place. In the course of a film, the projector shutter blocks out the picture for about 50 percent of the time, so that the audience is really sitting in front of a blank screen. During a two-hour film the audience will see 172,800 individual pictures (24 frames per second, 60 seconds per minute, for 120 minutes), but the projector shutter will have blocked off the light for about one hour of that time. During that time, the audience is watching the after-images.

Every film you see is, in a way, an optical illusion. The movement in movies comes from the combination of the slowness of your seeing process and the rapid movement of the film through the projector. Anyone who can push a camera button and thread a projector can make a movie.

Medialab

1. Look at the inside of a movie projector and find the place where the light passes through the film; also find the lens that magnifies the tiny picture and the claw that stops and pulls the film in jerks past the lens. Find the device that turns the sound track into sound.

2. Devise an experiment that demonstrates persistence of vision. Library research might be helpful in designing the demonstration.

3. *A Problem:* (a) What would happen if the camera used to make the film took 48 pictures each second instead of the normal 24? Note: the question is about the movie camera, not the projector. Assume the film will be projected at its normal 24 frame-per-second speed. (b) What would happen if the camera were run at 12 frames per second instead of 24?

How Pictures are Connected to Give Meaning

To make a film that people will enjoy, the film-maker has to know how to put together the thousands of pictures that make up the illusion of movement. Anyone who reads knows that a book is made up of words formed into sentences and then grouped into paragraphs. We could say this is the basic structure for a book. A person may have a huge vocabulary, but if he or she does not know how to put the words together into sentences and paragraphs, that person will never write a book. The basic structure of a film is less obvious but just as real and necessary.

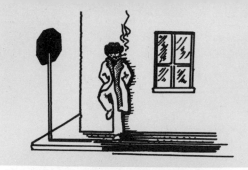

The basic building block of a film is the "shot." A "shot" is simply what happens in front of the camera from the time the camera starts until it stops. The "shot" is to a film something like the word is to a book. Just as words are put together to make sentences, shots in a film are put together to make "scenes." A "scene" is a single shot or a group of shots usually unified by time and place. Both a sentence and a scene are difficult to define but easier to demonstrate. Let's take a look at the making of just a few seconds of film that will eventually become part of a feature film. Here is the script for two scenes (numbers 114 and 115) from a film:

114 LONG SHOT—Bank building on busy street Entrance to bank is clearly visible. Pedestrians pass by, uniformed guard standing on left side of door. Charley is standing to the right of the revolving door.

Cut to

115 MEDIUM SHOT—Charley
Charley is chewing his ever-present toothpick and glancing around nervously. He checks his watch.

Cut to

CLOSE-UP—Charley
His hands move to his belt in a nervous gesture. We see a glimpse of the gun in his shoulder holster.

Scene 114 calls for only one shot—a long shot. A long shot is one in which the camera is set up a long way from the subject. This particular shot establishes the fact that Charley is standing in front of a bank and not just any downtown building. A long shot that "establishes" a location is called an "establishing shot." Establishing shots set the stage for the action to follow. The camera for scene 114 will probably be set up across the street from the bank or perhaps in a third-story window of another building across the street.

In the final film, scene 114 will last no longer than three seconds. To shoot the scene, however, the camera will be set up and as much as two to ten

minutes of film will be shot. From this the director or editor will select the best footage and decide if the pace of the film requires the long shot of the bank to be shown for two seconds or five seconds or maybe not at all.

Although this scene is very short and simple, it can be used to illustrate the work, cooperation and patience needed to make a full-length feature film.

For instance, if the ordinary people walking by the bank can be identified when the film is projected, they must give their written permission in the form of a "release" that allows their pictures to be used in the film. This is done to protect those who might find it embarrassing or somehow damaging to be recognized in a particular place by the public or those who simply wish privacy.

Most often the pedestrians and crowds you see in movies are paid to be there. They are called "extras" and are hired for films on a per-day basis. They are hired only to walk by a bank front, to stand on a corner, to carry a bunch of bananas through a fruit market, or to jump rope on a sidewalk. If the script called for a flock of pigeons to be on the sidewalk and to scatter when the hero approached, they too would be hired, from an animal rental specialist (for perhaps $100 or more a day).

If a film were being shot in your city, you might find an ad in the local newspaper asking for extras for crowd scenes. If you applied and were accepted, you might find yourself in a scene such as 114.

Long before actual shooting, the film's producers would have obtained the permission of the bank to film in front of it. The work would probably be done on a day the bank was closed. If the film is about a bank robbery, the bank might not like its name associated with the film. In this case the property department ("prop" for short) would have a fictional nameplate made so the bank would not be identified in the film.

72

As the actual shooting of scene 114 begins, the director yells, "Quiet on the set," and an assistant holds a slate in front of the camera reading "Scene 114, Take 1." The camera will run for several seconds or several minutes and then stop at the director's order. The slate board appears on the film as identification so that when the film is edited, a particular shot can be found easily. The actual film of the slate board is then discarded.

If the budget for this film is limited, the director might decide to save money by using a "stock shot" for scene 114. Film studios and special film libraries have large collections of footage of almost every conceivable situation, which they sell for use in films. If a director needs a picture of a house exploding, a ship sinking, a forest fire raging through thousands of acres, the skyline of Rome, a jet taking off or landing, these stock libraries will provide the needed footage.

One of the most commonly used stock shots, especially in television films, is the jet plane landing and taking off. These shots are used to indicate the movement or action of characters from one city to another. Some of these stock shots are supplied by the airlines, who realize that their name on the plane is free advertising.

So scene 114, one which will appear on the screen for a few fleeting seconds, requires much time and effort to shoot. Selecting just the right bank (which means first of all deciding whether the scene will be shot in a studio lot or "on location" on a public street); setting up the camera position; obtaining all the needed permissions; transporting the crew and actors to the right place at the right time; enlisting police permission to block off the sidewalk and perhaps the street (if the film takes place in the 1930s the director can't have 1970s cars driving past the bank); taking the light readings and supplying any artificial light needed; planning costumes and make-up; and finally directing the scene itself—all these take hundreds of hours of labor.

For scene 115, the camera will move closer to Charley, and again the filming will begin with the slate board. The director may decide to shoot this scene from two different angles and pick the best one later while editing the film. If so, the second angle will be slated as "Scene 115, Take 2." If, during the second take, Charley sneezes or a jet roars overhead or a member of the stage crew drops a

hammer with a loud clang, that take will have been ruined. It will then be started over, with the slate reading, "Scene 115, Take 3." The director's quest for perfection can result in scenes being shot and reshot four, six, or even twenty times.

After the entire film has been shot, the editing begins. The editor, or director, or both working together, select the best footage and make the crucial decisions of how long each shot should remain on the screen, which footage should be used and which thrown in the scrap pile, and in what order the shots should be arranged to tell the story best. The three shots in scenes 114-115 will pass across the screen in a matter of a few seconds. Few in the audience will appreciate the time, work, and effort that went into those few seconds of very ordinary filmmaking.

In our description of the structure of a film, we have compared a shot to a word and a scene to a sentence. The next larger division is a "sequence," which is a grouping of scenes joined by common purpose or setting. When people speak of the "chase scene" in films like *The French Connection* or *Bullitt*, they really mean the chase *sequence*. The two scenes used to illustrate "shot" and "scene" were part of a sequence informally called "Charley's Arrest." The arrest sequence will run in the film for about three minutes and will have about twenty scenes.

We can use the example of a football game to make these terms clearer. Let's say that a real football game is being filmed (or televised) as it happens—the director cannot control the action, so instead he must direct the cameras to cover what happens on the field. One of the sequences of the football game is the "Goal Line Stand."

SCENE 225—FIRST DOWN AND GOAL TO GO

Teams take positions with the ball on the six yard line.

LONG SHOT of players lining up.

Cut to

MEDIUM SHOT of quarterback barking signals and receiving the ball from the center. He steps back to pass and throws the ball.

Cut to

MEDIUM SHOT of intended receiver over goal line. The ball misses his fingertips by inches.

SCENE 226—SECOND DOWN AND GOAL TO GO

LONG SHOT— team huddle

Cut-away to

Cheerleaders

LONG SHOT—team breaks huddle and enters formation.

Cut-in to

EXTREME CLOSE-UP of football in center's hand.

Cut to

LONG SHOT—Ball is snapped to quarterback who is immediately tackled. Players untangle and the quarterback walks dejectedly back to huddle.

Scenes 227 and 228, we can guess, would show unsuccessful attempts at the third and fourth downs. Scene 229 would begin a new sequence, perhaps to be called "94-Yard Touchdown Drive."

Notice that scene 226 uses a shot called a "cut-away" and one called a "cut-in." A *cut-away* is a shift of attention from the main action to some related action. Shots of the crowd or the cheerleaders during a sports event on TV are cut-aways. They cut away from the main action. A *cut-in* directs the viewers' eyes to some very specific action or object within the main focus of attention. A close-up of a football sitting on the goal line or a close-up of a basketball hoop during a free-throw attempt are cut-ins.

Cut-ins and cut-aways are used in televised sports to provide visual variety. But they are also used in film because that is the way we look at things. If you attend a football game, your own eyes will spend most of the time watching the action on the field, but occasionally they will cut-away to catch some of the action in the stands. In a classroom you might cut-in to watch the teacher's hand as he or she picks up a piece of chalk. You might cut-away to look out the window at the passing clouds.

The cut-away is also useful to the director in manipulating time in a film. Film time and real time are different. If a film were made in real time, you would almost certainly find it boring. If the character were to fly from Chicago to Washington in a real-time film, you would have to watch the plane in the air for an hour—a scene that would quickly empty any theater. In a film-time film, you see the plane take off and a second or two later the traveler is standing beside the White House. Because you have learned to accept film time, this causes you no problems. Time in films is both compressed and expanded.

The cut-away is used to compress time. Take as an example a script that calls for a scene of a boat steaming up a river and docking at a wharf. In real time this action takes about 20 minutes, far too long for a film. The director solves the time problem by filming a long shot of the boat out in the river, cutting away to someone walking along the wharf to meet the boat, and then cutting back to the boat which is now in the process of docking. Viewers understand what has happened because they understand film language. Someone watching this sequence of shots who had never before seen a film would probably find it confusing and might even wonder if the boat docking is the same one that was out in the river just a second ago.

If the cut-away to the man walking were not used, the boat would be seen in one shot in the middle of the river and then would appear to jump magically to the dock. Viewers would not accept such a "jump cut." With the cut-away, the action appears smooth and logical.

Cut-aways are used in film because they are used in real life. This reduplicating of reality is also why there is a basic shot sequence in putting together films. The basic shot order is long shot, medium shot, close-up, and reestablishing shot. This order of shots was used in the "Charley's Arrest" sequence.

The long shot, also called the "establishing shot" (when it is used to establish where the action takes place), shows the main character or object in its general surroundings. The medium shot shows the main character or object in its immediate surroundings. A close-up includes only the main character or object or maybe even only a part of it. A reestablishing shot reminds the viewer of what surrounds the main character (or object). This technique is easy to see in this opening scene for a Western, which could even be used while the credits are being shown:

LONG SHOT—

Sunset over wide-open prairie land. The figure of a horse and rider trailing a cloud of dust can be seen in the distance heading toward a small town.

MEDIUM SHOT—

The man on horse rides along a crude trail.

CLOSE UP—

Now the man's face reveals a grim look of determination, with tightly clenched teeth; we see a sheriff's badge on his vest.

LONG SHOT—

(Reestablishing)—Another long shot reveals that the sheriff has reached the city limits just as the sun sets.

If this basic script were given to five different directors, each would film it in a slightly different way. Long, medium, and close-ups are only approximate terms for these shots. Some long shots are longer than others, just as some close-ups are closer than others.

This basic order of shots makes psychological sense because this is the way we see things in reality. Imagine entering a classroom on the first day of school. First you look around the room to establish where you are—a long shot. Then you begin to look around at who is in the room and to scan faces—your medium shot. Thirdly, you see someone you know and narrow in on an empty desk nearby—close-up. After you sit down you go back to examining the entire room again—reestablishing shot.

This basic order of shots is widely used, and you should be able to spot it easily in almost any film. You will also be able to spot many exceptions to this basic order, just as there are exceptions in reality. If your main concern as you enter the classroom is the rumor that your favorite teacher is teaching the course, you might look first to see who is standing in front of the room. In a film in which the person entering is concerned about the teacher, the first shot would then be an extreme close-up of the smiling (or scowling) teacher instead of a long shot of the room. A film director has to be part technician, part artist, and part psychologist to select the right shots.

In film there are as many "general rules" as there are exceptions to the rules. This basic shot order can even be completely reversed. Most often this is done for a shock effect. For example: An extreme close-up of a spider crawling; cut to a medium shot revealing that the spider is crawling on a person (shock number one); and finally a shocking long shot showing a cobweb-covered dead body complete with dagger. If this sequence were shot in normal order, the shock effect would be much less.

78

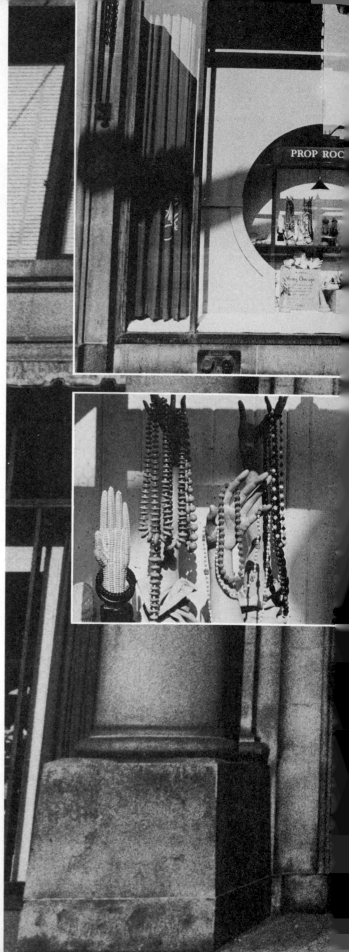

Editing

Every art form has some kind of "editing"—the process of selecting the best words, colors, lines, building materials or sounds and rejecting those that are less good.

When a film is finally shot, all the bits and pieces must be put together skillfully so the viewing audience will follow the story and be entertained. Putting together the bits and then selecting which are best is called editing. Editing in film can be done with a scissors and tape, but special editing machines make the job easier and faster.

The person editing the film works with a copy of all the footage shot, while the original is safely stored until the final steps of the editing process. (In making your own movies, you probably won't want to spend the extra money to have a copy of your film made.) The editor joins the shots into scenes, the

scenes into sequences, and the sequences into a film. He rejects film that is not exposed correctly, scenes that are poorly acted, or shots that contain too much or too little information. For professionally made films, ten to twenty times as much footage as is needed will be shot. To edit a one-hour film, the editor may have ten to twenty hours of film from which to select.

Just as the sentences and paragraphs of a book must be linked together by transitional devices, so a film must fit together according to the logic of its story. A film must be put together so the audience is involved rather than confused. For example, an editor putting together the scenes from our football game "Goal-line Stand" sequence could thoroughly confuse the viewers by changing the order of the shots. If the shot of the center snapping the ball were followed immediately by one of the pass receiver running after the ball, a confused audience would conclude that the center had somehow snapped the ball to the receiver.

Editing is the magic of film by which places hundreds of miles apart can be made to appear on the same street. Take a piece of film of a man looking out a window, join to that a two-second shot of ocean surf, and the viewer will conclude the man is looking out the window at the ocean. In reality, the man is in a Hollywood studio where there is nothing outside but a parking lot. The shot of the ocean probably shows a beach in Hawaii and was made three weeks later. Through the magic of editing, an audience will be led to believe he is on the ocean's edge.

There must be some logic to splicing one piece of film to another. If you were making a home movie of your baby sister and you first showed her crying into the camera, then followed with a shot of a huge black spider, the audience wouldn't know what connection there was between the spider and the baby. If, however, you showed your baby sister sitting next to a small tree and smiling into the camera; then looking toward the righthand side of the picture frame (where the tree is) and starting to cry; and then spliced on a shot of a spider crawling on a tree branch toward the left side of the frame (a shot you may have made years ago), the audience would assume the baby was being attacked by the spider. The act of looking toward the edge of the frame leads the audience to expect the next shot will be what that person sees.

A good many years ago a Russian director took a strip of silent film that showed an actor's face staring down. The director spliced this same shot in between a shot of a steaming bowl of soup, one of a dead woman in a coffin, and another of a child at play. His finished film was (l) face, (2) soup, (3) face same as in shot 1, (4) coffin, (5) face same as in shot 1, (6) child, (7) face same as in shot 1. Pretending it was a screen test for the actor, he screened the film for a small audience. The audience praised the unknown actor, commenting on his subtle expressions of hunger at the sight of the soup, grief at seeing the coffin, and amusement as he watched the child play.

This experiment illustrates the power of editing as well as its ability to make film acting much easier than stage acting. Even the world's worst actor can turn in an acceptable performance in a film if the editing makes it so. If his scene requires an expression of fright, our non-actor is told that he must look to his right and register an expression such as a person would have if he saw a 20-foot-tall rabbit outside the window about to eat the house. The director would have the actor (or non-actor) simply look to the right and express fright. If he cannot do even that, perhaps a well-timed and unexpected firecracker from a stagehand would accomplish the task. As edited, the actor's fright at the noise of the firecracker would be followed by a shot of the giant rabbit, and the audience would conclude that he is reacting to the sight of the rabbit.

When the editor works with the copy of the film, he or she cements together the bits and pieces of film that will eventually make a finished product. This glued-together film is then copied in a film lab into one complete piece of film. The magic of the movies has again been created out of skill, hard work, and patience.

1. While filming, you (a) shot a few seconds of a friend standing against a wall; (b) stopped filming but left the camera absolutely still, mounted on a tripod; (c) told your friend to walk away while the camera was not running; (d) began filming again without moving the camera. Describe the resulting film.

2. What would happen if, while filming, you did these steps? (1) You again pointed the camera at your friend standing against the wall. This time you ran the camera for as short a time as possible—ideally, advancing the film only one frame. (2) You stopped filming and left the camera absolutely still. (3) While the camera was not running, you told your friend to move four inches to the left. (4) You again ran the camera for one frame or as little as possible. (5) You stopped and had your friend move four inches to the left again. (6) Repeat this process until your friend is out of view of the camera. What would the resulting film show?

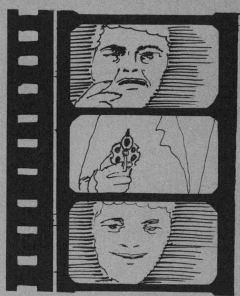

Face Filled
With Fear

Gun Pointed

Face With
Confident Smile

3. An editor can arrange the three shots described above in ways that will give the audience an impression of either cool courage or cowardice. Do you see how?

4. You are assigned to film a sequence in a railroad station. The script calls for the hero to kiss his leading lady, get on the train, and wave from the window as the train leaves. You arrive at the railroad station only to find that no engineer is available to move the train. No one else is able to drive the train and you cannot change the script. How would you solve this problem?

5. What would happen if a director arranged the following events? An actor located at A shoots an arrow as indicated in the sketch on the next page. The camera begins to film as the actor shoots the arrow and then quickly pans around and stops so actor B is in view. Actor B already has an arrow lodged in balsa wood underneath his shirt back. As the camera stops on him, he staggers forward and falls to the ground. How would this appear on the screen?

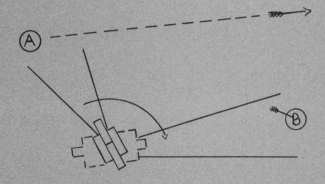

6. Using either a short film or a TV set in the classroom find clear examples of:
(a) An establishing shot
(b) A scene
(c) A sequence
(d) A shot
(e) A scene or portion of a scene in which a long shot is followed by a medium shot followed by a close-up.

7. Carefully study one scene or sequence in a film and see how it was made and put together.

8. Write a shooting script (no longer than one page) for the following action: A man approaches your house at night while you are asleep, leans a ladder against the house and begins to climb it. Halfway up his foot breaks through a rung on the ladder and awakens you suddenly from a deep sleep. Make your shooting script clear enough so that a director and actors could take it and actually make the scene from your directions. Number each shot and in-

dicate about how long each should last. The entire scene should last no longer than 45 seconds.

9. What effect on the meaning of the film would the elimination of shot 114 have in the example that began this section? Shot 114 was a long shot of the bank building on a busy street.

10. In the editing process one of the critical decisions to be made about each shot is how long it should be left on the screen. How would a shot that lasts too long affect an audience? A shot that is not shown long enough? Be aware that a shot left on the screen too long will have a different audience reaction than a shot left on the screen for too short a time.

11. Watch at least a few minutes of any kind of sport televised within the next week. While you watch, note to yourself the beginning of each new shot. Look for cut-ins and cut-aways. Be aware of the use of close-ups, medium shots, and long shots.

12. Prepare a rough draft of a shooting script (no longer than one-half page) that condenses time. Take any action that would normally take several minutes and condense it down to a few seconds. Your script should be clear enough for a director to use in making a film and should leave no doubt about what has happened.

13. Do you think the experiment of the Russian director involving the actor's face and the soup/cof-fin/child shots would work today? Remember that the people who viewed his experiment were very un-familiar with film.

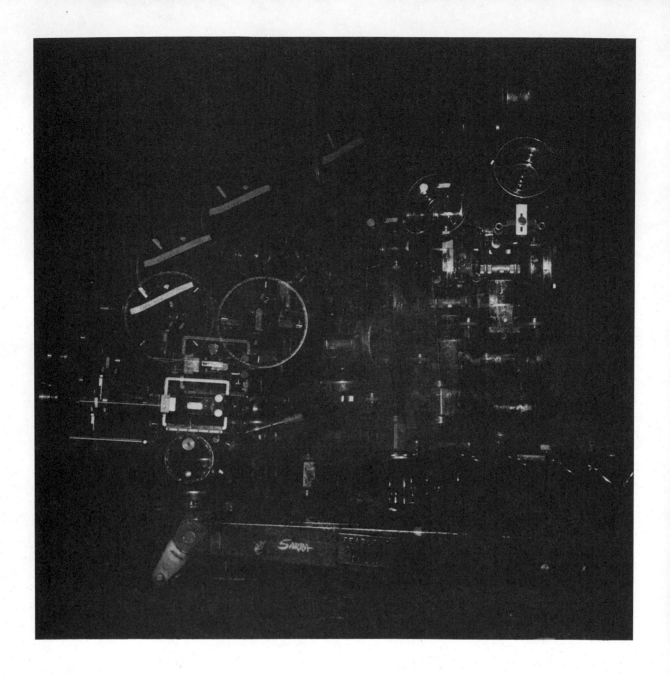

How the Camera Gives Meaning

Camera Movement

Movies move. Give a beginning filmmaker a camera, and he or she will move the camera back and forth, up and down, and play with the zoom lens like a new toy. An experienced photographer moves the

camera only when necessary and only after careful thought about how the movement will affect the viewer.

You should be able to recognize the most commonly used camera movements:

84

PAN

Pan: The tripod remains in place, but the camera swivels from left to right or right to left. The resulting shot duplicates a person surveying a situation by standing in one place and turning his head. A pan (short for "panorama") is used in film, as in reality, to survey a scene or to follow a moving object.

TILT

Tilt: A tilt shot is a vertical (up and down) pan. The tripod again remains in place while the camera pivots up or down. This seldom-used movement gives viewers a trip up or down a building, a person, or other tall object.

DOLLY

Dolly Shot: The camera rolls smoothly toward or away from the subject. In professional films the heavy camera is mounted on a special cart called a dolly. In amateur filmmaking the same effect can be obtained by moving the camera on a toy wagon, skate board, or any wheeled platform. The ground must be smooth for this shot to work.

TRACKING SHOT

Tracking Shot: Also called a traveling shot or a follow shot. This is a variation of the dolly. If you want to move the camera parallel to a fast-moving car, the camera can be mounted on a second car and moved alongside the car that is being filmed. If the camera is to move smoothly along rough or sandy ground (to follow two people walking on a beach, for example), a special wooden track is laid down and the dolly "tracks" along it for a smooth shot.

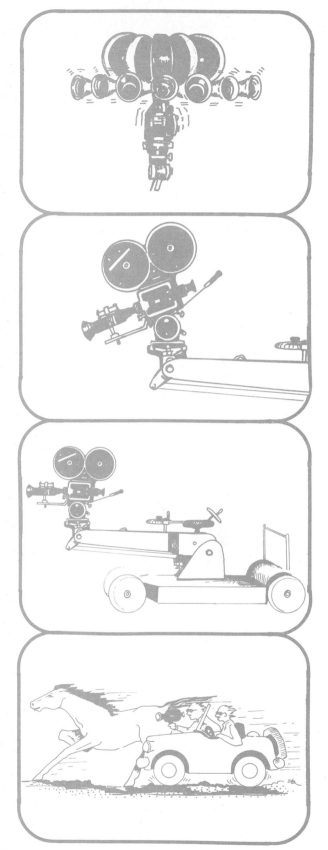

BOOM

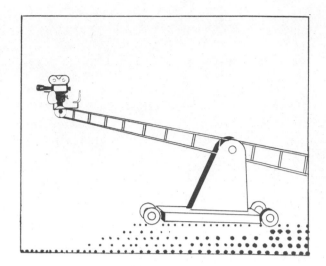

Boom Shot: This shot involves mounting the camera on a special and very expensive crane on the end of a hydraulic arm. The camera mounted on this "boom" can be moved very fluidly in almost any direction.

ZOOM

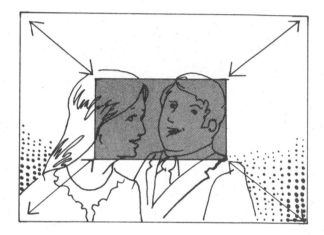

Zoom Shot: This shot is used for a dramatic or shocking effect. A zoom lens is manipulated while the camera remains stationary. The effect created is similar to looking through a telescope or binoculars and moving from the least to the greatest magnification (zoom-in) or the reverse (zoom-out). A zoom can be very fast or gradual. A zoom lens is available for home movie cameras and is much overused by amateurs. It is seldom used in professional films because there is no comparison to this kind of "seeing" in reality. Our eyes are not equipped with zoom eyeballs.

HAND-HELD

Hand-Held: All the previous techniques of camera movement depend on the fact that cameras are usually mounted on a tripod. But newer cameras are light enough to be carried by hand so that a film can be made by picking up a camera and walking around with it. This is most often done in documentary films and in filming for news.

A basic problem in any filming is where to place the camera. Part of that problem is solved by deciding what you want to appear on the screen. But the question remains, from what angle will you film?

Let's say you need a shot of a fighter standing alone in a boxing ring in an empty auditorium where tomorrow he will face the champ. Do you place the camera in one corner of the ring and look the boxer in the eye? Do you place the camera below the ring and look up at him, or perhaps even go into the rafters and look down on him? Each of these choices will produce a different emotional effect on the viewer. Your final choice will depend on the story line and on what you know about camera angle.

There are three basic camera angles:

You can place a camera rather normally so that you are looking at people or things from eye level.

You can place the camera below the person, looking up. This "low angle" shot is used when you want the viewer to "look up" to someone. A low angle shot will make a person appear strong and superior, even superhuman.

A "high angle" shot involves placing the camera so that it looks down on the subject being filmed. When we are above someone, looking down, we tend to feel superior to that person. So a high angle shot is used to make a person appear small, inferior, lonely, or looked down on.

If, in filming the boxer, we want to emphasize the fact that the boxer is small and alone in the face of the champ, the best camera angle would be in the rafters looking down. If the script calls for showing the boxer as superior and confident, then it would be best to place the camera below the ring, looking up at him.

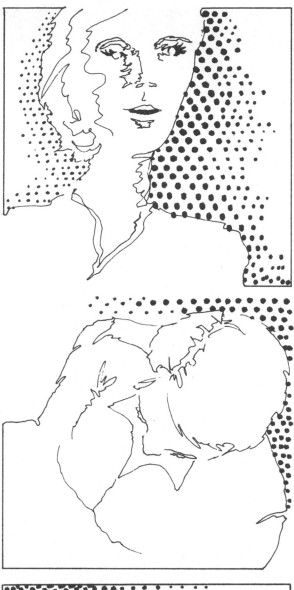

87

An awareness of how different camera angles make pictures look different is necessary to solve one of the basic problems of movies. Reality is three-dimensional, but the movie screen has only length and width. The problem is to give an appearance of depth to flat pictures. A movie camera is like a one-eyed person unable to see depth. If you close one eye and try to touch various objects a few feet from you, you will have difficulty because you can no longer see in three dimensions.

Camera operators rely on angles to give the illusion of depth. Consider these two pictures of the same face:

The picture below has more "depth" to it, because we see two sides of the face. The picture on top is "flat" and dull because it shows no depth. If you look at the faces in the ads in magazines, you will notice that rarely is a face shown straight on. A slight angle off to the side reveals more of the head and adds depth to the picture.

A movie screen, a TV picture tube, and a photograph all have only two dimensions and yet are called on to represent three-dimensional reality. Let's say your assignment is to take a picture of an automobile so that a person looking at it will have a good idea of what the car looks like from the outside. Where would you place the camera to take such a picture?

To give three-dimensional reality to static objects, you would use an angle-on-angle camera position. To use angle-on-angle positions, you take the film or picture from both an angle other than straight on *and* an angle other than eye level. If you look at pictures of products in ads, you will see that angle-on-angle shots are common indeed.

Straight On   Angle

89   Angle-On-Angle

Medialab

1. If there is at least one movie camera available for class use, make a film in the classroom with as many people as possible participating. The purpose of the film is to illustrate the various camera movements and angles discussed in this section. The film should contain examples of the following:

Pan from right to left
Pan from left to right
A tilt from bottom to top
A tilt from top to bottom
Dolly shot toward an object
Dolly shot away from an object
Tracking shot
Hand-held following a person or moving object
High angle shot
Low angle shot
Zoom—slow zoom *in* on an object
Zoom—slow zoom *out* from an object
Zoom—fast zoom *in* on an object
Zoom—fast zoom *out* from an object

These last four shots are possible only if the camera is equipped with a zoom lens.

Make no attempt to have the film tell a story or be *Godfather III*. Simply illustrate the above shots without making any attempt to connect one shot with the next. Use a film that needs no special lights.

2. When the illustration film is developed watch it as a class. Discuss the different effects of each shot. For example, does the pan from right to left feel any different than the pan from left to right? Does the "dolly in" towards a subject feel any different than a "dolly away" from a subject? What feeling does a zoom shot give? Judging from your own film, why do you think professional filmmakers seldom use a zoom shot?

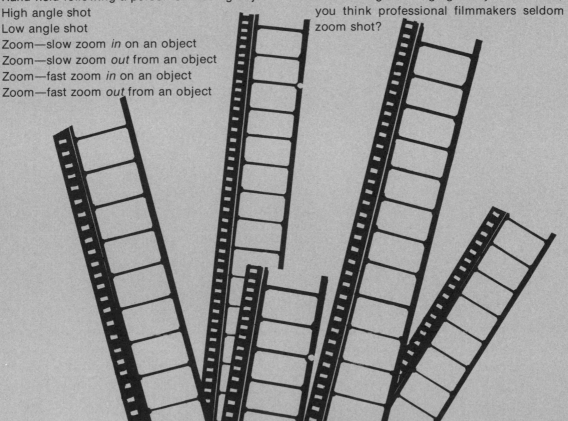

Meaning Through Color, Composition and Sound

A painter, a photographer, and a filmmaker all share a concern for the composition of a picture. Composition is how the parts of the picture are arranged, or "composed," within the frame. A poorly composed picture will look somehow "wrong" and will be distracting to the viewer. Seeing good composition in pictures takes a trained and knowledgeable eye. But even a beginner can quickly learn a few basic ideas of composition.

The kind of lines in a picture is important. If the film calls for a shot of the office of a strict army sergeant, the director will know that straight, angular lines should be part of the picture. Straight lines are masculine, curved lines feminine. The army sergeant would not have a round desk or rug or a chair with a curved back. But if the film calls for a shot of the bedroom of a female character presented as traditionally "feminine," the lines will be curved—oval rugs, paintings with curves, a vase. The choice of the kinds of lines in each room communicates to the viewer something about the kind of person who lives or works there.

If the director wants a quiet, peaceful sequence, he will compose using long horizontal lines. The horizontal line is restful, perhaps because it suggests the line of the body at sleep or rest.

Vertical lines inspire awe. The sight of a skyscraper as seen looking up from its base, the majestic vertical height of a distant mountain, or even the imposing vertical of a six-foot-tall adult as seen by a three-year-old are all awesome. If the director is filming a group of people sitting around a table and wants to show that one of the people is strong and determined, he might have that person stand up, thus creating a vertical line.

Diagonal lines suggest action and dynamism. If the script calls for a long shot of a racing car, the director will often make sure the camera is placed so that the car moves across the screen diagonally.

Pyramid Films

The angle of the raft makes this picture more exciting than if it were positioned parallel to the base of the photo.

From *400 Blows*.

The boy in this film still from *400 Blows* is trapped. The picture is composed in such a way that his head has little room to move within the frame. The fence also acts as a visual barrier adding to the feeling of imprisonment.

Pyramid Films

Low angle gives this character an added dignity and impressiveness. The contrast between the white face and darkness of the rest of the picture also adds interest.

Pyramid Films

A picture of a girl skipping rope sounds like quite an ordinary shot. But to make the picture more intriguing in this frame from the visual poem documentary *Jumprope*, the cameraman used an extremely low angle.

In this still from the film *Up the Down Staircase* the boy's leather jacket forms a massive dark shape filling nearly half the screen. His right arm extends directly across the other half of the frame suggesting a barrier. If the camera were placed where the three spectators are the idea of the huge dark shape blocking the way of Sandy Dennis would be missing. The boy with the jacket is not actually blocking the sidewalk but the careful use of shapes suggests that idea. The boy's head is also carefully placed in relation to the background. If the white wall with the graffitti were not placed where it is the picture would be much less effective.

The above still of Bette Davis and Joan Crawford is from the film *What Ever Happened To Baby Jane?* Analyze the shapes to see if they alone communicate something in this scene.

93

Color

Most of the film *Fiddler on the Roof* was shot through a camera lens covered by a piece of brown nylon stocking bought at a local department store.

Director Norman Jewison wanted the film to be filled with a warm and earthy feeling, befitting the peasant people and earthy location of the story. He found that a very sharp focus and bright colors gave a slick, too contemporary look. He also realized that "modern life is perceived sharply, but the moment you move into a period (of the past) it becomes, somehow, faded and a bit hazy. Your references to it are through old photographs and books and things. You don't see it quite as clearly as you see life today." To give the film the earthy look and to establish the mood of its taking place in the remembered past, the best solution was to shoot it through some kind of filter. The best results were obtained with a stocking that gave the film a subtle tint and softened the focus very slightly.

In addition to the unusual filter, nearly all primary colors were taken out of the sets used in the film. There are few pure reds, blues, or yellows in *Fiddler on the Roof*. The film gives nearly the "feeling" of black and white, although it was filmed in color.

Does the average viewer notice that certain colors are missing or call out to the projectionist to get that stocking off the projector? Of course not, but the techniques give the film a subtle reality it would not have had under more conventional shooting conditions. The careful use of color, composition, angles, camera movement and other film techniques should not be so obvious that they are noticed by the viewer, but they should influence the viewer. Film techniques work best when the audience is not aware they are working.

Special tricks are played with color in the film *Deliverance*, yet few viewers noticed them. When the film was developed, an extra degree of black was added. The effect is to give a sinister tone to the lush green color that marks most of the natural scenery. Director John Boorman felt that bright, lush green colors cause viewers to think "Isn't that pretty?" He wanted viewers to see the trees bordering the river not as pretty scenery but as a source of evil. He did this by adding black to the green.

The Godfather is carefully colored, and many shots are composed to resemble Italian chiaroscuro painting. This served to link this story of the Mafia with its origins and to give the picture a properly historical look.

Film directors do not take whatever color comes along. They realize that color, like composition and movement, influences the feeling the film creates in the audience. Often the color of a costume, an automobile, a room, or even an entire stage set is changed for a scene of a few seconds.

A film about a joyless future world that is run by a dictator and allows no personal freedom would not look right shot in "living" color complete with bright, gaudy splashes of color. Such a film would very likely be shot in a very subdued, almost colorless style, perhaps tending toward an overall bluish cast.

In the 1939 version of *Jesse James*, the James gang holds up a railroad train near sunset. Jesse leaps atop the train and runs along the top while it is still moving. The camera is alongside the train and shows James silhouetted against the darkening sky; below him the train windows glow with an orangish lamplight. Such care in filming was not done to make a "pretty" picture, but to point out through color the difference between the dangerous, cold world of the criminal and the comfortable, warm world of the law-abiding citizens.

A film director must be sensitive to colors and their effects on the mood of the audience.

Sound

Silent films always had sound—piano, organ, or orchestra accompaniment, along with the cheers and boos of the audience. Talkies have always had silence. The audio experience in any film is composed of these two elements—sound and silence. A creative filmmaker uses silence as much as sound. An amateur filmmaker looks with horror at holes in the soundtrack and fills them with noise or music.

Silence is what makes sound meaningful. Music can be considered a period of silence rhythmically interrupted. Without silence or at least a large variation in sound level, there can be no "beat," no rhythm. If notes never faded away into silence, music as we know it would not exist. Most musicians realize that most of their time "playing" is spent in silence, changing from one note to another.

Film sound can be either *synchronous* or *nonsynchronous*. Synchronous sound is the most common; the soundtrack includes the sounds that are being made by the people or things on the screen at that time. Two people talking, a gun being fired, the sound of marching as a military parade passes are all examples of synchronous sound. Background music is nonsynchronous sound; the viewer doesn't see the orchestra playing the music. Often scenes will contain a combination (or "mix") of both kinds of sound.

Some sound is recorded "live" on the location where the film is made. The camera is placed in a soundproof blimp so viewers will not hear the motor running. In documentary films when a hand-held camera is used, the blimp is sometimes discarded to increase portability. In these films, viewers can hear the sound of the camera running if they listen closely.

Much sound is dubbed into the film after the original shooting. In a fist fight, the appropriate crack of a fist hitting a jaw is added in a recording studio. In reality the actor probably missed or at least pulled his punch, making it silent. If all the thousands of fist fights ever filmed were to be run with live sound, the results would be more humorous than dramatic and exciting.

Dubbing is often used to produce natural sounds that add to the atmosphere. A lightning storm, the clanging of the jailhouse door, the crash of an overturning automobile, a squeaking floorboard, or a ticking clock are all added from a library of recorded sounds prepared for such occasions. The proper "mood" sounds can add suspense and realism to any film.

Actors Henry Fonda, Gary Lockwood, and Jack Elam are being "tracked" down by the camera in this scene from *Firecreek*. While the action continues, the director Vincent McEveety (in white trousers) leads the cinematographer William Clothier.

In the shot from *The Heart is a Lonely Hunter,* the director used a low-angle shot to emphasize the pleasure with which Alan Arkin's infantile friend accepted a cookie. In a figurative sense, he is smiling with his stomach as well as his face.

I. Much of what is said in this chapter about color, composition and camera angle is as true for still photography as it is for motion pictures. Find photographs or illustrations in magazines or elsewhere that illustrate each of the following:

(a) The use of a low camera angle to make a person or thing appear superior.
(b) The use of high angle to make a person or thing seem inferior or weak.
(c) A picture strengthened by verticals.
(d) A picture made restful with horizontal lines.
(e) Diagonal lines used to suggest excitement and dynamism.
(f) Curved lines and circles used to suggest femininity.
(g) Color carefully chosen to give added meaning to a picture.

2. View and discuss a number of short films using all that you learned in this chapter. Notice how the various techniques of editing, shot selection, camera angle and movement, color and composition are used to make the film work. Select one film and write a short paper pointing out how the filmmaker used these techniques to give the film meaning.

3. Take a short sequence from a film and play it for the class without sound. Have volunteers bring a tape or record they think would fit as a soundtrack for that sequence. Play the soundtracks while watching that sequence and notice how different sounds influence the meaning or feeling of the sequence.

4. The film techniques discussed in this chapter are often used to manipulate audience feelings during a feature film. By using the proper technique the director can create in the audience feelings of sympathy for the main character, even if he is a criminal. Every shot is carefully planned to produce the desired audience reaction. These same techniques can be used in television news camerawork, in documentary film designed to persuade the audience, in still photos used in magazines or newspapers, in advertising photography and TV commercials, or in educational films.

To illustrate how these techniques might be used to influence public opinion, discuss each of the following situations and how they could be presented in film to produce different audience reactions:

Situation 1: A man working on an assembly line at an automobile factory. Picture this man first as an example of the dignity and nobility of work; as the common man as hero. Then devise a way to picture the man as a slave of the assembly line, condemned to waste his life in a meaningless task.

Situation 2: An automobile as a magnificent example of the miracle of modern technology. Then picture the automobile as a wasteful piece of junk that pollutes the air and destroys the environment.

Situation 3: An ordinary man walking down an ordinary street. First use various film techniques to make the audience suspect he is a suspicious character and very dangerous. Then present the same man and the same street in such a way that the audience will respond to the man as a trustful, courageous sort of person.

5. View a film that was made to persuade. A TV commercial might work, even better is one of the many free-loan films produced by corporations and organizations to present themselves in a favorable light. After viewing the film discuss how the filmmaker used various film techniques to create a favorable impression and to persuade the viewers.

6. As a final project for this chapter, make a short film (one to three minutes). Write a script, plan your shots and scenes carefully and use some of the techniques learned in this chapter. Such a film can be made by one person or by groups of two, three or four students per film. Use film equipment from school or home and be sure to edit your film. When the films are all completed, have a class film festival and screen all the films. The crew of each film should be prepared to answer questions from the rest of the class.

Chapter 4
COMICS AND CARTOONS

All comedy is based on man's delight in man's in-
humanity to man.

—AL CAPP, creator of "Li'l Abner"

Cartooning is a *fairly* sort of proposition. You have to
be fairly intelligent—if you were really intelligent
you'd be doing something else; you have to draw
fairly well—if you drew really well you'd be a painter;
you have to write fairly well—if you wrote really well
you'd be writing books. It's great for a fairly person
like me.

—CHARLES SCHULZ, creator of "Peanuts"

The comic strip is one of the liveliest cultural off-
shoots of our slam-bang civilization. America and
the comic strip were made for each other.

—WILLIAM LASS, *Saturday Review*

HIGH SIERRA

CARTOONS THAT BITE

Every year Americans purchase about 300 million comic books. Comic strips are most people's first contact with a newspaper, and every survey about newspaper readership comes to the same conclusion—the comics are the most widely read part of the daily paper. For many adults comic strips are a daily ritual, and for many youngsters comic books are their main contact with reading.

Almost all newspaper comic strips are "syndicated." That is, a cartoonist draws one cartoon or strip a day (or one a week) and sends his work to a newspaper syndicate. The syndicate distributes the strip to those newspapers who subscribe, and the cartoonist receives payment through the syndicate from each subscribing newspaper. Gag cartoons

(one box rather than a strip) that appear in magazines are done by free-lance cartoonists who work in much the same way as free-lance magazine writers. The free-lancer works at home and sends cartoons to various magazines; if it is published, the cartoonist receives from $10 to $400 for publication.

Some comic strips are purely entertainment, while others give advice, preach, or make political and social comments. Many papers feature "political cartoons." These single-frame cartoons are editorials in pictures and therefore are most often found on the editorial page. The illustration shows some political or "message" cartoons from newspapers and magazines.

102

1. What comics—comic books, comic strips, magazines with cartoons—are read by class members?

2. Find out who syndicates some of the cartoons carried in your local papers.

3. Have each person select the comic strip or comic book that he or she reads most often. Write a brief article about the strip or book explaining why it is fun to read, what some of the cartoonists' favorite subjects are, what the comic says about life, and what kind of person probably would not enjoy that particular comic.

4. Look at the satirical cartoons on the preceding pages and determine what each one says.

5. Find political or "opinion" cartoons in your local papers or elsewhere and bring them to class. Collect them on a bulletin board; when there are enough gathered, discuss those that seem most effective.

6. If you have some artistic ability, draw your own opinion cartoon and add it to those on the bulletin board.

The Language of Comics

Each mass medium has its particular "language," one that most users of the medium understand but probably could not describe if they were asked. Film viewers know that a fade or a dissolve means a long passage of time, book readers expect a new chapter to mark a new time frame and location for the action, TV viewers know a station break does not mean the end of a program, and newspaper readers do not confuse the news with the ads. Why? Because users of each medium are familiar with each one's "language." They have learned these languages by experience with the media rather than through schooling or formal training. An adult who for some reason saw his first film at the age of 25 would no doubt find it utterly confusing and meaningless. The "language" of a medium is made up of the conventions, the rules, and the traditions that media creators use.

An adult who read a comic strip for the first time at the age of 25 would wonder what all those strange blobs are over the characters' heads. Of course, most comic readers learn the language when they are children. They learn that those strange blobs are dialogue balloons. Dialogue balloons show many examples of the conventional language of comics. The tail pointing to the speaker is one such example. If the balloon line is perforated, the character is whispering—the cartoonist need not print out "this person is whispering." Tiny letters in a huge balloon show the speaker is frightened or ashamed. A cry has a jagged outline, while a telephone voice has a zig-zag shape with an arrow going into the telephone.

If a balloon has little icicles underneath it, the words or thoughts are taken to be cold and cruel or filled with hatred. If the balloon has a series of small smoke-puff circles instead of a tail pointing to the character, the contents of the balloon are thoughts or dreams rather than spoken words. If the balloon has an arrow pointing outside the cartoon frame, the speaker is "off screen."

Swearing is expressed by "&#*@" or "! ! ! !." A lightbulb above a character's head means a bright idea, dark clouds signify depression, and musical notes symbolize music or singing. The boldness of the letters indicates the volume of the speaker's voice.

Speed lines indicate movement and sometimes are used to hide violence. A split panel can be used to indicate the passage of time without having to write "and several hours later . . . ."

These bits of the total language of comics are only a few examples of the hundreds of details that make up the grammar of the medium of comics. They are rules, but they are not strict and can be changed and modified in a great number of ways.

1. Go through a single comic book or a variety of newspaper comic strips and find examples of at least a dozen techniques of comic strip language. Include at least three that are not mentioned in this chapter.

2. Look at several comic strips and comment on the size of the head, hands, and feet. Explain what you find.

3. Comment on the different drawing styles used in various strips. In writing, attempt to describe the style of a particular cartoonist or strip.

4. Why do you think comics are so popular? In other words, what need do they supply to the millions who read them so faithfully? Do different comic strips satisfy different needs?

5. Cross-Media Study: Find characters who appear in comic books or comic strips and also in other media—television, film, records, radio?

6. Each person should bring to class (or be provided with) a comic book. Go through the comics and note visual techniques that are also used in films.

7. Prepare a research report on the history of comic books in the United States.

THE TECHNIQUES OF THE GAG CARTOONIST

A "gag" cartoon is a single picture, a comic strip is a row of pictures, and a comic book is a collection of stories told through comic style drawings. All these comic forms share the same language or drawing devices discussed earlier in this chapter. But the gag cartoonist has at his disposal the most finely developed bag of techniques to evoke laughter.

The following article explains these techniques:

From pp. 127-129 in *The Fourth Estate: An Informal Appraisal of the News and Opinion Media* by John L. Hulteng and Roy Paul Nelson. Copyright ©1971 by John L. Hulteng and Roy Paul Nelson. By permission of Harper & Row, Publishers, Inc.

To the real cartoon connoisseur, gag cartoons represent the ultimate in the cartoon art. A gag cartoon is to be savored, not just looked at and read. The subtleties of the art are considerable. Note that the whole point revolves around a single line printed underneath the cartoon, and everything within the drawing must substantiate that point. The gag cartoonist keeps his cast of characters down, his setting simple. He must make it clear at once, without benefit of balloon, just who within the drawing is doing the talking.

Sometimes he can put his gag over without a single word below. He does his gag in pantomime.

Unique among the cartoonists, he has no particular axe to grind. His objects of ridicule, when they are there, are hard to pin down, because he deals less in personalities and issues, more in general statements about mankind. He's never happier than when, in the words of Stephen Becker, he is "jabbing away constantly at our shams and illusions," in the end touching upon some social truths.

Gag cartoonists come onto their gags in a number of ways. Sometimes they dream up a scene and then try to think of a gag line to fit. Sometimes they start with the line and then try to imagine a scene that will make it funny.

Most gag cartoonists buy ideas from outside sources. They pay the writer 25 percent of what the cartoon earns and keep 75 percent for themselves. Only the cartoonist signs the cartoon.

It has been said that the novelist has only a few basic plots to work with. Similarly, the gag cartoonist has only a few basic ideas. The setting, the props, the characters change; the words in the gag lines vary; but the ideas stay the same. Perhaps you will recognize them:

1. *The cliché*. Most journalists avoid the cliché. Not the cartoonist. He can take a cliché and let a character act it out literally and get a laugh. Virgil Partch (Vip) is a master of this kind of gag. Vip shows a man lying dead on the sidewalk while a companion, unaware of the tragedy, turns to watch a cranky woman walk by. He says: "Boy! If looks could kill, eh, Steve?" Dana Fradon makes a slight change in a cliché in a *New Yorker* cartoon dealing with deteriorating telephone service. An executive leads a caller to the door and says: "Don't try to call me. I'll try to call you."

If you'd like to be a gag writer or cartoonist, see what you can do with these cliché lines:

"Mind if I smoke?"
"You'll only encourage him."
"You're putting me on!"
"Been waiting long?"
"Am I getting warm?"

2. *That's life*. This includes any gag that depicts life as it is, so that the reader will identify with it, and say, in effect: "Ain't it the truth!" Tom Henderson in *The Saturday Evening Post* shows a lazy, unshaven man reading the paper, the phone on a table at his side. His wife has just picked up the receiver after rushing in from in front of the house where she's parked the car. She's dropped groceries all the way in and knocked over a chair in her rush to answer the phone. She's saying: "Yes, he's here."

3. *Ridiculous situation*. The opposite of "That's Life." It just couldn't be that way! Jerry Marcus in *True* shows a worried woman driver with her husband sitting beside her. In back of her is a line-up of cars: a tow truck, a police car, and an ambulance. The husband says: "Relax, it's probably just a coincidence."

4. *Out of character.* Sweet little old ladies act like gangsters. Kids talk like grownups. Ministers sit in bars with wordly ladies. Mulligan in *The New Yorker* shows a perplexed man and wife looking at a painting of a haggard, hungry woman holding a baby with a frightened child at her side. The scene is stark, desolate. The painting is signed "Norman Rockwell." The man says: "Well, there must be more than one Norman Rockwell in the world."

5. *In character.* People act out their roles to the point of absurdity. B. Tobey in *The New Yorker* shows a young man smooching with a girl on a park bench. With his free hand, and without looking, he's reaching into a bag of popcorn and feeding a flock of pigeons and squirrels. An older couple is walking by, and the man says to the woman: "Now, there's a warm human being for you!"

6. *Understatement.* This is a favorite theme for the cartoonist; and British cartoonists have no corner on it. Jim Stevenson in *The New Yorker* shows an art expert examining a fine painting while the owner looks on. The expert has rubbed his finger across the painting; his finger is wet with paint. He says: "Well, this initial test suggests that the authenticity of your Rembrandt may be questionable."

7. *Exaggeration.* The opposite of understatement. Chon Day in *The Saturday Evening Post* shows a tired, middle-aged man asleep on a couch. His wife, a little portly, and a lady visitor are talking. The wife says:"He's had a bad back ever since he carried me over the threshold."

8. *Ingenuity.* When man solves some problem in an unusual way, readers—even readers of gag cartoons—appreciate it. Rodrigues in the *Saturday Review* sets up a situation in which a father tries to tell his side of the story to the rebel generation. He's fat, balding, middle-aged, well dressed; he stands on stage at a run-down coffee house, strumming a guitar. Hippie types sit watching him, frowning. He's singing:". . . Oh, my kid's twenty-three and he don't like to work/Oh he don't like to work/When I was twenty-three I worked very hard/Oh, I worked very hard . . ." You could classify it as "out of character" too.

9. *Stupidity.* This kind of a gag especially satisfies the reader, because the cartoonist always lets the reader know something a chief character in the cartoon doesn't know. The reader feels superior. Jerry Marcus again, this time in *The Saturday Evening Post*, shows a middle-aged couple already in bed, looking bored. Another couple, obviously visitors, stand nearby. The man, hat in hand, says: "Well, we really must be going."

10. *The letdown.* Some definitions of humor suggest this is the real core of humor. The reader is led to believe one thing, then finally disappointed. Jim Stevenson again, in *The New Yorker*. A guru sits in front of his high mountain cave. Around him are signs scrawled on the rock: "Smile and the world smiles with you, cry and you cry alone"; "Early to bed and early to rise makes a man healthy, wealthy and wise"; "A penny saved is a penny earned"; and so on. A disappointed, slightly hippie-ish couple has just arrived. The girl says to her male companion: "Something tells me we've come to the wrong guru." Again, classification can never be exact. This gag could serve as an example of "Understatement."

1. What is a "gag" cartoon?

2. Make your own gag cartoon. If you cannot draw, use existing drawings or magazine cut-outs. Or use an existing cartoon but change the "punch line."

3. Make a class collection of gag cartoons.

4. The article suggests ten types of "gags" commonly used in cartoons. Find examples of at least five of these techniques.

5. Are these same techniques used in other forms of humor? Find examples.

109

Cross Media Study:
Comics and Film

Learning about the techniques of any one mass medium often helps to understand other media. This is particularly true for films and comics. In a sense, comics were the first movies. Like films, they use a series of still pictures to tell a story. In film the movement is supplied by the camera and projector, while in comics the movement is supplied by the tricks of the artist.

The following article was written by Steve Gerber, who writes comics for the Marvel Comics Group and also makes his own amateur films. He is well aware of the similarities between film and comics. Since the previous chapter of this book was about film language, you should have little trouble applying film techniques to the world of the comic artist. So here, with a little help from Spider-Man, is "What Comics Can Teach You About Movies":

WHAT COMICS CAN TEACH YOU ABOUT MOVIES

On the most basic level, the creators of comics and of cinema are faced with an identical task: telling *a story in a series of still pictures designed to give the illusion of motion.* Visual narrative and movement are at the heart of both. And the similarity doesn't end there. Even the mechanics of the creative processes are remarkably alike for the two media. Much of the terminology is the same. Indeed, the only major differences between comics and film—with regard to storytelling, at least—are technological ones.

From: October 1974 issue of *Super 8 Filmaker* 145 E. 49th St. NYC 10017.

Otherwise, a comic book is essentially a film . . . in shorthand. And what comics teach about movies is something all film-makers, whether their interest is documentaries, sports reportage, or biblical epics, need to know: how to construct a dramatic event in pictures; how to make the pictures move.

Comics Writer as Screenwriter

A comic book begins as a typed synopsis in which the writer describes the action of the story page-by-page, often even panel-by-panel, for the artist. Every relevant detail is noted: what each character is thinking and feeling, the expression on his or her face, what they're doing with their hands, their physical appearances, and the settings, costumes, and props. Diagrams and sketches of these items may be attached to the synopsis. And snatches of dialogue are often included, along with ideas and suggestions for unusual artistic approaches and special effects. Fight scenes are choreographed. The need for an establishing shot here, a close-up there, is specified. And perhaps most importantly, the writer includes his estimation of how much space (one panel, one page, more?) each scene should require.

Thus, in form, style and content, the writer's synopsis for a comic book bears a distinct resemblance to a story treatment for a film. In the case of a silent Super-8 short, it could even suffice as a shooting script. Chances are a film will require *more* separate shots than a comic book, but consider the advantages of planning your shooting on paper as tightly as I plotted the following sequence (shown in Illustration One) for a comics story called "The Return of the Living Mummy."

Scene One: Four-panel opening page with sequence as follows: (1) A wooden crate resting on the floor of the Egyptology Room of a New York museum; the room is dark except for moonlight streaming in from a skylight in the ceiling. (2) Same shot, but a bandaged arm is smashing out from inside the crate. (3) Entire crate flies apart as Mummy breaks out. (4) Large panel; long shot of Mummy looking around him, seeing the various Egyptian art objects, etc.

Now let's look at the techniques involved in creating these panels. A picture of a wooden crate in a dark room (panel 1) is not particularly exciting in itself, but it poses a mystery immediately. And the lighting, a single shaft of cold silver from above, casting stark, shifting shadows, at once establishes a mood. Without a word of dialogue or sound effects, we've made it clear that whatever is inside the crate poses a threat.

To create the same mood in a film, you might open with a long shot of the Egyptology Room, with the crate standing upright in the center of the shot. (Actually, the panel shows you where to position the crate and your camera.) You might dolly in slowly, silently, until the crate dominates the scene. Then you halt, holding the same shot for several seconds. Next, the crate itself rocks ever so slightly, creating the first sound of the film. Suddenly, one arm smashes out, splintering the wood; then you cut to the other arm, as it comes through the opposite side of the crate; then a foot, a knee—each shown separately in a series of quick cuts. Then you take a long shot as the entire crate flies to pieces, revealing the full, fearsome figure of the Living Mummy.

The point here is that the storytelling techniques of comics are directly translatable into cinema *if* you, the screenwriter, remember that the comic book is presented in visual "shorthand." That "if" cannot be overemphasized because the image on the movie screen is constantly changing. The viewer isn't able to flip back a page or reread a panel to see if he's missed something. This means that the "information gap" between panels in comics can be much wider than the gap between shots in film; every action need not be detailed in comics. Nevertheless, the technique of getting from "point A" to "point B" in the plot is virtually identical.

Comics Artist as Filmmaker

Working from the writer's synopsis, the comics artist draws the story in pencil, breaking down each page into an arrangement of panels, composing each individual drawing, deciding which panel, if any, should dominate the page. In so doing, the artist also contributes to the overall rhythm and continuity of the story, and performs functions similar to those of the filmmaker.

The *size* of a panel drawn by the artist, for example, is roughly analogous to the *duration* of a shot—but only roughly. In this respect, comics are somewhat more flexible than film. The artist is not bound to a rectangular frame of predetermined size for his panel; the filmmaker, obviously, is. Then too, the effect on the audience of certain approaches to a scene are different in comics. For example, a page consisting of, say, nine small panels, may either elongate a scene, if the content of those panels is calm, or produce a staccato effect, if the content is rapid-fire action. A series of short, quick shots in a film is almost always likely to produce the staccato effect, regardless of content.

Aside from these differences, though, the function of the artist is like that of the filmmaker who does all the shooting, as well as directing and editing. The artist, in effect, sets up the shots, blocks the actors' movements, and generally provides the print equivalent of shooting and cutting. Dialogue and captions are added later by the

AN ORDINARY SHIPPING CRATE --IN THE NIGHT-DARKENED *EGYPTOLOGY* WING OF A NEW YORK *MUSEUM.*

A NOT-SO-ORDINARY *FIST*--

--SWATHED IN *BANDAGES*, CAKED WITH THE DUST OF AGES, SMASHING *THROUGH* THE CRATE.

NO MORE CRATE!

BUT AMID THE JAGGED WOODEN *SHARDS,* ILLUMINED ONLY BY THE PALE *MOONLIGHT* THAT STREAMS THROUGH THE CEILING WINDOW--

--STANDS A *MAN* (OR A STIFF, WITHERED *CARICATURE* THEREOF) WHO HAS LIVED FOR *3000 YEARS.*

FOR ALL BUT A BRIEF *INSTANT*-- A FEW SHORT DAYS LESS THAN ONE YEAR AGO--

--HE HAS SPENT THE PAST THIRTY CENTURIES *ALONE*-- ENTOMBED --AND YET-- *HE STILL LIVES!*

Illustration One: Comic-book as shooting script for opening sequence of mystery thriller; four panels outline storytelling techniques.

comics writer, much the same way background music and voice-overs might be added to a silent film. As a rule, the tighter the writer's synopsis, the more likely it is that the artist will draw what the writer had in mind.

This principle can be applied to cameramen and screenwriters, too. Take, for example, the 3-panel sequence shown in Illustration Two. Matt Murdock—the blind attorney who is secretly Daredevil—hears a voice from "off-screen." We cut immediately to the source of that voice as Matt perceives it with his radar sense, the unique power that compensates for his lack of sight. For the comics artist, Sal Buscema, each of these panels required written description down to the last detail. The direction from which the voice is heard, the "radar sense" special effect, the matched action from the "real" shot to the "radar" shot, and, of course, the urgent emotions and movements of both characters all had to be carefully written out for the artist to render the sequence correctly. For the cameraman/filmmaker the same tightly written directions are useful. If you construct your shooting scripts meticulously, the chances of making the film you set out to make are greatly enhanced.

At the same time, a certain flexibility is desirable. Just as the comic artist may visualize a shot differently than the comics writer, you-as-cameraperson may discover possibilities that you-as-screenwriter never anticipated. For example, look at Illustration Three, which shows the final comic-book scene of a drama

Illustration Two: Comic-book version of off-screen voice, special effects, and matched cuts.

about a clown who commits suicide in a swamp. The monster you see is Man-Thing, here returning to his home. The scene is composed of three panels (note the vertical dividing lines that do not completely separate the panels), and is the comic-book equivalent of a "tracking shot." The idea for this scene was entirely the creation of artist Mike Ploog. My own unimaginative little ending for the story had Man-Thing wander off into the marshy swamp in a typical "wide angle" type panel. Mike, on the other hand, created a more powerful image by depicting the monster in two stages of movement: standing fairly straight, and

then slouching deeper into his swamp.

The monster seems to lumber towards the reader. If you were filming him, he'd be moving closer to the camera even as you move it, tracking him from left to right. Meanwhile, the characters who are delivering their final lines about the clown's suicide, seem to recede in the background. Of course, this type of scene should be carefully planned *before* it is shot on location, but you should also give yourself room to maneuver once you get there. Lots of good ideas come at the last minute from unexpected sources.

114

Illustration Three: Comic-book equivalent of a tracking shot; the monster is shown in two stages of movement across three panels.

Besides sharing responsibility with the writer for visualizing the overall flow of the story, the comics artist shares a concern for using a variety of panels. Nothing is duller in comics than a page made up entirely of close-ups (or long shots, or medium shots). In breaking down a page, the artist again plays the role the filmmaker and film editor play in shooting and cutting a scene—all the same rules apply. The shots must be varied, but they must come together to form an integrated whole. And just as the overuse of "trick shots" is to be avoided in film, overly fragmented layouts are shunned in comics. If the cinematic technique is to be effective, it must be "invisible." It must not distract the viewer or it defeats its own purpose.

We turn to Matt Murdock again—this time in his Daredevil outfit (see Illustration Four)—for a lesson on placing diverse shots together. Gene Colan drew this fight sequence using several separate panels arranged to present a coherent picture of the action. First you see the scene from street level (low-angle shot); then from the air (vertical dolly shot); then from the points of view of the villain, the hero, and the spectators. The result is a fast-paced action sequence (it *had* to be fast paced, we ran out of pages), in which the reader alternately sees the fight as if he were a participant and an observer. Comic books are filled with sequences like this one; for the filmmaker, they are the perfect guide to new framing techniques and the provocative use of various camera angles.

Summing up, then, it seems clear that the problems to be solved by the comics artist and the filmmaker are very nearly the same. How best to tell the story? Convey the mood? Follow the action? To find answers to these questions, you can study the work of the best comics artists: Jack Kirby, John Buscema, Rich Buckler, Jim Starlin, Will Eisner, as well as those whose work is displayed here. Their names are usually listed in the credits which appear at the beginning of each comic-book story.

How Comics and Movies Differ

Despite all the parallels, comics are not movies, and understanding their dissimilarities is equally vital to learning about one from the other. First, and perhaps most crucial, even though the goals and the creative mechanics of the two media are analogous, the technologies involved are vastly different.

Given a little imagination and a sharp pencil, the comics writer-and-artist team can tackle anything from a sock hop to an intergalactic war. Most Super-8 filmmakers, it's safe to assert, will probably have to content themselves with the more mundane end of that spectrum. So it's wise not to let yourself be influenced by the subject matter of the comics, enticing though it may be. Don't attempt the sequel to ''2001'' as your first film—or even your second.

But realize, too, that it would be far more difficult to portray the sock hop scene in comics than it would be in movies! The finite areas of space on the comic-book page, the limited number of pages in each book, and the relative unsophistication of the four-color printing process, make subtleties extremely difficult to achieve, both in dialogue and illustration. Generally speaking, the artist gets only one chance at each panel. The printer has a range of only thirty-two shades. If the writer writes too much copy, he covers up the picture.

The filmmaker has a far greater range of moods, textures, and colors to work with. He need not rely on archetypes and stereotypes as substitutes for real characterization. (True, the comics are maturing, coming out of that phase, but it's still possible to tell the hero from the villain by the color of their respective long-johns.)The themes that film can explore are much richer, much more complex. And they can be dealt with, even by the novice, with a pretty fair degree of success.

Illustration Four: Comic-book version of fight sequence; the series of panels shows how to place together different camera angles and points of view.

1. Make two columns on the blackboard and list ways in which comics and films are alike and ways in which they differ.

2. Could an intelligent person who has never seen a comic strip in his life understand a Spider-Man comic right away, or would it take some learning first?

3. Which do you think would be most difficult to become—an expert creator of comic books or a film director?

4. Find examples in comics that would match the following devices in films: a frame, a scene, low angle, high angle, camera movement, subjective camera, color used to influence feeling, lighting used to influence feeling. Make a scrapbook of examples, labeling each one and explaining why each particular technique is used.

On the opposite page is a copy of the Code of the Comics Magazine Association of America. Publishers who are members of the association agree that their comics will conform to this code.

Similar professional codes exist for films, advertising, radio, and television.

Compare the comics code with the code of the Motion Picture Association of America. Which do you think is stricter and why?

If you were a comics publisher would you agree to abide by this code?

Do you disagree with any of the items in the code? Are there other items you would want to add?

CODE OF THE COMICS MAGAZINE ASSOCIATION OF AMERICA, INC.

Adopted on October 26, the enforcement of this Code is the basis for the comic magazine industry's program of self-regulation.

CODE FOR EDITORIAL MATTER

General Standards Part A

1) Crimes shall never be presented in such a way as to create sympathy for the criminal, to promote distrust of the forces of la and justice, or to inspire others with a desire to imitate criminals.

2) No comics shall explicitly present the unique details and methods of a crime.

3) Policemen, judges, government officials and respected institutions shall never be presented in such a way as to create disrespect for established authority.

4) If crime is depicted it shall be as a sordid and unpleasant activity.

5) Criminals shall not be presented so as to be rendered glamorous or to occupy a position which creates a desire for emulation.

6) In every instance good shall triumph over evil and the criminal punished for his misdeeds.

7) Scenes of excessive violence shall be prohibited. Scenes of brutal torture, excessive and unnecessary knife and gun play, physical agony, gory and gruesome crime shall be eliminated.

8) No unique or unusual methods of concealing weapons shall be shown.

9) Instances of law enforcement officers dying as a result of a criminal's activities should be discouraged.

10) The crime of kidnapping shall never be portrayed in any detail, nor shall any profit accrue to the abductor or kidnapper. The criminal or the kidnapper must be punished in every case.

11) The letters of the word "crime" on a comics magazine cover shall never be appreciably greater in dimension than the other words contained in the title. The word "crime" shall never appear alone on a cover.

12) Restraint in the use of the word "crime" in titles or sub-titles shall be exercised.

General Standards Part B

1) No comic magazine shall use the word horror or terror in its title.

2) All scenes of horror, excessive bloodshed, gory or gruesome crimes, depravity, lust, sadism, masochism shall not be permitted.

3) All lurid, unsavory, gruesome illustrations shall be eliminated.

4) Inclusion of stories dealing with evil shall be used or shall be published only where the intent is to illustrate a moral issue and in no case shall evil be presented alluringly nor so as to injure the sensibilities of the reader.

5) Scenes dealing with, or instruments associated with walking dead, torture, vampires and vampirism, ghouls, cannibalism and werewolfism are prohibited.

General Standards Part C

All elements or techniques not specifically mentioned herein, but which are contrary to the spirit and intent of the Code, and are considered violations of good taste or decency, shall be prohibited.

Dialogue

1) Profanity, obscenity, smut, vulgarity, or words or symbols which have acquired undesirable meanings are forbidden.

2) Special precautions to avoid references to physical afflictions or deformities shall be taken.

3) Although slang and colloquialisms are acceptable, excessive use should be discouraged and wherever possible good grammar shall be employed.

Religion

1) Ridicule or attack on any religious or racial group is never permissible.

Costume

1) Nudity in any form is prohibited, as is indecent or undue exposure.

2) Suggestive and salacious illustration or suggestive posture is unacceptable.

3) All characters shall be depicted in dress reasonably acceptable to society.

4) Females shall be drawn realistically without exaggeration of any physical qualities.

NOTE: It should be recognized that all prohibitions dealing with costume, dialogue or artwork applies as specifically to the cover of a comic magazine as they do to the contents.

Marriage and Sex

1) Divorce shall not be treated humorously nor represented as desirable.

2) Illicit sex relations are neither to be hinted at or portrayed. Violent love scenes as well as sexual abnormalities are unacceptable.

3) Respect for parents, the moral code, and for honorable behavior shall be fostered. A sympathetic understanding of the problems of love is not a license for morbid distortion.

4) The treatment of love-romance stories shall emphasize the value of the home and the sanctity of marriage.

5) Passion or romantic interest shall never be treated in such a way as to stimulate the lower and baser emotions.

6) Seduction and rape shall never be shown or suggested.

7) Sex perversion or any inference to same is strictly forbidden.

CODE FOR ADVERTISING MATTER

These regulations are applicable to all magazines published by Members of the Comics Magazine Association of America, Inc. Good taste shall be the guiding principle in the acceptance of advertising.

1) Liquor and tobacco advertising is not acceptable.

2) Advertisement of sex or sex instruction books are unacceptable.

3) The sale of picture postcards, "pin-ups," "art studies," or any other reproduction of nude or semi-nude figures is prohibited.

4) Advertising for the sale of knives, concealable weapons, or realistic gun facsimiles is prohibited.

5) Advertising for the sale of fireworks is prohibited.

6) Advertising dealing with the sale of gambling equipment or printed matter dealing with gambling shall not be accepted.

7) Nudity with meretricious purpose and salacious postures shall not be permitted in the advertising of any product; clothed figures shall never be presented in such a way so to be offensive or contrary to good taste or morals.

8) To the best of his ability, each publisher shall ascertain that all statements made in advertisements conform to fact and avoid misrepresentation.

9) Advertisement of medical, health, or toiletry products of questionable nature are to be rejected. Advertisements for medical, health or toiletry products endorsed by the American Medical Association, or the American Dental Association, shall be deemed acceptable if they conform with all other conditions of the Advertising Code.

COMICS MAGAZINE ASSOCIATION OF AMERICA, INC.

300 PARK AVENUE SOUTH   NEW YORK, N.Y. 10010

Chapter 5
NEWS MEDIA

No experiment can be more interesting than that which we are now trying, and which we trust will end in establishing the fact, that man may be governed by reason and truth. Our first objective should therefore be, to leave open to him all avenues of truth. The most effectual hitherto found, is the freedom of the press. It is therefore the first shut up by those who fear the investigation of their actions.

—THOMAS JEFFERSON

All government handouts lie. Some lie more than others.

—JOSEPH ALSOP

Every government is run by liars.

—I.F. STONE

I think the inherent right of the government to lie—to lie to save itself when faced with nuclear disaster—is basic, basic.

—ARTHUR SYLVESTER

Why should freedom of speech and freedom of press be allowed? Why should a government which is doing what it believes to be right allow itself to be criticized? It would not allow opposition by lethal weapons. Ideas are much more fatal things than guns. Why should any man be allowed to buy a printing press and disseminate pernicious opinions calculated to embarrass the government?

—NIKOLAI LENIN

The mass media cover Blacks as a matter of routine only on their sports and crime desks. And this situation will remain until more Blacks are hired, promoted and moved into ownership positions in the media.

—LIONEL C. BARROW, JR.

UPI Telephoto

What Is News?

I think news is... _____

Before you read this chapter, spend a few minutes thinking about your own definition of "news." In one or two sentences, write a definition of what you think "news" is. Do this now before reading any further.

If you were to ask a dozen professional news people for their definition of news, you would collect a dozen different opinions. The dictionary definitions are most unsatisfactory. For example, one dictionary's first meaning for "news" is "recent events and happenings, especially those that are unusual or notable." Yet the fact that you cleaned up your room yesterday for the first time in two years would fit the definition, but would hardly make the morning paper or the evening television newscast. The dictionary proceeds, realizing perhaps that the first definition was inadequate, and describes news as "new information about anything previously unknown." Yet when you walk into math class and learn for the first time how to factor a quadratic equation, that is new and "previously unknown" information to you. But again your math class would not make the news. So what is news? Can it be defined?

For you and me, the consumers of news, news might be defined as what newspapers and newscasters decide is newsworthy. But the people who run the papers, write the stories, and edit the news have to decide what is news and what is not. They do this partly by following tradition and partly by making educated guesses about what the reading, viewing, or listening public wants to know.

If a man eats a fish that is not news, but if a fish eats a man that is probably news. If a fish eats a man in your town, it will certainly be news in your town. If a fish eats a famous person, it will probably be news all over the world. News favors the unusual. NBC-TV news commentator David Brinkley explained: "If an airplane departs on time and arrives on time, it isn't news. If it crashes, regrettably, it is." Walter Cronkite of CBS-TV was once asked by a college student why so much coverage of college students is devoted to their misbehavior. She asked why there wasn't more coverage of the students who quietly go to class instead of the others who demonstrate, riot, or stage wild fads. That, Cronkite explained, would be "a little bit like having to report all the cats that aren't lost that day."

The desire of journalists to report the unusual (a desire encouraged by their readers' attraction to the out-of-the-ordinary and the bizarre) explains why so much news is "bad news." People often ask why newspapers and TV newscasts dwell on tragedies, accidents, crimes, and generally negative human events. Since planes are so safe, people are usually honest, buildings rarely burn, and criminals are only a small part of the population, such negative events are precisely what is *unusual*. It is normal for things to work fairly well and for people to lead their lives with a certain degree of contentment. A society in which the good news would be out of the ordinary would be a sorry place to live.

But all that is unusual is not news (cleaning your room, for example) nor is all news unusual. There are other qualities that make items newsworthy.

Timeliness

News should be new. There is no such thing as old news; only history. Instant news has become the standard.

Significance of the Event

This news value demands the most personal judgment on the part of the news editor. News events must be events that are important in some way to the audience.

Closeness to the Audience

A fire in the house next door would certainly be news in a neighborhood paper, or even a city paper. But the fire would not be news on national television since it would not be "close" enough to most viewers. A national election in Afghanistan might not even be mentioned in American papers, but the national election in America will fill several editions of most American papers.

Importance of the People Involved

If your next door neighbor were famous, the fact that his or her house burned down might make national news. A speeding ticket is rarely a newsworthy event unless the person speeding is well known.

Drama of Human Interest

The news has to be interesting (some say entertaining) or the audience will not read or watch it. Some stories are included with the news because they are particularly dramatic or have "human interest" value; this news value can make an otherwise minor event into real news. If the fire in your neighbor's house happened on Christmas Day, for instance, the "human" values in the story might make it national news.

Medialab

What is News?

1. Examine each story in the first three pages of your local paper and determine which news value or values it embodies. By doing this, you will be answering the question "Why is this news?" Apply the five news values mentioned earlier in order to make your judgment. Do the same for the first three stories carried on local TV news.

2. Decide if each of the stories on the first three pages of the paper fits the definition of news you wrote at the beginning of this chapter. After doing this, you might want to change your definition of news.

3. Discuss the various definitions of news proposed by class members and try to find one that most of the class agrees is valid.

4. *Debate or Discuss:* News reports should place more emphasis on good news than on tragedy and violence.

124

Where Do People Get the News?

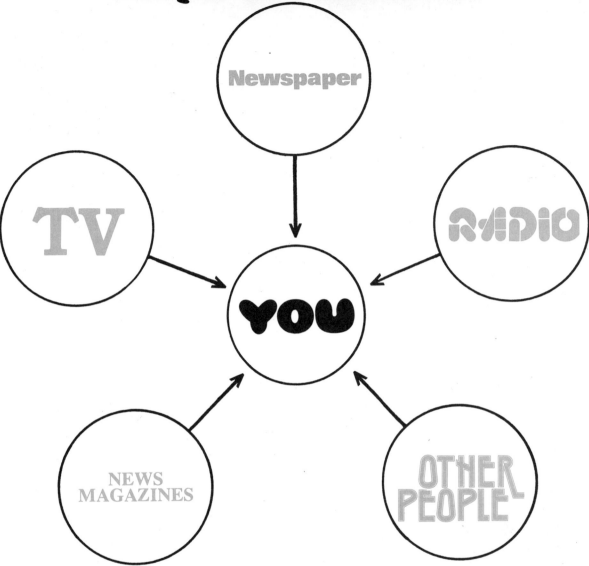

The diagram above shows the various sources of news available to most people. Conduct a study among the class, asking each person, "Where do you usually get most of your news about what is going on in the world today?" Compile the answers and determine which of the five sources is the most important to the class. Each year or two the Roper organization conducts such a survey across the nation asking a sampling of people the same question. Their results over recent years are:

Source of most news:	12/59	11/61	11/63	11/64	1/67	11/68	1/71	11/72
	%	%	%	%	%	%	%	%
Television	51	52	55	58	64	59	60	64
Newspapers	57	57	53	56	55	49	48	50
Radio	34	34	29	26	28	25	23	21
Magazines	8	9	6	8	7	7	5	6
People	4	5	4	5	4	5	4	4

1. Compare the results of your survey with that of the Roper study. Try to explain any differences you find.

2. Discuss how people's answers have changed through the years. What do you think the survey reveals about how well-informed people are about world affairs?

3. Survey the class to determine *which* newspapers, magazines, and television and radio newscasts provide news to the class as a whole.

4. Find out who owns the news sources in your city—television and radio stations, and newspapers. Does one owner control several sources—say, two newspapers or a newspaper and a TV station?

How Do the News Media Differ?

Each news medium may report the same news, but the words, the images, and their effects on the news consumer are different. Let us consider how the four major news media (TV, newspapers, news magazines, and radio) differ in their presentation of the news.

Television, and to some extent radio, have one or two individuals who present the news. The television viewer sees a person who is regarded as trustworthy or hears a radio announcer with a voice that rings with authority. Newspapers and news magazines lack this element of personality and instead must depend on the printed word. Television news commentators are often highly paid public celebrities. Some TV newscasters are not reporters at all; they are announcers with a favorable public image. Newspaper editors are seldom recognized on the street and rarely become celebrities.

Television can present a strong visual image. A written news story about poverty will probably make less of an impression on a reader than a powerfully filmed story of a starving family. A live telecast of some important happening is far more memorable and emotionally powerful than a series of printed words in the newspaper. Television news is at its best when it can show what is happening as it happens —the moonwalks, Congressional hearings, wars, disasters, and sports news. But the national networks require events of great national interest before they will preempt regularly scheduled programs for a live telecast.

Another form of network news presentation that is almost as powerful as the live events is the documentary. These 30- or 60-minute network "specials" have included in-depth programs on topics such as poverty, the law, the Pentagon, migrant workers, pollution, football injuries, and hundreds of other subjects. Such documentaries are usually about topics of national interest and are probably produced by one of the three networks for nationwide broadcast rather than by a local station about topics of local concern. Documentaries are expensive to produce and invariably lose hundreds of thousands of dollars for the networks. They also do rather poorly in the ratings but are still seen by millions of people and sometimes have a noticeable effect on government agencies and future legislation. It is in these documentaries that television is at its best in providing in-depth news coverage. In 30 or 60 minutes, a documentary can give the depth lacking in the evening news as well as present powerful visual images to influence opinions.

For the majority of viewers TV news *is* the evening network news. A television newscast allows viewers less selectivity than a newspaper allows its readers. A newspaper reader scans the headlines first and reads complete stories only if the headline promises a story of particular interest. Television news is usually watched in its entirety. The TV viewer is not as free to select which items he or she will watch. NBC reporter John Chancellor explains: "Many middle-aged people who are opposed to television news are people who had not been subjected to serious news, seriously presented, until they got a television set and until television in the mid-fifties began to develop serious news programs. Before that people read daily newspapers. They read the sports page, the comics page; they glanced at the front page. If people didn't want to read about an ax murder, they didn't have to read about it. If they didn't want to read about the race problem, they didn't have to read about the race problem. Then came television, and the problem with television is that to see any news you pretty much have to see it all. It's a very brutal way to get the news. You can either accept the news that comes off the tube or turn it off completely. You can't pick and choose."

Another unique quality of television is that the presence of film or TV cameras at an event can change what happens there. In the presence of a camera we all become actors, and the TV news is then a stage on which we can act out our viewpoint. Some members of Congress objected to the idea of television for Congressional hearings (during the Watergate hearings, for example) on the grounds that the presence of TV cameras would create a "circus" atmosphere. Such fears turned out to be groundless, but the TV camera does have far more effect than a newspaper reporter with a notepad or even a radio reporter with a small tape recorder and microphone.

Still another aspect of television news not shared by the other media is that a person who looks and sounds believable can influence viewers' opinions. The same person's statement in printed form might be far less convincing. However, the opposite can also be true. This importance of the "image" a person can project over television has become an important factor in political campaigns.

For the most up-to-the-minute, quickest, and most frequent news, no medium currently does better than radio. Many stations carry news every 30 minutes; most, every hour. Radio is available anywhere in the country, thanks to transistors and radios, which have become almost standard equipment in automobiles. Using a telephone, a radio station can present news almost as it happens. A newspaper has to wait at least until the next edition, and television has to wait (with the exception of special bulletins) until the next evening news. Radio serves the nation more as a headline service. Many radio news broadcasts are what is called "rip and read." The disc jockey (the same one who announces songs and reads commercials) is given paper news reports ripped off the wire service teletype machines and reads them for five minutes.

Better radio stations, usually in large cities, have news departments and reporters out looking for stories. But radio news today functions best as a headline service, as a first alert for important news and as the best source for recent weather information. There are a few stations in the country that broadcast only news, but they have yet to make a serious contribution to the advancement of news broadcasting.

The physical problems associated with publishing a newspaper make the news at least a few hours old by the time the paper hits the street. But of all the news media, newspapers offer the reader the greatest variety and the greatest personal choice.

THE SAME NEWS... RE

Each newspaper reader is his own editor, selecting the news that he thinks important and ignoring what he thinks is not. Newspapers have been in the news business far longer than any of the electronic media and have the most people working on gathering and writing the news.

Newspapers and news magazines provide the most in-depth reporting while radio and television (with the exception of documentaries) go into comparatively little detail. The news magazines often provide the most detail about national stories but are a few days or a week behind the newspaper in getting the news to the readers.

There are currently three national news weeklies with a large circulation— *Time* with over 4 1/2 million readers; *Newsweek* with about 3 million; and *U.S.News and World Report* with about 2 million circulation. The news magazines report the news with a more entertaining and lively writing style than the newspapers. They have more time to prepare in-depth stories since they are not under the pressure of putting out a daily publication. However, both *Time* and *Newsweek*, which are printed on a Sunday, can publish a story about an important event that happened on Saturday in time for the newsstand copies available Monday morning. *Time* is printed in seventeen printing plants around the world and begins selling each edition on Sunday night and Monday morning in 185 countries.

The news magazines provide the most retrievable form of news. Radio and TV news is gone once the show has ended. A listener or viewer cannot go back and check what was said or find the text of the news broadcast at a public library. A newspaper is more retrievable, but its size and inexpensive paper make it hard to store without the inconvenience and expense of microfilm. News magazines are readily checkable in any library or in the basement piles of back issues in thousands of homes. A news magazine also is on sale for at least a week, while a newspaper disappears from newsstands within twelve hours. Because of this longer sales period and the relative permanence of the news magazine, magazines have developed a policy of stressing facts and checking their accuracy.

News magazines (as well as other magazines that use factual articles) have full-time "checkers" whose only job is to verify the facts reporters mention in their stories. The checkers also are charged with filling in facts that reporters leave out. A story might come to a checker with a line such as "The 00-man Sudanese army . . ." It will be up to the checker to fill in the "00". Other news media are careful about reporting facts accurately, but none treat even the least important facts with the passion of news magazines. The presence of insignificant, but often colorful facts is one of the aspects of news magazine writing that distinguishes it from newspapers. A news magazine story might begin: "Flowers were in bloom on the crumbling towers of St. Hilarion, and hawks turned soundlessly high above Kyrenia." A newspaper story, on the other hand, would begin simply by noting "Strife-torn Cyprus was reported quiet today with only sporadic outbreaks of shooting."

News magazines present the news in the form of dramatic stories. Unlike newspapers, they have no tradition of reporting unbiased news and restricting opinions to columns and editorials. They often present opinionated news and interpretations of events, sometimes in articles signed by the writer. News magazines present their opinions as part of the news; newspapers keep opinion pieces separate; television editorials are clearly labeled on the local level, while interpretive documentaries are presented on the national level. The presentation of news in a TV documentary is somewhat similar to that in a news magazine.

PORTED DIFFERENTLY

1. Construct a news media comparison chart using the general form given here. Before filling in the chart, discuss exactly how the questions should be answered, the amount of detail desired, the time spans to be used for comparison, and any other points of possible confusion about the chart. Either individuals or small groups can fill in the charts.

2. Compare charts with others in the class (or other groups) and discuss reasons for your answers. Draw the chart on the blackboard or overhead projector and fill in the boxes with answers that reflect general agreement (where possible) among the class members.

3. Draw two general conclusions from the charts.

	RADIO	TELEVISION	NEWSPAPER	NEWS MAGAZINE
1. How much time or space does each medium devote to actual news?				
2. How much detail about each story does each medium provide?				
3. How fast does each provide the news? Which is fastest and which slowest?				
4. Which media depend on advertising to make a profit and thus stay in business?				
5. Is the news part of the medium economically profitable?				
6. Which are the best known nationwide suppliers of news in each medium?				
7. Which are the local news suppliers in each medium?				
8. Which do you think has the strongest emotional effect on the audience?				
9. Which do you think most influences people's opinions?				
10. What is the strongest point of each?				
11. What is the weakest point of each?				
12. Which covers each of the following best: sports local politics human interest in-depth news stories world events events at your school tragedy weather financial news				

How Are the Various News Media Alike?

The news media are all united by their concern for reporting the news and by their need for an audience. They are all dependent on advertising and the need to show a profit; they all rely on the Associated Press and United Press International as main sources of news; and all have a "gatekeeper" who controls the flow of news to the public.

News, in the United States, is a product that is sold to consumers. In some countries news is whatever the government wants the people to believe. The fact that the government does not run the news media gives them a certain independence and a willingness to point out flaws and to criticize the government. This ability of the press (both print and electronic) to criticize government and industry is essential to freedom of the press. It is quite natural for governments to at least bend the truth they give out. It is the mission of the press to dig for the whole truth. For this reason many politicians, from mayors to presidents, are antagonistic toward the press. If the press were subject to the government, it would do little but print whatever the government told it to. The Watergate scandal would never have been uncovered (*Washington Post* newspaper reporters were the first to report it); mistakes made in Vietnam would still remain hidden (it was the *New York Times* who first published the "Pentagon Papers"); and scores of dishonest politicians and businesses would still be in power preying on the ignorant and uninformed.

But the press must pay a price for this freedom. Since no news medium is supported by taxpayers' money, the high cost of gathering and spreading the news is assumed by advertisers and the news-buying public.

Another little-known similarity among the news media is their reliance on the wire services of the Associated Press (AP) and United Press International (UPI). If you were to walk into the nerve center of news-gathering activity in any TV or radio station, newspaper, television network, or even news magazine, you would see teletype machines noisily typing out foot after foot of news from all over the world.

AP and UPI are the two largest and most influential news-gathering organizations in the world. In spite of their importance, the general public knows relatively little about their work. The Associated Press has more than 3,000 employees throughout the world, while UPI operates 240 bureaus in 62 countries and employs over 10,000 people.

If you look for the symbols (AP) and (UPI) on the pages of your local newspaper, you will see how important these two wire services are. The symbol at the beginning of a story indicates that the story was provided by the wire service and sent via teletype machines to the newspaper.

Newspapers and news departments of broadcast stations subscribe to or join the wire service. Each subscriber pays a fee to the wire service and also agrees to supply it with coverage of local events that might have national interest. The reports from the wire services arrive on the teletype 24 hours a day. AP and UPI reporters all over the world phone or send stories to the New York headquarters. From there the stories are sent to subscribers who can print them as news, rewrite them, use them as a research source, or ignore them. A sample of news as poured from the teletype machine is shown on page 149.

An average newspaper contains more news from the wire services than from its own reporters. The smaller the paper, the truer this is. Many small-town papers are little more than a collection of wire service reports and syndicated material. The average radio news broadcast is at least 90 percent wire service material. Edward Jay Epstein in his five-year study of network (not local) TV news concluded that the source for 70 percent of NBC-TV's Nightly News was wire service reports. There is no way that the news consumer can tell the source of a TV or radio news story.

A third similarity all news media share is the use of a "gatekeeper." A news medium could be pictured as a funnel. Into the wide and always open mouth of the funnel flows a steady stream of news. Since there are nearly 4 billion humans on earth, there are potentially billions of news stories happening every day. Someone has to make the decision as to what is worth giving out to the public and what belongs in the wastebasket or on the floor of the film-editing room. The person who performs this function has different titles in each news organization. In many places he or she is called the managing editor or simply the news editor or news director. Social scientists use the term "gatekeeper" to describe this person, since he or she acts as a kind of doorman for the news, deciding which items make the paper or the broadcast and which do not gain entry.

Although gatekeepers are extremely important to the news process, they are usually unknown to the general public. They do not get by-lines on newspaper stories, nor do they read the news on television. The gatekeeper is a powerful ongoing influence, but when decisions are made on important stories, the publisher of the paper or the director of the TV or radio station may step in. But the sheer volume of news that flows into news media headquarters and the limited amount that comes out means that the gatekeeper is the one person most influential in deciding what is and is not news.

In newspapers the gatekeeper uses only about one in five stories that come in; in television and radio the number is probably closer to one in ten or twenty. On large city newspapers, news pours in so fast that only one in ten items scanned by the gatekeeper makes the paper. The gatekeeper is given a certain amount of air time or magazine space or newspaper pages to fill. This number is determined by the amount of advertising available. A large amount of advertising means less news, less advertising gives the consumer more news. Because ad space has already been committed, it is figured first, and the news must fit in the space that is left over.

1. This section suggested only a few similarities among the news media. List several other qualities they all share.

2. How do you think news in the United States would be different if it were government controlled and paid for from tax money?

3. Find some current examples showing the news media and the government in conflict.

4. Do you think it is dishonest for a government agency, a corporation, or an individual to release news about itself that presents it in the best possible light?

5. How much advertising does each news medium generally contain? Use a single issue or broadcast as an example. Express all answers in terms of

percentage. For example, time a 30-minute TV newscast; use a stopwatch to count the exact number of minutes and seconds of news. Count the number of minutes and seconds of ads during that half hour. If there are 20 minutes of news and 2 minutes of advertising, then you can say that 10 percent of the news time is devoted to advertising. For newspapers, measure in terms of column inches.

6. Draw two conclusions from the statistics on the amount of advertising in each news medium.

7. Do you think the need to show a profit and to sell advertising influences the kind of news the various media will report?

8. Determine what percentage of all the news in your local papers is provided by AP and UPI.

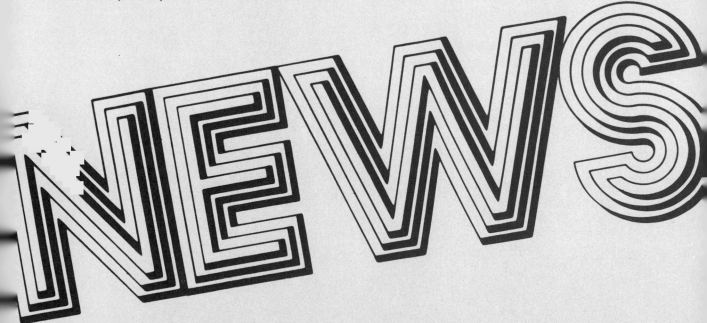

9. Prepare a written or oral report on the Associated Press or United Press International (or any other wire service).

10. Does anyone serve as "gatekeeper" for the school paper?

11. Compare the major national news magazines for the amount and quality of their news coverage. Compare the opinions or biases you find in their coverage.

12. How do television, radio, newspapers, and news magazines differ in their approach to news?

13. Draw up a list of "Some things I would like to see in newspapers that are not there now."

14. After comparing and judging the local newspapers, do the same with the *local* newscasts of all the TV stations in your area. Arrange a class project to compare and rate the local newscasts. One way to do this is to time exactly how many minutes and seconds of a nightly 30-minute local newscast is news, how much is advertising, how much is sports and weather, how much is chatter among the announcers. Find out which station gives the most news. Which station uses news film best? Which station gives the most detailed coverage of local events?

15. If you have the chance to attend some event that is covered by the media, be sure to read, watch, and listen to all the media reports on that event you can. Compare them with the experience you had at the actual event.

16. Have a student or group report on a comparison of the three major news weeklies—*Time*, *Newsweek*, and *U.S. News and World Report*.

17. Have a small group find examples of the same news item reported in the local papers, papers in other cities, news magazines, radio, and TV. Compare the treatment each medium gives the story.

Chapter 6
NEWSPAPERS

Who Owns the Newspapers?

To publish a newspaper, a machine is needed that will print large quantities of words at a relatively low cost. Such a machine could not exist until the 15th century when Johann Gutenberg invented a system of setting type that used movable, reusable type. But one hundred years after the invention, newspapers were still almost unknown. Why the long delay between the invention and its application?

Two major obstacles existed for the would-be newspaper publisher—most people couldn't read, and the local king or ruler controlled the flow of information. Although the necessary technology was available, two "social" inventions were needed in order to establish newspapers as a mass medium—democracy and literacy.

Democracy was necessary because a free press is a threat to a king or dictator. Knowledge is power, and to give everyone the knowledge of news is to give everyone a share of the power. Literacy was needed so that there would be enough people willing to buy and read papers, and it is only in the past three generations that literacy has become common in the United States. It was only natural that the first popular democracy—the United States—would be the birthplace of the popular free press. Today, one out of every five newspapers printed is published in the United States, and about 20 percent of the world's news readers are in the U.S., even though the United States has only 6 or 7 percent of the world's population.

American newspapers began with bulletins hung on tavern walls or printed sheets from the local postmaster or printer. Anyone could start a newspaper, and this fact was important in the development of a free press. Most schools have small newspapers that cover only events in school, but there is no legal reason why these papers could not be expanded to become neighborhood newspapers. On the other hand, a school radio or TV station cannot broadcast to the public without a government license. New, inexpensive offset printing systems make it possible for anyone with a few hundred dollars to produce a small newspaper with a circulation in the thousands.

In spite of the ease of producing a paper, very few new newspapers founded in recent years have successfully competed with already established dailies. Underground papers and papers for minority groups have performed an extremely valuable community service, but these have not been papers for the majority.

Today there are about 1,750 daily newspapers in the United States, about the same number as existed in 1920 and actually fewer than in the late 19th century.

Newspaper ownership has recently become increasingly concentrated, with a smaller and smaller group of people owning the nation's newspapers. All the owners of newspapers in the country could assemble in an average-size high school gymnasium or auditorium. This increasing concentration of owners means there is less competition between papers. Competition among papers, as among any business, helps ensure the news consumer that the papers will try to do the best possible job of finding and reporting the news.

Without local competition, a single paper can establish a news monopoly in a city and can succumb to the temptation to turn out a paper that is a collection of wire service items, press releases, and syndicated material. Such a paper will give a certain amount of news and information to the people. But it will not ask the newsmakers hard questions, or send reporters to dig around for the truth behind the press releases, or attempt to expose corruption in local government or business, or spend large sums of money for investigative reporting. Very likely it will not attract the best possible talent in reporters and editors.

A paper with a local monopoly can make a substantial profit from advertising without making any effort to actively pursue local news. The people in that city have then, for all practical purposes, lost freedom of the press even without censorship or government restrictions. A local monopoly does not always lead to this situation, but it is all too common, especially in small American cities.

Journalism Quarterly studied a city in which a news monopoly was established and then looked at how it changed when a strong competitor started business. The study found that the original monopoly paper gave 41 percent of its nonadvertising space to local news (local news is the most expensive to obtain since it requires reporters, travel, and time). When the competing paper began operation, the percentage increased to 51 percent—the people in the town got more news, thanks to the competitor. But when the competitor failed and went out of business, the amount of local news slipped back to 43 percent.

How common are newspaper monopolies? In 1880, 61 percent of all newspaper towns had competing dailies. By 1930 that figure had dropped to only 21 percent; in 1940 it was only 13 percent, and today fewer than 3 percent of newspaper towns have competing dailies. There are only fifteen cities left with competing papers published at the same time of the day (for example, competing morning or evening papers). Some cities have two papers but one is sold to those who prefer a paper in the late afternoon and the other to those who prefer a paper in the morning. Some cities have two papers owned by the same person or company; such papers do not really compete.

About half of the nation's daily papers are owned by "chains," companies that own more than one paper. The largest chains include the Chicago Tribune, Scripps-Howard, Hearst, Newhouse, Knight, Gannett, and Ridder papers.

The decreasing amount of competition and the increase of concentrated ownership is not necessarily a bad influence on news, but the tendency in such situations is that both the quality of the news and the variety of opinions available to the public will decrease.

1. Try to find some foreign newspapers and compare them with American papers. Even if the paper is not written in English, it can be compared in terms of appearance and advertising. Some libraries and large newsstands carry foreign papers.

2. Find out which local paper most of the families of class members subscribe to.

3. Take a survey of class newspaper reading that will show how many people in the class read a paper daily, which sections they read most, and how much time a day they spend reading a newspaper. Expand the survey to include the families of everyone in the class.

4. Find copies of "national" papers such as *The Wall Street Journal*, *Christian Science Monitor*, and *National Observer*. Have a class member report on them, or make the papers available for class reading.

5. Find out if your city has competing papers or is a newspaper monopoly. Who owns the local paper or papers? Find out what other communications businesses the owners run (for example, do they own any other papers as part of a "chain," or do they own radio or TV stations?).

6. Who are the "gatekeepers" at your local paper or papers? Find out the names of all the local publishers, too.

7. Make a careful study of your local papers and discuss various opinions about them. Do they do a good job of providing news?

How News Is Published (The Process)

From More Language That Needs Watching by Theodore M. Bernstein. Copyright ©1962 by Theodore M. Bernstein. Reprinted by permission of Atheneum Publishers.

It is mid-afternoon and the office of the morning newspaper is quiet except for the typewriters of a few rewrite men tapping out short stories of routine events. The man covering police headquarters phones the city desk to report a rather large theft of uncut diamonds from a dealer's office—"Looks like a pretty fair story." Should he cover it or does the city desk want to assign another reporter to the story? He is instructed to remain on his beat. Arnold Dittenhouse draws the assignment. He is told the nature of the story and goes to work.

From the headquarters man Arnold picks up the basic facts by phone. A diamond merchant, Gregory Lee, has reported the loss of $100,000 worth of uncut stones from the safe in his office at 1661 Sixth Avenue. Lee says the stones were there the previous afternoon but were gone this morning. The police have questioned everyone in the office except a clerk ("Haven't got his name, but the precinct cops can give it to you"). The clerk has not been questioned because he left on a two-week vacation last night and no one seems to know where he is.

Arnold next travels to the precinct station house and buttonholes a detective on the case. He learns that the clerk is Julius Feinguy, 22 years old, who rooms with a family named Fickett in Queens Village. He also discovers that the F.B.I. is investigating because of a suspicion that the diamonds may have been transported across state lines. Do the police suspect anything phony about the case—a staged theft to collect insurance or anything like that? No, they do not. Was the safe jimmied open or blown open? No, there were no signs that it had been tampered with in any way. Then it looks like an inside job, doesn't it? The police are offering no theory about it just yet.

A visit to Lee's office seems to be in order so that Arnold can at least get some idea of the physical layout. At the Sixth Avenue address the reporter is fortunate enough to find Lee in his office. He thus is able, in addition, to gather a few details about the personal appearance of the distraught, bespectacled, round little man who has suddenly found himself a figure in the news. Arnold is curious about how the safe was opened. Lee suggests the possibility that he may have left it open and un-watched very briefly the previous afternoon when he stepped into another room to answer a phone call. He has nothing else to add to what Arnold already knows.

At this point the reporter phones the city desk to report how the story shapes up and to see whether the office has any further information that would require outside checking before he returns. Time is getting shorter now, and he is told to come in.

Back at his desk, Arnold knows there are still one or two angles to be explored. There is also one piece of routine that he senses he must still perform, but for the life of him he can't recall what it is. He phones the F.B.I. press officer, but, as he expected, learns nothing except that the investigators would like to question Feinguy. No, they cannot say where they are looking for him.

Next he searches through the phone book for the Ficketts. (What is that piece of routine he has overlooked?) Mrs. Fickett tells him what she knows about her roomer, Feinguy, which is not much. No, she doesn't know his home town or where he went on vacation.

Ah, yes, that piece of routine.

Send to the newspaper morgue to see if there are any clippings on Feinguy. Not very hopeful, but you never can tell. While he is waiting, he organizes his notes. At last the copy boy hands him the slim folder from the morgue. It contains a single small clipping: A five-year-old dispatch from St. Louis relates that Julius Feinguy, 17, won a city-wide essay contest. St. Louis? An angle, perhaps.

It is getting late, but Arnold now has a couple of more phone calls to make. First he checks back to headquarters. Are the police looking for Feinguy in St. Louis? The police won't say. Arnold drags out a St. Louis phone book. There's a chance. Feinguy is an unusual name. He finds a number and puts through a call. Yes, this is Julius Feinguy's mother. No, Julius hasn't been there. No one else has phoned, but a detective did visit her to ask the same question. What is it all about? Thanks, Mrs. Feinguy.

Arnold decides to let his paper's resident correspondent approach the St. Louis police and puts in a call for him. Meanwhile, he has a story and probably an exclusive angle. It is time to begin writing. He checks with the city desk to in-

form the editors about the story and to get instructions about how much to write. He returns to his desk, feeds some paper into his typewriter and begins. He must hurry, he knows. The deadline is an hour and a half away. But it will take him perhaps an hour to write the story. And it has been drumm-ed into him that every story that is to appear in the paper cannot go to the composition room at the deadline, because if that happened the paper would never be printed. So he writes as rapidly as he can, sending the story to the desk in short sec-tions, or "takes." He pauses only to consult his notes and to take a call from the St. Louis correspondent. Out rolls the story, take after take.

What has happened up to this point is the exercise of the creative faculty of newspaper-ing. The city desk and the reporter combine to bring the story into being. The reporter, now working at top speed, is almost completely preoccupied with his subject matter. Many fine points of writing, of presentation, even of accuracy may escape him. But he is backstopped. The critical facul-ty is now brought into play on the copy desk. His story is pass-ed to a copy editor. Except for the news editor and his assistants, who oversee in a general way everything that goes into the newspaper but obviously cannot read closely all the thousands and thousands of words, the copy editor exercises final responsibility.

Let's call him Harold Aufseher. The diamond story is now in his hands. He has been told by the city desk how long the story is to be. As a practiced editor, Hal knows that Arnold probably will exceed his limit (most reporters understandably do that) and so he is on the alert to trim out the soft spots as he proceeds. In addition he will try to tighten the wording wherever he can to save precious space. When the reporter writes, "one of the employees," Hal will condense it to "an employee"; when the reporter writes that the police "rushed to the scene," Hal will strike out the phrase as an unnecessary and self-evident detail. In the second paragraph he discovers an involved fifty-word sentence; he breaks it into two short, clear sentences. When he reads that "the tray with its little bags and boxes of stones were missing from the safe," he almost automatically corrects the grammatical error. He sends the lead to the com-

posing room and picks up the next take.

Here he finds that Arnold has inadvertently begun to refer to Gregory Lee as "Mr. Gregory." Rather than interrupt the reporter he checks in the phone book to make sure of the man's name. However, when he notes that there has been no elaboration of the statement in the lead about $100,000 worth of uncut diamonds, ranging up to nine carats in weight," he decides he will have to interrupt the reporter. "Who made the evaluation—the dealer, the police, the insurance company?" He returns to his desk and inserts the necessary information.

Next he deletes a quotation from Mr. Lee: "I always thought there was something a little shady about Feinguy." Libelous. He also deletes a quotation from Mrs. Fickett: "He was careless personally—fingernails always dirty and that sort of thing." Poor taste and irrelevant.

Smoothly and swiftly, his critical faculties always on the alert, Hal makes his way through the story. As he goes, he writes subheads in the copy—those little headings of

boldface type that are inserted to break up long stretches of gray type. And as he goes, he is trying to resolve in his mind what the headline should say. When the story is finished, he tackles the head. His job here is to condense the main news of Arnold's 600-word story into half a dozen words.

Arnold has been writing under pressure; Hal has been editing under pressure. Each has a multitude of things to keep in mind. The story, as it presently appears in the paper, is as accurate as they can make it; it is a smooth, lucid job of narrative and exposition, and it may even have some literary quality. Both have worked hard, if hastily, to make it a finished piece of news writing. For Hal, incidentally, it is only one of a dozen or more stories he has processed before deadline. He has had to switch his attention rapidly from robbery to rocketry, from budgets to bullets, from grand slams to great slums, from racket busters to filibusters. Is it extraordinary, then, that something has eluded him, that he has allowed a mistake to slip into print? It is perhaps not excusable, but it is at least understandable.

THE NEWS PROCESS

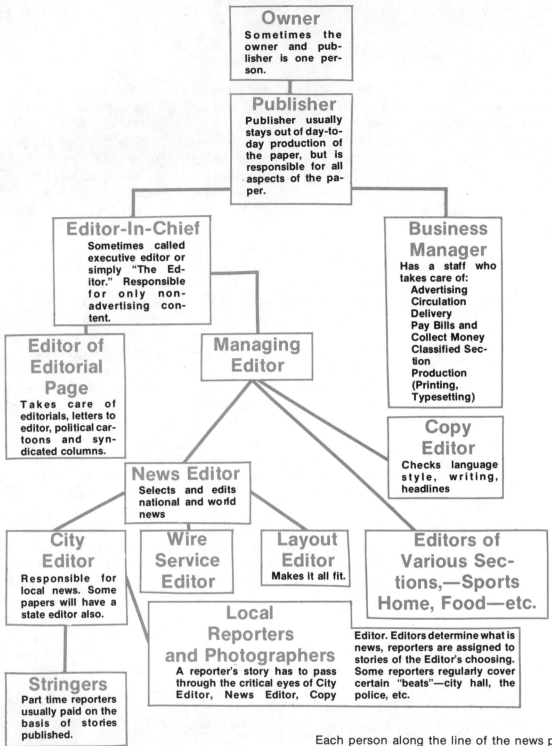

Owner
Sometimes the owner and publisher is one person.

Publisher
Publisher usually stays out of day-to-day production of the paper, but is responsible for all aspects of the paper.

Editor-In-Chief
Sometimes called executive editor or simply "The Editor." Responsible for only non-advertising content.

Business Manager
Has a staff who takes care of:
Advertising
Circulation
Delivery
Pay Bills and Collect Money
Classified Section
Production (Printing, Typesetting)

Editor of Editorial Page
Takes care of editorials, letters to editor, political cartoons and syndicated columns.

Managing Editor

Copy Editor
Checks language style, writing, headlines

News Editor
Selects and edits national and world news

City Editor
Responsible for local news. Some papers will have a state editor also.

Wire Service Editor

Layout Editor
Makes it all fit.

Editors of Various Sections,—Sports Home, Food—etc.

Local Reporters and Photographers
A reporter's story has to pass through the critical eyes of City Editor, News Editor, Copy Editor. Editors determine what is news, reporters are assigned to stories of the Editor's choosing. Some reporters regularly cover certain "beats"—city hall, the police, etc.

Stringers
Part time reporters usually paid on the basis of stories published.

As you can tell from the chart, a newspaper has many editors. The people most associated in the public mind with a newspaper are the reporters, yet their job is at the bottom of the totem pole of the news process.

Each person along the line of the news process makes decisions about the news, and each is subject to possible veto by the boss. The owner of a paper is the most removed from the paper's daily operation, perhaps visiting the paper only occasionally. Yet the owner can influence the kind of news the paper prints by making basic policies it follows.

Meedaab

How the News Is Published

1. In Bernstein's story, what is the main force that prevents the reporter from doing a thorough report on the crime?

2. Would your local paper rely on the police report of the gem theft or would it assign a reporter to dig up facts?

3. What is the newspaper "morgue"?

4. What does "libelous" mean?

5. In the chapter on the news media, the word "gatekeeper" was explained. Who, on the newspaper chart, acts in any way as a gatekeeper?

6. Who are the publisher, the editor, and the managing editor of your local papers?

7. What could be some of the bad effects on the news if the business manager (on the chart) were the boss of the news editor?

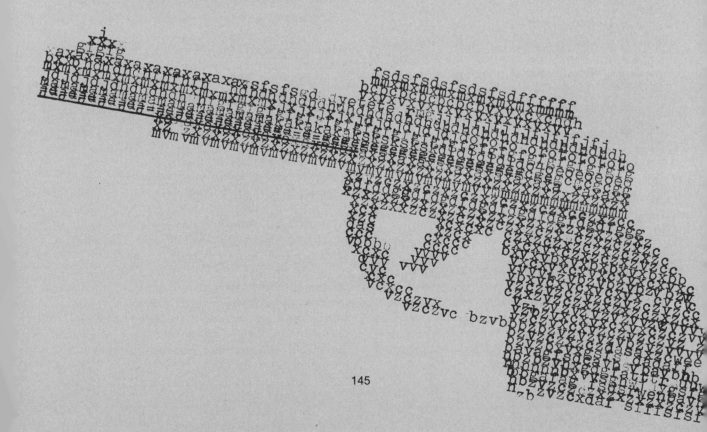

What News Is Published: (The Contents)

Unless you live in a town with a number of competing papers and have compared them carefully, you may not know whether your local paper does a good or a mediocre job of reporting the news. To make such a judgment, you must be able to compare it with other papers in cities the same size as yours, and you must be able to tell where the news comes from and have some idea of the bias of the paper and the values on which it makes news judgments. In order to make a news judgment on your local paper, or on any paper, it helps to know what is inside the paper and where it comes from. Let's take a close look at the contents of a newspaper.

The "masthead" gives the name of the paper and other details such as the date, number of pages, etc. Often the name of the paper will be printed in an old style type simply because that style used to be the darkest kind available; often it has become a kind of "trademark" for the paper. Many papers have redesigned their front pages to look more modern.

The edition of the paper is usually listed in the upper right-hand corner. Editions are called "three star final," "suburban," "market final," etc. Large papers publish a number of editions during the day, each basically the same but with more recent news and details than the preceding edition. Small papers publish only one edition a day.

The edition's most important story or "lead story" is the one with the largest headline. It usually starts in the upper right-hand part of the front page.

Newspaper headlines are traditionally written in the present tense, even if the story happened in the past.

Since newspapers are folded in half for sale on newsstands and in boxes on the street, the top half of the front page is often designed with the most attractive, dramatic, or saleable parts on it.

Headlines in newspapers are written to fill a certain amount of space. (In magazines a headline or title is written first, and then editors decide how much space to give it.) Newspapers are partly responsible for nicknames applied to public figures such as the President. Since space is so limited, a newspaper headline will often use shortened forms like Ike (for former President Eisenhower), JFK, or LBJ. Any President with a long last name will find himself renamed to fit the headlines.

A second and smaller headline (usually one column wide) below the story's main headline is called a "deck."

Photographs are often referred to in the newspaper business as "cuts" from the days when illustrations were made from woodcuts. The description or explanation given with a newspaper photo is called a cut-line. In the magazine or book business it is called a caption.

146

Chicago Tribune

THE WORLD'S GREATEST NEWSPAPER

Sunday, April 13, 1975

Final Edition

Vol.—No. 1 t • © 1975 Chicago Tribune 14 Sections

50¢

New Cambodia aid effort

U.S. drops supplies to Phnom Penh

...tyne Price

...e wanted to be
...usic teacher

...ontyne Price went on to
...at the Juilliard School of
...in New York City and
...is a living legend in the
...tic world. She talks about
...oaring rise to fame in
...*le.*

...at happened
...obs for all?

...1960s — remember —
...al leaders and econo-
...alike talked about "full
...yment." It was a nice
..., conjuring up visions
... cars in every garage, a
...eck for everyone, pros-
...Whatever happened to
...oncept? Read Bill Nie-
...report in Perspective.

...paring for
...ual meetings

...ears the annual stock-
...s meetings were dull
...gethers dominated by
...oning voices of execu-
...But then social and po-
...issues crept into the
...gs and the tone of the
...ings changed dramati-
...How corporations pre-
...or today's annual meet-
... outlined by James
...in Business.

...ool districts
...d elections

...ary and high school
... elections were held
...t the Chicago suburbs
...y. Results of many of
...ces and the results in
...community college dis-
...appear on *page 12.*

Ford will renew his fund plea

From Tribune Wire Services

THE UNITED States Sunday began air dropping supplies into the beleaguered Cambodian capital of Phnom Penh, a White House spokesman said.

President Ford's press secretary, Ron Nessen, said that the United States has enough funds from earlier Cambodian appropriations to continue the U.S. emergency airlift of food and ammunition for 10 days to 2 weeks. Commercial planes from Saigon have been ferrying the supplies to Phnom Penh. Nessen's announcement was the first that this country was dropping supplies by parachute.

In Washington, President Ford, apparently surprised at the decision of Cambodia's leaders to remain in Phnom Penh, renewed his request Saturday for $122 million in emergency military aid to Cambodia.

Nessen restated Ford's aid request—and said it had never been withdrawn.

U. S. SOURCES in Saigon had reported earlier that the airlift had been suspended after the U. S. Embassy in Cambodia was closed and Americans ordered evacuated by the President.

Cargo planes, flown by civilian pilots, had been running into rocket attacks when landing and taking off at the Cambodian airport. One DC-3 crashed on being hit by a rocket Thursday, killing the pilot and three other crew members.

In a phone report to Saigon Sunday, a New York Times correspondent said the situation in Phnom Penh is calm and there is no sign of Khmer Rouge troops entering the city.

THE TIMES reporter, Sydney Schanberg, who stayed behind when Americans and other foreigners were evacuated Saturday, said there had been no significant change in the military situation since the departure.

Speaking from Le Phnom Hotel over a crackly phone line, he said, "There is no sign of any increased activity by the Khmer Rouge, either by artillery or by ground troops."

Meanwhile, Cambodia's armed forces commander announced he had taken over the leadership of the government with the sanction of the National Assembly.

GEN. SAK Suthsakhan, the armed forces chief of staff, announced in a radio address that the National Assembly, Cambodia's chief legislative body, had suspended its activities for three months and empowered a committee of four army men and three politicians, including Premier Long Boret, to run the government to "cope with the present military and political situation."

Gen. Suthsakhan listed the makeup of

Continued on page 16, col. 1

With American Marines providing cover, Americans and Cambodians flee to helicopter Saturday for airlift out of Phnom Penh.

AP

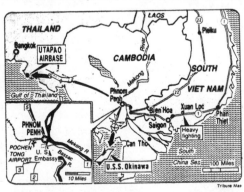

Tribune Map

Communist troops pin down a 3,000-man South Vietnamese relief brigade in heavy fighting at Xuan Loc near Saigon. Page 2.

South Vietnamese refugees tell why they have fled the Communists. Page 2.

Israel's defense minister says events in Viet Nam prove that the United States does not keep its promises. Page 2.

How much longer will South Viet Nam's President Thieu be "Washington's man in Saigon."—an article by Donald Kirk in the Perspective Section.

Hanoi hawks and dov... debate Saigon's fate— siege, or bloodbath?

By Philip Caputo
Chicago Tribune Press Service

SAIGON—A heavy North Vietnamese attack on this city is expected soon from Binh Duong Province to the northwest. And there are indications that Hanoi is abandoning its plans to force the South Vietnamese government into negotiations by laying siege to the capital, military sources said Saturday.

"It looks as tho the hawks in Hanoi may be winning out," one of the sources said. But he qualified this assessment with a comment that "psychological pressures" may still compel North Viet Nam to merely surround Saigon and refrain from seizing it by storm.

There is enough evidence to support both theories, and, as in any analysis of North Vietnamese intentions, the

News analysis

possibility that Hanoi may ou... opponent with an unexpected m... to be taken into account.

THE EVIDENCE pointing to... sault on the city is as follows:

● In the last 10 days North V... ese combat forces in Military R... —the Saigon area—have in... from 80,000 to 100,000.

Most of the increase is accou... by the transfer into Region ... bulk of the 5th Division from t... and the arrival of the entire 3... sion, one of North Viet Nam ... divisions—it is more than twice...

Continued on page...

Newspaper Advertising

Few people would answer the question "Why do you watch television or listen to the radio?" with the reply "For the advertising." But many people do buy and read newspapers because of the advertising. Only in newspaper advertising is the potential consumer told exact prices and places to shop and given coupons to reduce the purchase price. Only newspapers carry ads for neighborhood stores and tell what is on sale tomorrow. Magazine and television advertising is concerned more with motivation and persuasion; newspaper advertising gives information. The classified section contains almost pure information, with little of the psychological techniques and trick-working of the kinds of ads discussed in the advertising chapter. Newspaper advertising is most often cited by people as being useful and reliable.

Not only is advertising a service to the public, but it is also the way the paper makes a profit. The subscription or delivery price of a newspaper helps to pay expenses but is not sufficient to make an attractive profit. A full page of advertising space will cost from a few hundred to many thousands of dollars, depending on the paper's circulation. Space in the paper is sold by pages, half pages, column inches or, as in the classified section, by the column line. Sixty percent of the average paper is advertising; this helps account fot the fact that newspapers as a business enterprise are among the most profitable in the nation.

In this chapter we will consider over a dozen different kinds of "news" items that are printed in a paper. But from the viewpoint of the publisher and editor there are only two kinds of space—advertising space and the "newshole." The "newshole" is the amount of space left to fill once all the advertising is accounted for. Still, not everything that goes into the "newshole" is "news."

Wire Service Material

The newshole in the average paper is 40 percent of its total number of pages. About 37 percent of that space is filled by wire service material. Such material is clearly marked:

NCAA makes only minor football rules changes

ARLINGTON, Tex. [APn—The N.C.A.A. Football Rules Committee, refusing to temper with what outgoing chairman John Waldorf called the "finest game we've ever had," made only minor rules changes Wednesday.

Of the 40 or 50 minor changes made in the rules book, Waldorf, supervisor of officials in the Big Eight Conference, said only six were significant.

• Players not wearing their mouthpiece will cost the team a time out.

• If a jersey is torn, it must be replaced in 25 seconds or the player will have to leave the game or call time out.

• Referees can suspend play when weather or riot conditions warrant.

• The football will be a natural tan with two white stripes.

• The sideline area boundaries for the teams will be the 30 yard lines instead of between the 35 yard lines.

• The "free ball rule" is changed so that a team cannot lose possession if a penalty occurs while the ball is free on a punt, field goal attempt or kickoff.

Sometimes the wire service report is rewritten, sometimes it is published as it is received.

Time to get out
Yanks warned in Viet

SAIGON [UPI]—American and South Vietnamese officials Wednesday began the final stages of the evacuation of "nonessential" American personnel and their families within 24 hours. The initial plan involved retired American military personnel.

United States officials said they would bypass Vietnamese emigration procedures, which are replete with red tape.

There was no indication how

AVENUE, THE SHORT BIKE JOURNEY FOLLOWED SLOAN'S

MARKING THE LAST SIGN DELINEATING THE ROUTE.

ROCKFORD EXPLAINED THE TRAIL WAS OPEN ONLY FROM 8 A.M. TO 6 P.M.

ON SUNDAYS AND WOULD BE PATROLLED BY POLICE TO KEEP PYLONS IN

PLACE TO SEPARATE CYCLISTS FROM MOTORISTS. THE TRAIL WILL BE OPEN FROM

THIS SUNDAY THROUGH SEPT. 28.

1136PM MG 7-1

FIRST GRAF CHICAGOBOKE TRAIL CORRECT TO READ CHICAGO BIKE TRAIL

CNB 52   REARDON DICTATION TO HENNESSY

INSERT C

THOMPSON CONF

MAYOR RICHARD J. DALEY WAS NOT AT CITY HALL THIS MORNING AND

WAS NOT EXPECTED TODAY, ACCORDING TO HIS PRESS SECRETARY, FRANK SULLIVA

ASKED IF DALEY WOULD HAVE A STATEMENT CONCERNING THOMPSON'S

DECISION TO RUN FOR GOVERNOR, SULLIVAN RESPONDED, "NO, THERE WON'T."

1140AM MG 7-1

Syndicated Material

Syndicates are another source of material for newspapers. Feature syndicates supply comic strips, cartoons, columns on topics from cooking to politics, and longer "feature" stories. Syndicates do not supply "hard" news. The material arrives by mail at the newspaper ready for printing or typesetting. Papers pay for what they use on the basis of circulation—the larger the paper's readership, the higher the fee for using the item. Some of the larger syndicates include King Features, North American Newspaper Alliance (NANA), Religious News Service, and United Feature Syndicate. Some syndicated material is marked with the name of the syndicate for copyright purposes. About 10 percent of the entire average paper (about one-fourth of the newshole) is taken up with syndicated material.

Most newspapers feature one or more syndicated columnists. A good paper will serve its readers a varied diet of columnists with different viewpoints. Since columnists can write about whatever they please, they are usually very opinionated and biased. It is their purpose to argue strongly for their viewpoint rather than to present straight news reporting. Many columns are political, but others are about religion, bird watching, gossip, or almost any conceivable subject.

A newspaper editor can select only very conservative or very liberal columnists or only those he personally agrees with. But such a limited selection does not serve the needs of the readers. One way to evaluate the slant or bias of any paper is to study the viewpoints of its regular columnists and other syndicated material.

Sections and Departments

On larger papers each of these sections might have a full-time editor and staff. Such sections can provide readers with news, valuable how-to information, consumer advice, and features. In cities with competitive papers, these sections have great influence on which paper people will buy.

Almost every daily paper has a sports section and many have either pages or separate sections for society news, food, family features, entertainment (movies, theater, music, etc.), books, business and finance, real estate, and travel.

Unfortunately, there is a tendency to allow these sections to become little more than disguised advertising. A real estate section, instead of giving news about real estate trends in the city, will be filled with articles written by realtors advising people to buy a house now or by developers extolling the beauties of their latest suburban housing tract. A food section or department can provide, for instance, economical and creative recipes, shopping advice, articles on how to tell and select quality meat, advice on which foods are good buys and which are not. A good section could report on sanitation conditions at local food stores and restaurants and even give comparative prices. On the other hand, a food section can print recipes supplied by advertisers (using brands advertised a few pages later) or ads disguised as articles from public relations groups for butter producers (or prunes or coffee or frozen food or whatever) telling how healthful and inexpensive their product is.

The temptation for the paper is to keep the advertisers contented. An article in a real estate section about the shoddy building at a local housing project is hardly likely to make that builder spend money to advertise in the paper. An article warning consumers that a certain supermarket has a confusing labeling system for meats might be uncomfortable for the supermarket—which spends thousands of dollars a year for newspaper advertising.

Filling special sections and departments with press releases is tempting because they are free and already written, and they pour into the newspaper office by the thousands. *The New York Times*, the nation's largest newspaper, throws away 168 bushels of wastepaper every day, according to one of its associate editors. And much of the wastepaper is press releases.

The Editorial Page

One section of the newspaper where editors can exercise some influence on the city is the editorial page. It is on this page that the paper, or its editors or owners, can speak its mind. On page one the newspaper has the obligation to present the facts, but on the editorial page it can indulge in argument and opinion. On this page it also often prints letters from readers. The editorial page should offer a variety of opinions and a fair sampling of the mail it receives.

Press Releases

Every large corporation, as well as government agencies, large institutions (like universities) and other groups, has a public relations ("PR") department, whose aim is to tell the community about the good things the organization does and to create a favorable public image.

One of the jobs of the PR director or department is to send "press releases" to newspapers, radio, and TV stations. The press release is usually written so that it can be reprinted almost word for word in a newspaper or magazine. Such press releases, or slightly rewritten versions of them, form the basis for many items in newspapers. This news item is an example of a story based on a press release:

New Shopping Center to be Constructed on Northwest Side

J.D. Bosch, Inc., today announced plans for a new three-million-dollar shopping center to be constructed on the city's northwest side near Newburg Park. It is scheduled to open for business next April with nearly 85 stores.

The new complex will be designed by R.G. O'Brian and Company and built by the Atlas Construction Company of Rochelle. Mr. Gerald Bosch, chairman of the board of J.D. Bosch, Inc., proclaimed the new shopping center a welcome addition to the northwest side community. He said the new center will enable area residents to shop without the long trip downtown and will provide about 900 parking spaces.

Bosch promised that the new center will be the most modern shopping facility in the entire area.

The problem with press releases is that they are a form of "managed news." They are usually truthful, but most often the "truths" are carefully selected to give a favorable impression of the company, government agency, or other organization responsible for the release.

An average large city newspaper receives about a hundred press releases daily. They are either thrown out, rewritten and used, used as is, or used as a lead for a reporter to investigate and supply more objective details.

An example of news by press release:

NEWS

TEXAS MOBILE HOME ASSOCIATION
P.O. Box 4397
Austin, Texas 78765
Area Code 512 476-1669
LESLIE M. BEARSS, Executive Director

Release Date: Immediate

Contact: Les Bearss

Grover Mitchell

MOBILE HOMES TO BE ANCHORED

AUSTIN, (TX), July 6—Texas Mobile Home Owners will soon have the responsibility and expense of properly blocking and anchoring their homes as a result of an act recently signed into law by Texas Governor Dolph Briscoe, according to E.L. Murray of Corpus Christi who is Chairman of the Board of Directors for the Texas Mobile Home Association.

The law becomes effective 180 days following the effective date of the minimum standards which are to be established by the Texas Performance Certification Board, the policy-making body for the Mobile Homes Division of the Texas Department of Labor and Standards. Only mobile homes purchased after this effective date will be required to be blocked and anchored in accordance with this law. Exempted are mobile homes located more than 300 feet from any other occupied or inhabited building or structure.

Actually, two sets of standards will be in effect: Mobile home dwellers within the first two tiers of coastal counties in Texas will be required to block and anchor their homes to withstand hurricane force winds and throughout

(more)

AUSTIN, Texas—Mobile home owners will soon have the responsibility and expense of properly blocking and anchoring their homes as a result of an act recently signed into law by Texas Governor Dolph Briscoe, according to E.L. Murray of Corpus Christi, chairman of the board of directors for the Texas Mobile Home Association.

The law becomes effective 180 days following the effective date of the minimum standards which are to be established by the Texas Performance Certification Board, for the policy-making body for the Mobile Homes Division of the Texas Department of Labor and Standards. Only mobile homes purchased after this effective date will be required to be blocked and anchored in accordance with this law. Exempted are mobile homes located more than 300 feet from any other occupied or inhabited

The Houston Post
Columbia Journalism Review

1. Find out how much your local paper or papers charge for advertising space. This information can be obtained from the newspaper or the library.

2. What percentage of your local papers is advertising? The national average is 60 percent—comparare your paper(s) to this average.

3. Which local advertisers pay the newspaper the most money for advertising? Your answer will probably have to be an educated guess based on an examination of as many editions as possible. In some cities, a few large stores contribute half or more of a newspaper's advertising revenue.

4. What percentage of your local paper's average edition is the "newshole"? To measure it, subtract the answer to Item 2 above from 100 percent. (The average paper comes in with 40 percent news.)

5. Which wire service does your local paper(s) use the most? What percentage of its newshole is filled by wire service material? How does this compare with the national average?

6. Find examples in your paper of syndicated material other than comics or cartoons.

7. Which syndicated columnists are available in your local newspapers? What is the subject matter and viewpoint of each?

8. Does each local newspaper offer a variety of syndicated columnists or does it favor those with a particular political viewpoint?

9. Assign to individuals or small groups the task of evaluating various sections and departments of local papers—sports, finance, real estate, etc. Report the findings to the class. Be sure to determine whether much of the material in the sections is "puffery"—press release material praising certain products or companies.

10. Does your paper have an editorial page? If so, does it express a consistent viewpoint? Does the editor tackle important local and national issues?

11. Does your paper print letters to the editor? If so, do they represent a fair cross-section of opinion or are they limited to those who agree with the editor?

12. Find one or two examples in your paper of what seems to be a press release. Discuss the pros and cons of printing press releases.
Does your school send out press releases?

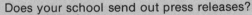

Local News

Each newspaper needs its own reporters, especially to handle local events that the national news services will not cover. Reporters are either part of a general reporters' "pool" assigned to stories as they break, or are given regular beats such as city hall, the police, the state legislature, etc. A small paper, of course, will have only a few reporters to cover everything.

Reporters write their own stories, which are then subject to rewrite by various editors. For a last-minute important story, a reporter may phone the information directly to the paper, where a rewrite editor takes it down and hurries it into an acceptable form for the paper.

A reporter covering a story never knows whether the event will be considered newsworthy enough to make the paper or how much space it will be given. For this reason, news reporters write in what is called "pyramid style." They arrange the news item so that the essential details are all in the opening paragraph. Each paragraph thereafter is more general and less important. A good reporter writing in the pyramid style will answer the questions *who*, *what*, *where*, *when*, *how*, and *why* in the first paragraph. This done, the news editor can fit the story into any available amount of space. A reporter might write 1,000 words on a story and have only 100 used in the paper. You can see the difference between the pyramid style and other writing styles by reading a front page newspaper story and stopping after any paragraph—the story still seems complete. If you try this with a magazine article, the item will not seem complete and will very likely lack some essential information.

A by-lined story carries the reporter's name. Most reporters are unknown to the general public and receive few by-lines. The reporter's job is sometimes exciting but involves many long hours of boring meetings, writing and rewriting, and simply waiting.

One common reporting assignment is to cover a speech, airport arrival, dedication or whatever, by a famous person—a newsmaker. This is more common in large cities than in small towns where few newsmakers put in an appearance.

NEWSMAKERS

"Newsmakers" are people who make news when they talk, marry or divorce, date, write, or do almost anything. They are politicians, celebrities, media heroes, people in the public eye. What they do often is not terribly important or newsworthy, yet it somehow ranks as "news." Some newsmakers, such as the President of the country, do things that are really news. But they can also make news by doing ordinary things such as walking the dog, talking to people on a street corner, or attending church services.

You are probably not a newsmaker. If a news-

Pseudo-events are events designed to produce news favorable to the person or persons planning the event. The success of a pseudo-event is measured by the amount of space it succeeds in capturing in the news media. Such events are planned with the convenience of the news media in mind and would often be meaningless without news media coverage.

Press releases are one special form of pseudo-events. Other, more ordinary pseudo-events include anniversary celebrations of companies or institutions; dedications or ground-breaking ceremonies or ribbon cuttings; press conferences, interviews, "leaks" and trial balloons, prepared statements, and speeches; demonstrations and picket lines; hunger strikes; symbolic actions of various sorts; banquets; some law suits (filed only to gain publicity); tree plantings or parades.

The news item shown below could well have begun at a meeting of the board of directors of Crandall Brothers Department Store. The board perhaps noticed a decline in sales and so called in a public relations consultant to boost sales. The PR consultant suggested that the store stage a celebration of 40 years of existence. The event is, in actuality, no more newsworthy than the store's 39th or 38th year of business, neither of which was reported in the local press. All the newspapers and radio and TV news departments were invited to the ribbon-cutting, which was scheduled in the morning to allow plenty of time for pictures in the evening paper and film on the 5:30 local news. At the ribbon-cutting, a press release was given to all media people there. That evening the following story appeared in the paper:

maker were caught shoplifting a typewriter from your local department store, the event would be news. The more important the newsmaker, the bigger the story. If you were caught trying to steal a typewriter, the story would not be news unless you live in a very small town.

The term "pseudo-event" has been coined to describe a certain kind of event that often receives space in newspapers and in radio and television news broadcasts.

CRANDALL BROTHERS MARK FORTY YEARS OF SERVICE

Crandall Brothers Department Store in downtown Rochelle today began its week-long celebration of 40 years of service. In a ribbon-cutting ceremony dedicating the newly remodeled store, William Crandall, son of founder Malcolm Crandall, pledged better service and continued efforts to serve the needs of Rochelle. Events planned for the week include the distribution of free candy to all children who enter the store, a vacation sweepstakes, reduced prices, and a two-day Downtown Days Sale in which all auto traffic will be stopped, turning the street into a pleasant mall for pedestrians. A circus will be held in the evening of Downtown Days on State Street, with admission free to all.

CRIME AND DISASTER

Another common kind of local reporting covers the disaster or crime story. The story of a deadly accident, a fire, or a crime is the staple of the newspaper. Why these tragedies are so important as news is hard to understand. But they remain important to papers because people like to read them. The same subjects—crimes, fires, disasters—are important in novels, movies, and television programs as well as in news reporting.

Some sociologists claim that people like to read about the tragedies of other people to gain assurance that their own lives aren't so bad after all—things could be worse. Others guess that people like to read about crime and tragedy because they are exciting, something to break the ordinary and sometimes dull routine of daily life.

One veteran Chicago reporter writing about crime in the news pointed out, "We still satisfy curiosity, not social purpose. All murders do not make good newspaper stories. Murders among black people are called 'cheap' by the downtown papers; 'Suburban girl slain' is always a headline story, because the suburbs are the residence of the 'better' people; and deadly brawls among 'cheap' people are not news, unless the resulting murder is bizarre."

some situation and reveals facts not previously known. Often investigative reports reveal corruption in government or business. A newspaper might investigate the local ambulance services, for example, to look for corrupt practices, kickbacks, hidden charges, and the like. Or it can check on city workers to see if the taxpayers are receiving a full day's work for a day's pay from those employees paid by tax money. A paper can investigate short-weighting and other dishonest practices in grocery stores; unsanitary conditions at restaurants and hamburger stands; housing conditions among the poor of the city; or political influences in the city school system.

Such reporting takes time, money, and courage.

Investigative reporting in the early 1900s eventually resulted in the passage of the Pure Food and Drug Act when reformers and writers like Upton Sinclair described unsanitary packing houses and meats filled with waste and dirt. Ida Tarbell's investigative reporting on the Standard Oil Company led to its break-up into a group of smaller companies. Such reporting was once called "muckraking" and is still called that by some newspeople today.

Investigative reporting takes a great deal of time to do well, and many papers unfortunately consider it a luxury. It is true that investigative reporting sometimes leads to lawsuits, political pressure, threats, and loss of advertising revenues.

Human Interest Stories

A newspaper that reported only the facts, only the world's most important events, only the actions and ploys of world leaders and criminals, might soon find itself without the large number of readers it needs to stay in business.

Most newspapers include what are called "human interest" stories. Sometimes these are local stories written by staff reporters; other times they are provided by the wire services. Human interest stories are about non-newsmakers, about the troubles or heroics of the ordinary person. Whether tragic or humorous, they are often moving and dramatic.

Investigative Reporting

There are many papers whose pages have not seen an investigative news report in twenty years. Even the best papers can manage only a few a year. An investigative report is one that looks deeply into

1. Try to arrange with a local paper to have a reporter talk to the class. Be ready with questions to ask about the newspaper business and reporting.

2. Look at the front page of any newspaper and notice the pyramid style of writing. Take one of the following events (make up your own details) and write a four-paragraph news report about it:

A fire at the school

Your teacher has won a state lottery of one million dollars

A student at school has broken the world record for sleeping without waking

The first (lead) paragraph should contain the who, what, where, when, how and why of the event. Each following paragraph should be more general and contain less important information. The story must be complete whether the editor decides to use one, two, three, or all four paragraphs in the paper.

3. Check to see if your paper uses reporters' by-lines—never, sometimes, or usually. What kind of stories are usually by-lined?

4. Find a story in the paper either on the local or national level that involves a newsmaker (other than a politician). Discuss the value of such news in the paper.

5. List the currently best-known newsmakers. Are there some qualities that most of these people have in common? Why do you think the news media and their readers are so fascinated with the powerful, the rich, and the beautiful?

6. Was Evil Knievel's attempt to jump the Snake River Canyon on a motorcycle a pseudo-event? Find examples of pseudo-events in newspapers.

7. Devise some kind of pseudo-event that would (a) give your school favorable publicity; (b) call the attention of the people in your city to some local problem; (c) call the attention of the country to some problem or event that the class agrees on.

8. As an ambitious class project and an experience in obtaining the news media's attention, attempt to gain news space or time on TV or radio by staging a worthwhile pseudo-event. Make the event an attempt to gain media coverage for some cause the class believes deserves attention.

9. A fairly large percentage of news that makes up the main section of a newspaper is crime: murders, robberies, arson, riots, etc. What do you think is the effect on readers of the news decision that "crime is front page news"? Do you think crime should be so important? What kind of crimes are rarely reported?

10. Where does most of the information about crimes come from? How does the source influence the story?

11. MURDER VICTIM FOUND IN GARBAGE CAN

The body of an unidentified 28-year-old woman was found last night, stuffed in an alley garbage can on the 1300 block of West Front Street on the city's east side.

The partially clad body was discovered by James Hanson, a resident of the block, after he had parked his car in a nearby garage. "I saw a leg sticking out of the garbage can," Hanson told police, "and looked in

and saw the body. I rushed home and called the police."

The victim had been stabbed repeatedly and had a cord tied around her neck, according to police. The body has not yet been identified, and police have no suspects in custody.

Why do you think people read stories like the one about the murder victim? Do they enjoy it? How do they feel after reading it? One way of looking at this kind of news story is that it is included as a sort of violent form of entertainment. Certainly no paper would be justified in keeping such a story secret. Do you approve or disapprove of the way the details of the murder and the finding of the body are presented? Are they necessary? What purpose do they serve? How else could the story have been written?

12. If you live in a large metropolitan area, your newspaper probably does not report all crimes. Certainly it does not give the same amount of space to each crime. What do you think determines how much space is given to a local crime story?

13. Judging from the "human interest" stories you have read what qualities does an editor look for in such an item?

14. A human interest type story is featured on this page: "Steve's a stand-up type." Speculate why the story was interesting enough to warrant AP attention and to be used by many newspapers. Rewrite the "Steve's a stand-up type" story so that it is an editorial. You do not have to use all the details in the story, but do use the item as a basis for some kind of expression of opinion.

Steve's a stand-up type

PHILADELPHIA (AP)— Stephen Tolvish has the only residence on the block with a folding door.

He lives in a telephone booth in northeast Philadelphia.

"It's nice and it's warm and I keep it clean," said the former mailer for a printing firm.

Tolvish, who is 54 and mostly unemployed and has never been married said he has been living in the telephone booth "off and on for a year."

He stores his suitcase and clothes atop the booth. Tolvish does odd jobs for people in the neighborhood, and the "boys on the corner" take him home sometimes so he can get a bath.

He dines out, when he has the money. He sleeps standing up for obvious reasons, and getting a good night's sleep is often difficult.

"When people want to use the phone," Tolvish said, "they knock on the door. I wake up and get out."

15. Find out what kind of investigative reporting your papers have done recently. If they have done none, write a letter to the editor and ask why.

159

Opinion vs. Objectivity

To be objective means to eliminate personal opinion and prejudice from reporting. Some say that a completely "objective" story is not humanly possible; individuals can only express their viewpoints. They feel that each reporter expresses his opinion as well as possible and that if people read these various viewpoints, they will then be able to reach their own decisions. Others say that this gives the reporter too much power; only the facts should be presented, and opinions left up to the reader.

Newspeople themselves are undecided about the problem of objectivity:

David Brinkley, well-known as the NBC-TV evening news anchorman, said this: "A person presumably is expected to go on the air and be objective, which is to say that he's to go on the air and to have no likes, no dislikes, no feelings, no views, no values, no standards—to be a machine. If I were objective, I would have to be put away somewhere in an institution, because I'd be some sort of vegetable. I make no pretense at being objective. Objectivity is impossible to a normal human being. Fairness, however, is attainable, and that's what we strive for."

A.M. Rosenthal, who was managing editor of the most powerful and well-known newspaper in the United States, the *New York Times*, has said that objectivity is " . . . the determination to write and edit with the elimination of as much personal bias as humanly possible, to present facts and situations as close to reality as possible, to avoid our own pejorative phrases or comments, to give accused people or institutions the right of immediate reply, to present all shadings of opinion and counter argument, and most of all, to keep examining ourselves day by day and story by story to see if we are being as objective as we can."

A good headline must be immediately clear to the reader. If a headline is ambiguous—that is, if it has two possible meanings—it will leave some readers confused. Sometimes ambiguous headlines are simply confusing, other times they can be humorous. Some ambiguous newspaper headlines appear on the opposite page.

Headlines

Headlines serve a number of purposes. They are a convenient way for a newspaper reader with only a few minutes to learn what has happened in the world. Sometimes the headlines are written to entice readers to purchase a newsstand copy. When this practice of using headlines to sell papers is carried to an extreme, it is called sensationalism. A paper might report a murder with a huge headline reading, "Mad Murderer Rampages Through City." Few papers practice such outright dishonest sensationalism any more, mainly because it is poor journalism and because most readers have the paper delivered to their homes rather than purchasing a copy from the newsstand. A more responsible headline for the same story might read "Man Found Murdered in Hotel."

Headlines summarize the news. Some newspapers employ one or more people whose only job it is to write headlines. They must be accurate, must contain the most important facts of even complex stories, and must fit into a certain number of spaces.

The Lower case

Fish & Game To Hold Annual Elections

Berkshire Courier
Great Barrington,
Massachusetts 12/24/74

Between 9:00 and 5:00, the noise was audible even over the daily street din, though apparently not enough to rankle the day people, who could only have heard it during brief forays from their insulated office buildings. Just we full-timers rang our hands in despair, for at night the roar was all ours.

New Times
1/24/75

A favorite piece by Tchaikovsky is highlighted as Andre Kostelanetz conducts the National Symphony Orchestra IN PERFORMANCE AT WOLF TRAP Monday, Dec. 23 at 8:00 p.m. on PTV. IN PERFORMANCE AT WOLF TRAP is made possible by a grant from Atlantic Richfield Company.

Aroostook Republican, Caribou, Maine 12/18/74

Ford Signs Privacy Act, Taps Lynn

Sentinel Star, Orlando, Florida
1/2/75

IN SUNDAY'S COURIER-EXPRESS Rita Smith writes about a teen-age prostitute who refuses to change her way of life despite the pleas of her anguished mother. For home delivery phone 847-5500.

Courier Express, Buffalo, New York
1/11/75

CIA Reportedly Sought to Destroy Domestic Flies
San Francisco Chronicle 1/10/75

The sources also said that the President would probably be likely to move to a top spot on the White House staff.

The New York Times
11/4/74

Stolen Painting Found by Tree

The (Philadelphia) Evening Bulletin 12/17/74

The breaking down of most prejudices and discriminations has lifted women from mental work to important management and top professional positions.

The Scranton Tribune
1/14/75

Only a third of state's voters went to polls on Nov. 5

One-third of the registered voters in Massachusetts stayed home Nov. 5, nearly a record for absence at polls.

The Boston Globe
11/26/74

The license fee for altered dogs with a certificate will be $3 and for pets owned by senior citizens who are altered the fee will be $1.50.

Santa Barbara News-Press
1/13/75

Computer center turns on students
The Daily Transcript
Dedham, Massachusetts 1/10/75

Bland Music Contest Set For Feb. 23
Page News and Courier, Luray, Virginia
2/6/75

462C UNIPRESSERS:

TO ALL OF YOU AND YOUR FAMILIES, MAY THIS BE A MOST PLEASANT HOLIDAY AND MAY THE NEW YEAR BE BRIGHT AND PROSPEROUS.

UPI 12-25 02:09 PPS

EDITORS: PLEASE DISREGARD 462C UNIPRESSERS. IT WAS INADVERTENTLY TRANSMITTED ON THIS CIRCUIT.

UPI 12-25 02:21 PPS   UPI 12/25/74

Edmisten Seeking Injunction Against Damn Construction
The Maiden (North Carolina) Times 1/8/75

Bell says Gravitt tried sex in the air
San Antonio News 1/8/75

A headline can be written so that it summarizes a story accurately and clearly, or it can be written to express a "slant" or "bias"— an opinion about the story.

For example, a gathering of a large number of people in Washington, D. C:, for the purpose of encouraging Congress to pass legislation favoring abortion could receive either of the following headlines:"7,000 Gather to Urge Women Be Given the Right To Decide on Abortion" or "Mob Invades Washington To Push For Abortions."The use of a "loaded" word like *mob* in the second headline would tend to influence readers against the gathering. The use of the word *right* in the first headline could be taken as a word loaded in favor of the action. A more neutral headline would be "7,000 Demonstrate For Abortion Legislation."

These two headlines appeared in two Chicago newspapers, both referring to the same event:

GANG MEMBER SHOT BY POLICEMAN

VIETNAM VETERAN SHOT IN SCHOOL

Both headlines are true; the man was both a veteran and a gang member. But the first calls the dead person by a negative term while the second uses a more favorable label. Each headline has a different effect on the reader.

Newspapers can be quite objective and present a wide variety of viewpoints or they can consistently give readers slanted or biased news. Newspapers often are labeled conservative or liberal, or are known as pro-business or pro-labor, or have certain viewpoints they stress constantly. For example, a newspaper editor who favored gun controls might use every story he could find in which innocent people were killed because of the careless use of guns. A newspaper can present opinions in many ways:

Editorials or items clearly labeled "opinion."

Slanted headlines.

"Loaded" words in stories.

Careful selection of what to print and what to omit.

Selection within each news item of details.

Placement of the stories (placing an item on the front page says it is more important than if it appears in the back pages of the paper).

Bias and Opinion

1. Examine your local paper or papers to see if you can find any particular bias. Usually you will need to study more than one issue to make the bias clear. Ask adults who have been reading a certain paper for many years if they have found any viewpoint or bias. Do they object to it, or is it one reason they read that paper? Do you think newspapers should try to be objective or should they allow their own opinions to show in their news coverage?

2. The following "news item" is fictional, but it is based on an actual event. Read it and then go on to the questions.

DICK GREGORY ASSAILS U.S., GETS $1,250 FOR COLLEGE TALK

Dick Gregory, who apparently has switched from comedy to militancy, delivered a lashing lecture Friday against almost everything. He spoke at Fremont Community College.

More than 1,500 persons, most of them young students, crowded the auditorium to listen to Gregory attack America as a "sick, degenerate country run by a bunch of insane fool maniacs."

Gregory was paid $1,250 for his talk with money taken from the Student Activities Fund.

He was invited to speak by the Culture Committee of the college. Dr. Wilfred Bauman, college president, said the huge lecture fee did not include any tax money. "Gregory's fee was paid by students from the Student Activities Fund and by an admission charge," he said.

Gregory attacked the " . . . white racist system of the United States," and then flew back to his comfortable Chicago home. Dr. Bauman said he heard part of the lecture but was then called away on other business.

This "news story" not only presents news, namely the fact that Dick Gregory spoke to students at the Community College, but it also reveals the opinions of the newspaper or, at least, of the writer of the story.

Find specific words, phrases, and selection of details that reveal the writer's opinion about Gregory and the talk.

Rewrite the news item (you can make up additional details) to show how it might have been written by (a) someone who wrote a fair and objective news story without revealing his or her personal opinion; and (b) someone who agreed very much with Gregory's opinions and expressed that agreement in the news item. Your rewrite should also include a new headline.

3. Rewrite some headlines in your paper so they are biased. Then rewrite the same headline with a different bias.

4. If you find any example of biased or slanted headlines, bring them to class—start a bulletin board of them if enough are found.

1. The contents of a typical American daily newspaper are as follows:

Advertising 60%
Wire service material 15%
Syndicated columns and items..........10%
Sports, society and special
Departments and sections 10%
Local news from reporters 5%

Compare your paper with these statistics and draw some conclusions.

2. If your town has competing papers, obtain copies of each for the same day. Examine them carefully and decide which gives the most news, which is the most objective, and which the most interesting. Which one would you subscribe to and why?

3. Newspapers today are a mix of the tragic and the humorous, the historical and the insignificant. An axe murder is placed next to the weather map, and both are followed by an ad for bananas at 9 cents a pound. In a talk to newspaper editors, Robert Hutchins told them that newspapers "should do as well as they can the things they can do best, and should leave to others the responsibility of entertaining the public." Do you agree with Hutchins or do you find other factors at work that make it necessary for a newspaper both to entertain and to inform?

4. You are the travel editor for a newspaper. A large international hotel chain offers you and your family or a friend a week's free vacation (including air travel) to the Bahamas along with 300 other reporters. Do you accept the offer? Justify your position as an unbiased reporter of the news. You should be aware that such press "junkets" are quite common. Some newspapers have a policy forbidding the acceptance of such offers, while other papers allow reporters to accept. Such junkets usually include a press packet complete with prewritten stories and photos.

5. What are the policies of your local papers on identifying juveniles who are arrested? Some papers treat juveniles as adults, while others refuse to print their names. Is it more important to publish such names to alert the larger community or to protect a young person from being given a possibly undeserved bad reputation?

6. Using a crayon or marking pen and the main section from a local daily paper, mark the following according to the numbers given here:
   1. Wire service story.
   2. Syndicated material.
   3. Pseudo-event.
   4. Press release item.
   5. "Newsmaker" story that is included only because a newsmaker was involved.
   6. Loaded headline.
   7. Adjectives in news stories that convey bias or opinion.
   8. Editorials.
   9. A photo with a message.

7. Some newspapers perform valuable service to their community while others survive nicely by printing a minimum of news and a maximum of advertising. Every year or more *Time* magazine compiles a list of "The Ten Best American Dailies." In 1974, that list was as follows (in alphabetical order):

   1. *The Boston Globe*
   2. *The Chicago Tribune*
   3. *The Los Angeles Times*
   4. *The Louisville Courier-Journal*
   5. *The Miami Herald*
   6. *The Milwaukee Journal*
   7. *Newsday*
   8. *The New York Times*
   9. *The Wall Street Journal*
   10. *The Washington Post*

In order to compile this list *Time* evaluated 1,760 dailies according to this standard: "They [the ten] make a conscientious effort to cover national and international news as well as to monitor their own communities. They can be brash and entertaining as

well as informative. They are willing to risk money, time, and manpower on extended investigations. Through 'Op-Ed' [opinions and editorial] pages and dissenting columns they offer a range of disparate opinions."

You might be lucky enough to find your own paper on this list. Obtain as many of these papers as you can (from a newsstand, or by writing to the papers and purchasing a copy through the mail) and examine them to see why they are considered superior. Remember that the list would be different if made up by a different group of people and that it reflects subjective judgments and opinion.

8. Using all you have learned in this chapter, make an intelligent evaluation of your local paper or papers.

9. Is your newspaper providing more or less news now than a few years ago? A way to measure this is to count the total number of columns devoted to advertising for six days, Monday through Saturday. Then count the total number of columns of non-advertising material (the "newshole") for that same six-day period. This measuring task could be divided among several class groups. This will give you a ratio of news to advertising—50/50 or 60/40 or whatever. Then using either your library or the back issues of the paper at the office of the newspaper itself, compare the recent count with that of a similar week, three, five, and ten years ago. If you find that there is less news today and more advertising than in the past, chances are you are not getting all the news you should. If your paper provides about 100 columns of newshole per day or less, it ranks low in comparative news space. If it provides 140 columns or more a day, it is giving a good amount of news. This column count is based on an 8-column paper (each page has 8 columns across). If your paper is four columns wide, cut the numbers in half; if six, divide by 3/4.

Since this measurement with the past is time-consuming, divide the work among the class and reach a conclusion about the recent history of news coverage in your city.

10. Spend at least one day of class time examining some newspapers other than dailies. These would include papers such as the *National Enquirer* sold in grocery stores, newspapers for ethnic groups and racial minorities, and the "underground press." Collect as many of these papers as possible and pass them around for reading and discussion.

11. A commission of 22 national authorities in law, education, and journalism studied high school newspapers throughout the country and concluded that most are "house organs" or public relations tools for the school administration. The commission found that "Censorship and the systematic lack of freedom to engage in open, responsible journalism . . . is a matter of school policy—stated or implied—in all areas of the country." Discuss your own school paper as an exercise in learning about the news. Is censorship the rule? Should school papers be public relations instruments or a chance for students to exercise freedom of the press?

Chapter 7
MAGAZINES

A Short History of

Perhaps more than any of the other mass media, magazines offer a wide choice of subjects that appeal to small groups of people with special interests. The thousands of magazines published today offer something for almost everyone from comic book fans to crossword puzzle lovers to classical scholars. Many magazines, in fact, are so specialized that it is hard to think of them as *mass* media. Yet even these can exert strong influences on their readers, who in turn influence others.

Benjamin Franklin is credited with starting the first American magazine, a monthly with the ponderous title of *The General Magazine and Historical Chronicle for all the British Plantations in America*. His first issue, in February 1741, made media history and gave many others the idea of publishing a magazine. Franklin's magazine and its early competitors were almost solid print and would be unlikely to receive a second glance from today's reader, who is accustomed to attractive magazines that depend heavily on the modern inventions of photography and four-color printing.

Within fifty years of Franklin's venture, there were almost one hundred magazines in the United States, including *The American Magazine* published by Noah Webster (better known today for his dictionary than his magazine). Webster and Franklin and their colleagues were among early magazine publishers in the United States. The *publisher* is the person who starts the magazine—the person (or group of peo-

ple) with the idea and the money needed to make the magazine work. The publisher hires an *editor*, who finds articles for the magazine and has the general responsibility for the content of the magazine. The actual writing in the magazine is not usually done by the publisher or by the editor but by writers, both free-lancers who write for a number of publications and full-time staff writers, employees of the magazine.

In the mid-nineteenth century, magazines were read mainly by the educated elite. During this time magazines such as *Atlantic Monthly* and *Harper's* were started as intellectual journals. But even as early as 1840 there were signs of what we today would call mass circulation magazines. One of the most popular, *Godey's Lady's Book*, was edited by Sarah Hale to instruct women about manners, proper housekeeping, and fashion. Even during the Civil War, *Godey's Lady's Book* distributed 100,000 copies and was probably read by four times that many people. Included in its pages were stories and poetry by writers now found in today's textbooks of American literature—Edgar Allan Poe, Nathaniel Hawthorne, and Henry Wadsworth Longfellow.

Many new magazines were started around 1880, after Congress passed a bill granting magazines special mailing privileges. Magazines were given a kind of government subsidy because they were "published for the dissemination of information . . . or devoted to literature, the sciences,

SMALL GROUPS...

the American Magazine

arts or some special industry." This mailing privilege still exists, in modified form, today. Five to ten magazines can be mailed for the cost of a single first class letter.

The completion of the first railroad line across the entire United States in 1869 made the national magazine practical. Also, as education spread, more and more Americans were able to read, and the potential audience for a magazine was greatly increased. In the 1880s and 1890s, *Ladies' Home Journal*, *Good Housekeeping*, *McCall's*, and *Cosmopolitan* began. *The Saturday Evening Post*, founded in 1821, became the most influential and powerful magazine in the nation after it was bought by Cyrus Curtis, who also published *Ladies' Home Journal*. Curtis made the *Post* a reflection of American life and presented in it the image of pro-business, "America for Americans." The *Post* published writers such as P.G. Wodehouse, Sinclair Lewis, F. Scott Fitzgerald, William Faulkner, and Ring Lardner.

The Saturday Evening Post had no serious competition as the largest magazine until 1932, when a small black-and-white magazine was issued from a Greenwich Village basement. It was *The Reader's Digest*. The *Digest* promised an article for every day of the month and caught the public's fancy almost immediately. Today that magazine, founded by Lila and DeWitt Wallace, has the second largest circulation in the world with over 18 million readers in dozens of different languages.

In 1923 Henry Luce published the first issue of a weekly news magazine called *Time*. The magazine helped the news make sense; it provided clear summaries of the succession of confusing events called "news." *Time* was a success and gave rise to later successful imitators such as *Newsweek* and *U.S. News and World Report*. In 1936 Luce started *Life* magazine, a magazine that brought vivid pictures of World War II into the homes of Americans in that pre-television era. *Look*, with a similar slant, began publication the next year, and both thrived on superb, vivid photography.

From the end of World War II until the late 1960s, magazines attempted to be a truly mass medium, appealing to everyone. But then well-known and successful general circulation magazines, such as *Saturday Evening Post*, *Life*, and *Look* shocked their readers by announcing they were going out of business. Magazines that attempted to appeal to everyone found it increasingly difficult to compete with television as a general entertainment media. The great circulation race slackened to a slow walk. Instead of a few gigantic magazines reaching tens of millions, the current trend in magazine publishing is the specialized magazine for a small but interested audience. Increases in the cost of paper, printing, and postage have made magazines too expensive for advertisers who want to reach most of the nation with their sales message.

SPECIAL INTERESTS

MAGAZINES TODAY

So many magazines are published in the United States that no one knows exactly how many exist. Every day at least one new publication is born and another dies. There are currently at least 20,000 different magazines published, ranging from *The Biscuit and Cracker Baker* and *Auto and Flat Glass Journal* to *Reader's Digest* and *Sports Illustrated*.

Most magazines are sold by subscription and/or through newsstands. Neither the subscription rate nor the newsstand price is sufficient alone to enable a magazine to survive and show a fair profit. Magazines make much more money from advertising than they do from what the readers pay for each copy. A few publications, usually intended for very specialized audiences such as doctors or schoolteachers, are actually given away. These "controlled circulation" magazines assure potential advertisers that their message will be delivered to a guaranteed number of doctors or history teachers in the country. At the other extreme are specialized magazines and newsletters that contain no advertising and are supported completely by subscription prices that run to more than $100 yearly.

The majority of magazines contain both advertising and editorial content such as articles, columns, and cartoons. In this way, magazines resemble newspapers, television, and radio. All these media have some kind of "content" (shows, news, music) mixed with and economically supported by advertising.

The editorial content of magazines is created by their own full-time staff, by free-lance writers, or by both. Some of the publications written by a full-time staff are *Time*, *Newsweek*, *The National Enquirer*, and *Mad*.

However, a completely staff-written mass circulation magazine is the exception. Most magazine articles are written by free-lance writers. Publications receive thousands of manuscripts through the mail; their writers range from professional, often-published authors to students who submit school assignments that a teacher considers worthy of publication. In one year *Playboy* received over 12,000 unsolicited and unagented fiction stories as well as thousands of additional nonfiction

Tips to Writers from Writer's Market

ARGOSY, 205 E. 42nd St., New York NY 10017, Editor: Gil Paust. For the "adult male, with at least high school education, interested in outdoors, nature, adventure, exploration, camping, hunting, fishing, travel, history, automobiles, sports." Monthly. Circulation: 1,400,000. Rights bought "depends on individual arrangements." Buys 100 mss a year. Query first. Reports in 1 month. Payment in 3 weeks. Enclose S.A.S.E. for reply to query.

Nonfiction: Articles of personal adventure—humor, offbeat and exotic travel, treasure hunts, unusual outdoor stories—everything of interest to the active, intelligent male except overly sexy material. Must be documented and authentic. "We like to feel that the author was actually on the scene. We don't need anything on the movies or for our regular columns." Length: 2,500 to 3,000 words. Pays $500 to $3,000.

Photos: Major areas for photo stories are outdoor adventure, leisure, and recreation. "Before submitting, photographers should thumb through back issues of *Argosy* to see the type of stories we run." Send color transparencies as well as black and white contact sheets. Pays $100 a page for b&w, $150 for color, and from $500 to $750 for a cover. "But we will pay much more for exceptional material." Photographer is responsible for identifying and explaining his photos. Send pictures; queries cannot describe photos fully. Expenses, if any, must be arranged specifically for each assignment. Picture Editor: Bernie White.

Fiction: Needs good fiction material, 4,000 to 5,000 words, novelettes of 12,000 to 16,000 words and novel condensations of 25,000 words by top fiction authors. Fiction should also emphasize the smart male slant and deal with outdoor subjects: Man against nature, animals, the sea, mysteries, war—everything except boy-girl romances. Prices vary from an average $600 for novelettes, $1,000 and up for novels. Fiction Editor: Bruce Cassiday.

How To Break In: "To break into the pages of *Argosy* for the first time, a new writer would first have to submit a story idea that we like. It could be just two or three paragraphs. And he would also have to include the possibility of good photos. If he's a photographer himself, this would be to his credit. Then, if his story idea is accepted, we would ask him to do the piece on speculation, obviously because we have no idea of how well he can write since, as a beginner, he will have no samples of published stories. In *Argosy* there is no such thing as a small sale; we run only full-length features, no shorts."

manuscripts. Of these 12,000 stories, *Playboy* published only four. The odds are always against the free-lancer, yet thousands of free-lance articles are published each year. ("Unsolicited" means that no one at the magazine asked for the article—it simply arrived in the mail. On many occasions a magazine will originate an article idea and "solicit" an author to write it. "Unagented" means that no literary agent was involved. Professional writers often use a literary agent—a person, usually located in New York, who knows the best markets for articles. Agents sell manuscripts to publishers and receive for their services 10 percent of whatever the author is paid.)

Anyone can submit an article or an idea to any magazine and hope for publication. If the article or story is published, the writer will be paid anywhere from $20 to $2,000 depending on the circulation of the magazine and its payment policies.

Most writers who send in unsolicited articles receive a standard form letter called a rejection slip; sometimes an editor will send a letter with the rejection. Rejection by one magazine does not mean that the idea or manuscript is unpublishable. There are many other reasons for an editor's rejecting it. Many articles have been successfully published after having been rejected by dozens of magazines.

REDBOOK MAGAZINE, 230 Park Ave., New York NY 10017. Issued monthly. Buys first North American rights. Reports in 2 to 3 weeks. Pays top rates, on acceptance. Enclose S.A.S.E.

Nonfiction: Robert J. Levin, Articles Editor. Narratives and exploratory factual pieces are always wanted; conditions which affect the magazine's readers, who are young married women in the 18- to 34-year-old group, and about which they can do something. Inspirational pieces are welcome if they are written from the point of view of an individual or family. Also interested in submissions for "Young Mother's Story" and "Young Woman's Story" features. "If you have had some experience in your family, social or marital life that you feel may be particularly interesting and helpful to other young mothers or young women, we would be interested in seeing your story. Please don't hesitate to send it because you think your spelling or punctuation may be a bit rusty; we don't judge these stories on the basis of technicalities and we do make minor editing changes. For each 1,000 to 2,000 words accepted for publication, we pay $500. Mss accompanied by a stamped, self-addressed envelope, must be signed (although name will be withheld on request), and mailed to: Young Mother's Story or Young Woman's Story, c/o Redbook Magazine. Stories do not have to be typed, but we appreciate it when they are legibly written." Length: articles, 3,500 to 4,500 words; short articles, 2,000 to 2,500 words.

Fiction: Mrs. Neal G. Thorpe, Fiction Editor. Uses a great variety of types of fiction, with contemporary stories appealing especially to women in demand. Short stories of 3,500 to 5,000 words are always needed. Also short-shorts of 1,400 to 1,600 words. Payment for short-shorts begins at $750, and at $1,000 for short stories.

From *Writer's Market '75*, 9933 Alliance Road, Cincinnati, Ohio 45242.

Publishing An Article

If you have an idea for a story or an article for a magazine, how can you go about getting it published?

The first step is to decide which magazine is best for the idea. If you have an idea for an article about horseback riding, for instance, you certainly would not submit it to *Popular Mechanics*, any more than you would submit an idea about your custom car conversion to *Horsemen's Journal*.

The best way to select the proper magazine is to read that magazine frequently and become familiar with the kind of articles it publishes. Another helpful guide to finding the best magazine market for an article idea is a book called *Writer's Market*, revised yearly and available at most libraries. This book lists magazines and their addresses, and tells what kinds of articles the magazine needs and how much it will pay per word or per article.

Once the writer has picked a magazine, the typed manuscript can be sent along with a "cover letter" explaining that the article is being submitted for possible publication. (If you want your article back, also send along an envelope addressed to yourself, plus the postage needed.) Another approach is to send a "query" letter. A query letter explains the article idea, presents an outline, and perhaps includes a sample of a portion of the article. If the magazine responds positively, the writer completes the article and then submits it to the editor. Very often the editor will return the manuscript, suggesting minor or major changes before it is finally accepted for publication. Once accepted, the article will probably be published anywhere from one to eight months later.

1. Prepare a query letter to some magazine with which you are familiar and propose an article suitable for its audience. Select one or two alternates that would also be suitable.

2. Either as part of this media course or in connection with a writing course, send query letters and/or manuscripts of high quality to magazines in an attempt to have some student writing published. Through some kind of screening process, make sure that only the class's best efforts are sent out to magazines. Avoid the major magazines and concentrate your efforts on the smaller, more specialized publications. High school students can and have published magazine articles, and many classes have been successful in this project.

3. Using either *Writer's Market* or another reference source, find the name and address of a magazine that interests you. The magazine should be one you have not read before, perhaps one that is not readily available in your town. Write for a sample copy—be sure to send the amount listed for a single copy price. Keep the magazines in a classroom collection for the duration of this course so others can see the variety of magazines that is available.

4. Find out if any magazines are published in your city (use the *Yellow Pages*). If so, find out what kind of magazines they are. If possible, invite someone from a magazine to talk to the class or arrange a tour of the editorial offices.

5. The *Reader's Guide to Periodical Literature* is a handy index to magazine articles published in hundreds of popular magazines. It is a valuable research tool but does not index even 20 percent of all the articles written each year. Many other periodical indexes exist to cover more specialized fields. There is an index for magazines in the arts and humanities, one for film magazines, and dozens of others. Find out which indexes are available at the largest public library in town and examine them. For each one, describe the kind of magazine included and the kind of articles indexed.

6. *Debate:* Magazines should or should not have special mailing privileges.

7. *Debate:* Magazines are more or less valuable and useful than newspapers.

Magazines and the Marketplace

Advertisers often choose magazines rather than other media because of the specific "demographics" that magazines can provide. "Demographics" is the measurement of the kinds of people who read the publication—their age, income, interests, and the like.

If, for example, you wanted to sell a kit that could be used to chrome-plate an automobile engine, the best place to advertise would probably be in a special-interest magazine. You could select from the many magazines read by people interested in cars—for example, *Hot Rod*, *Motor Trend*, or *Car & Driver*.

If you advertised on television or radio or even in a general magazine such as *Time* or *Reader's Digest*, your money would be spent to reach millions of people who wouldn't want to chrome-plate their engines even if you supplied the kit free. Magazines, by limiting their audiences to specialized interests, create the best possible "market segments" for advertisers.

Mass circulation magazines used to engage in circulation wars to obtain as many readers as possible. The more readers a magazine had, the more it could charge for each advertising page. But magazines with millions of readers, such as *The Saturday Evening Post*, *Look*, and *Life*, went out of business because, with their general appeal, they couldn't offer advertisers the specific kind of audience they wanted. On the other hand, magazines could not compete with television in the "numbers game" — the millions of viewers who might see one commercial. These magazines, then, did not stop publication for lack of readers or because of poor quality in the editorial content, but because of too little income from advertising. While mass circulation magazines aimed at "everybody" have been going out of business or struggling to survive, specialized publications have prospered.

In order to fill as many pages as practical with advertising, magazines themselves advertise to the business community. Some of these ads give an idea of the aims of magazines that relate to both the editorial content and the advertising.

The ads shown here, for *Rolling Stone* and *Scientific American*, are typical of those that most large magazines use to attract new advertisers.

The box in the lower left-hand corner of the *Scientific American* ad is an example of the findings of demographic research. Such research is very important to advertisers. *Reader's Digest*, for example, knows that men influence 49 percent of the purchases of salad dressing and 46 percent of the purchases of frozen orange juice. *Reader's Digest* also knows and boasts that about one-third of all purchases of goods in the nation are made by *RD* readers. *Architectural Record* magazine knows its readers are responsible for over 90 percent of the total dollar volume spent on architect-planned buildings. In order to attract its yearly $100 million in

advertising, *TV Guide* knows that it must maintain its current position of being looked at each week by about 30 percent of the American population.

The magazines young people read are equally well researched. *Rolling Stone* knows that it can offer a prospective advertiser (willing to pay $4,500 for a full black-and-white page or $6,800 for a full color page) two million readers with an average age of 22. They know that the average *Rolling Stone* reader buys $72 worth of books and 57 LP record albums a year and goes to the movies 22 times; 74 percent of *Rolling Stone* readers have camped overnight in the past year, 26 percent own electric guitars, 11 percent own motorcycles, and 78 percent are male.

Such specific demographics are crucial to the magazine business.

"ATOM" SMITH.

Or How Corporate Ads Can Capitalize on Our Unique Chemistry.

The venerable prophet of profits never foresaw what's going down today.

Economics used to be as stately as the Emperor's Waltz. The workers toiled, and the mills of profit ground predictably. Often they ground exceedingly large.

No more.

Today, more of us work with our heads than our hands; we produce services (60% of the GNP), rather than products.

Today, it's knowledge that raises the bread. Organized, systematized knowledge.

The fuel for our trillion dollar service economy. And that's where we come in.

SCIENTIFIC AMERICAN.

Our readers and writers are the do-ers, the need-to-know-ers, the avantists and the knowledge organizers who lead this revolution, a revolution producing a new kind of society.

Social scientists call it a knowledge society. It's a society of education, affluence, new lifestyles and new headstyles, where net income often runs second to psychic income. The environment. Consumerism. Job enrichment. Quality of Life. It's a society of new media, new formats, new audiences.

That's why calling corporate media plays the old way is like quarterbacking in Pudge Hefflefinger's leather helmet.

The Leadership Game.

We've all been taught to file leaders

Adam Smith

They're the real opinion leaders.

The energy crisis, the environment, resources, population, health care. With those issues who else *could be* the opinion leaders?

They see problems coming decades before anyone else, so they are "the experts" the media interview. They give the testimony that shapes legislation. And they supply the Federal Government with administrators, regulators, advisers—as well as opinions and attitudes. (Want a for-instance? Look in our May issue at an article "Nuclear Strategy and Nuclear Weapons", written by a lawyer and former DOD analyst. He reports that two *very* top cabinet officers...oh, you know who we mean... had their noses in it almost before it was off the press.)

Aides of one called the author for more dope, and senators used the piece for some verbal nukes of their own in floor debate.)

A convenient label for such leaders is pro/tech.

Scientific American has the highest concentration of them of any TGI-measured

medium.

Small wonder.

We're not a mirror magazine that tells its audience what they already know.

We're the discovery monthly—a magazine of new ideas and original information.

This is where our leaders read and write about issues *before* they become issues.

So it's where you can talk to these influentials *before* problems—and opinions—go public.

Get The Kiddies Off "The Street."

But putting our advertisers in touch with the opinion leaders isn't the only way we protect their futures from future shock.

We help them on "The Street". It's changed too. No place for amateurs. Big money going after big earners.

Where do we fit in?

As Wall Street's early warning system for the profitable technologies that keep these giants big.

What better place to tell corporate prospects a dynamic growth story than in the pages of Scientific American, where the financial world shops for future profits.

Corporate advertising in Scientific American. The formula for communications synergy.

You can bank on that.

How our leaders stack up against their leaders as corporate prospects						
	Business Week	Smith- sonian	Fortune	Time	SCIENTIFIC AMERICAN	S/A Rank
Age: 18-34	40.2	34.2	38.9	45.4	51.7	1
Education: Graduated from college	35.9	43.1	52.6	34.4	53.5	1
Occupation: Managers/Professionals	36.3	31.7	43.4	28.1	44.1	1
Professional/Technical	19.5	23.5	26.2	19.2	38.4	1
Individual Employment Income: $20,000+	16.2	10.5	20.7	7.7	11.7	3
Ever written to an elected official	25.4	24.0	28.6	21.6	28.7	1
Source: 1974 TGI						

under professional/managerial.

Today's leaders are filed under another address: pro/tech. They are the men and women who discover knowledge, who invent it. They take these discoveries and turn them into new products. New markets. New solutions to old problems.

SCIENTIFIC AMERICAN

THE HUMAN POPULATION $1.25

September 1974

THE KNOWLEDGE SOCIETY

Magazine Advertising

1. What is your reaction to the *Rolling Stone* ad?

2. Do you see any way in which advertisers might influence the content of magazines?

3. Find out which magazines are the most popular with members of the class. Why are these the most read? What kinds of ads do they contain?

4. Have each person in the class select a different magazine and do a "profile" of it. To "profile" the magazine, find out the following information by using issues of the magazine. *Writer's Market*, and the library's copy of the *SRDS* magazine volume:

Title.
Subscription and newsstand price.
Frequency of publication.
Does the magazine accept free-lance articles?
If so, what is the pay?
What kind of articles are published?
Who is the intended audience?
How much does a full page of advertising cost?
How many pages are there in a typical issue?
How many ad pages are there in a typical issue? (Add up partial pages and include the cover ads in your count.)
What percentage of the total magazine is advertising?
What is the estimated yearly income of the magazine? (To estimate income, multiply the subscription price by the number of subscribers. Add to this the estimated amount spent in the magazine by advertisers.

What kinds of products are advertised most?
What is the publishing philosophy that governs the choice of articles?
What does an advertiser pay to reach one person when a single full-page ad is bought?

After you have spent many hours of writing your great magazine article, and weeks or months of waiting for a reply, the answer might come back clipped to your manuscript and looking like this.

Please include return postage, or manuscripts will not be returned if rejected.

Health

American Osteopathic Association

212 East Ohio Street

Chicago, Illinois 60611

Thank you for letting us read your manuscript.
We regret that it does not meet our current needs,
but we express our continuing interest in quality
contributions in the field of health education.
The Editors

Chapter 8
RADIO

BEGINNINGS

In 1919 radio was a hobby for a few hundred people who played with the new invention. There was no broadcasting, and few people owned radio receivers. An engineer for Westinghouse, Dr. Frank Conrad, built a little radio station in his Pittsburgh garage in 1920—and radio was born. Conrad wanted to experiment with broadcasting equipment, so he went on the air three times a week and asked anyone who heard him to send a postcard. After he ran out of things to talk about, he placed the speaker of his hand-cranked Victrola next to the radio microphone and became the first disc jockey.

He received enough mail to interest a local department store in using the broadcasts to advertise radio receivers. The radios sold out, and the basic pattern for commercial radio broadcasting was established. Frank Conrad's station later became KDKA, which still operates today.

Early radio stations broadcasted election results, professional fights, and entertainment programming. Only when television took away people's favorite radio programs did the airwaves move toward today's heavy emphasis on music.

In less than 60 years radio has developed into a mass medium that truly blankets the nation. Today the average home has five radios, and there are *100 million* more radios in the United States than there are people. More than 96 percent of Americans over the age of 12 listen to radio during the course of a week, and the average listener logs three and one-half hours of radio listening a day.

From a hobbyist's weekend toy, radio has grown into big business. There is perhaps no better way to see the change in radio than to consider the behind-the-scenes operation of a large metropolitan radio station.

Avoid the dread tune-out!

Out of the science lab and into the air waves comes the new cry of sledgehammer radio

by Mike Lenehan

Test subject No. 8: Linda Mae Bellings. Female. 17 years old. Caucasian. Upper middle class. Urban. Junior in high school. Automobile owner.

She is seated outside of, and slightly below, a glass-enclosed control room in a stainless-steel and black-formica-modern classroom/laboratory affair, in the psychology building of Texas Women's University in Denton, a few minutes' drive from Dallas. Perched atop her head—momentarily disturbing the graceful set of her hair—are headphones through which she will receive the input test material. Strapped across her chest are belts that will measure her heartbeat and respiration rates. Her pudgy hands rest in molded cups arranged in such a fashion that her palms will relay to metal sensors every slight change in the electrical conductivity of her skin.

In the pale fluorescent light that bathes the control booth, she catches a glimpse of the presiding scientist. He is Dr. Thomas Turicchi, mathematician, musicologist, psychologist. From his vantage point behind the knobs, lights and switches of his monitor/control panel, he perceives that everything is in order. A tape recorder is set in motion. An ink stylus that will record the changes in Linda Mae's bodily functions starts its slow, erratic trace across a roll of graph paper. The test begins.

The input starts with a record by The Jimmy Castor Bunch. The record is called "Troglodytes." It is rock and roll music stripped to its essentials—a cacophony of various electronic and percussive instruments resounding to the primal beat. If all goes according to plan, it will set 17-year-old Linda Mae on edge.

One chord, then a simplistic monolog shouted in a hysterical voice: "Gotta find a woman, gotta find a woman." As its first strains pulsate through the thin wires and into Linda Mae's audio reception system, her hands take on a certain clamminess, and the electrical conducting capacity of her epidermal tissues increases. Her heart begins to beat a little more rapidly now; her chest is rising and falling with the new rhythm of accelerated breathing. Linda Mae is pleased. She likes this song about the Troglodytes.

When the testing of Linda Mae and her 27 fellow subjects is completed, Dr. Turicchi and Lew Witz, general manager of Chicago's most successful rock and roll station, WCFL, will sit down and pore over the test results to decide the big question: Will "Troglodytes" be played on Super CFL?! If Linda Mae's responses are not nullified by those of a 22-year-old male, who represents the plum in WCFL's target-audience pie, the record will be assigned a value on the high end of Tom Turicchi's 1-50 numerical response scale.

And if that number is high enough, Lew Witz will play the record, and you will hear it played on WCFL. Witz may not be particularly fond of the record himself—in fact, whenever it comes on, he may turn off the monitor that carries his station's signal into his Marina City office. But he'll play it anyway, absolutely secure in the knowledge provided by Dr. Turicchi that in any average quarter-hour time period on any typical schoolday afternoon, the rhythmic thumping of that bass, the primal beating of that drum, the primal cry of that raspy-throated singer ("Gotta find a woman, gotta find a woman") will set approximately 65,000 teenage bodies into an ecstasy of palm-sweating, heartbeating and heavy-breathing.

The testing technique, called "psychographics" by Dr. Turicchi, is the latest wrinkle in the radio programming game; but it is based on a fairly common idea—that a particularly pleasant or unpleasant reaction to any stimulus increases certain physiological functions of the body. If this reaction is favorable, galvanic skin response, heartbeat and respiration rate rise more or less smoothly to a peak. If the reaction is unfavorable, the rise is sudden and sporadic—it comes in spurts and shows on a graph as a jagged line. With the psychograph—which is essentially a souped-up lie detector—Turicchi measures and records emotional responses. He then interprets the raw test results by assigning numerical values to the pleasures he sees on the machine-produced graphs. Thus, a subject's subconscious, emotional response to a record—or to a commercial, a jingle or a bit of disk-jockey patter—can be evaluated quantitatively. Radio programming has now become . . . a science!

As Witz tells the story, WCFL was a "mess" when he took over its managerial reins in 1968. Progress was unspectacular until one morning in early 1972 when he happened to voice some dissatisfaction over the station's "sound" to an acquaintance

at TM Productions, the Texas-based company that produces WCFL's singing jingles. Witz was then introduced to Tom Turicchi. In February 1972, Dr. Turicchi began to test WCFL's programming material, and the following May, psychographic testing became an integral part of WCFL's emergence as "Super CFL!"

. . . In the spring of 1972, WCFL was pulling approximately 8,100 male listeners between the ages of 18 and 34 in a typical late-morning quarter-hour listening period. WLS, the station that had held Top 40 predominance in Chicago for as long as anyone could remember, had about 20,000 listeners in the same period. Just one year later, by the end of May, 1973, Lew Witz had succeeded in turning those numbers around: 32,000 for WCFL, 14,000 for WLS.

If the significance of those figures escapes you, consider this: In May of 1972, WCFL could get about $90 for one minute of afternoon drive-time (rush period) advertising. Today, that same minute brings about $120. At 12 minutes of commercial time per hour, four hours of drive time per day, that comes out to $1,440 increased revenue *per day* in afternoon drive time alone. . . .

Bill Drake, a California-based programmer, became a radio legend in the mid-1960s by eliminating the irritants. His format, which he sketched out in a restaurant on a tattered napkin, kept commercials to a minimum; it got rid of long, annoying jingle tunes; it compacted the weather report, streamlined the news, shut up the rambling disk jockeys. It gave listeners as few reasons as possible to tune out. And it was an instant success, picked up by every Top 40 station in the whole thumping country.

To understand why, you've got to remember that, for purposes of programming a Top 40 radio station, the archetypal listener is envisioned as a teenager in an automobile. This is not the person the stations want most to reach, in terms of delivering audience to advertisers, but he is the one who must be satisfied. He is attack objective Numero Uno.

Why? Because he is a fickle little !"$*&! The tools of decision lie immediately at his fingertips. With one flick of the wrist, he can pass judgment on the most carefully planned program—either by reaching for a

184

volume knob to turn his radio louder when he is pleased, or by punching the push-button station selector—the dread tune-out!—when he is irritated. (This whole situation, by the way, is duplicated by Tom Turicchi in another form of psychological testing—Operant Preference Testing—in which the test subject can select any of four different stations on a pushbutton console.)

So, the enlightened theory holds, you must constantly guard against the tune-out. You've got to imagine that every listener can slough you off with one nearly imperceptible flick of the wrist. Keep that fickle !"$✱&! and you've got everyone. To keep him, you've got to *eliminate those irritants.*

That's why the traditional ways of judging listener response to a particular song are perhaps no longer the best ways. The traditional ways—juke boxes, sales surveys, request lines—all represent conscious, overt acts on the part of the potential listener. They are fine for telling what the listener will like, but they can't tell what he *won't* like. And in Top 40 radio, what he won't like—the irritants—are of primary concern, especially in the case of relatively new and untested records.

Of course, there are many radio programmers who prefer the old ways. In Chicago, only WCFL and WMAQ-FM, as far as Lew Witz knows, use any form of psychographic testing. Of all the stations in the country, Witz estimates that a mere 200 have been influenced by psychographics somewhere along the line. That means that for every station that uses it, there are about 30 that don't. . . .

At WCFL, jingles, records, announcements, weather reports and all the rest are programmed to build what Lew Witz calls "calibrated emotional waves." Programming elements are chosen and placed to take the listener on an emotional ride—slow at the start, building through the middle, socko at the end, and then back down to an emotional ebb from which the whole thing starts all over again. (By the way—in case you were wondering—your peak moment of attention is right between records. And that's where you're likely to hear the broadcaster's most important message: his call letters.) Even commercials are programmed

for maximum emotional impact. Some—those that receive particularly poor scores on the psychograph test—are rejected or re-produced. Others are placed according to the edicts of a five-page procedural manual.

. . . Radio programming is a "philosophy based in psychology," says Jim Loupas, WCFL's 34-year-old chief of engineering. "People are going to listen to the station that's easiest to listen to." At WCFL, Loupas says, even technical matters of transmission and signal quality are designed to support the programmer's quest for that elusive subliminal response. Loupas and his staff of 25 engineers maintain a complex array of transmission and limiting devices; one of them automatically "holds up" the tail end of a record so that the emotional flow of programming will not be interrupted by a fading vocal or instrumental line. Sound is balanced over 16 discrete ranges of audio frequency. (Your home stereo probably allows you to balance two: bass and treble.) Transmitter tuning is changed periodically to accommodate the fast-changing trends in popular music—this, because the walking bass lines of the Pointer Sisters require equalization different from the old brass sound of groups like Chicago and Blood, Sweat & Tears. "We're constantly adjusting the sound of our signal," Loupas says. "We keep this station tuned up like a piano." . . .

A station's call letters and dial position also can be important in the subliminal preferences of listeners. "We learned two very important things from psychographics," Lew Witz says. "One was that we were giving listeners a lot of reasons to leave our signal. The other was that even when they were listening, they didn't know it. We could see from a subject's graph that he had been listening to WCFL, and yet when we asked him what station he had listened to, he'd give the name of the other station." (At both WLS and WCFL, the competition is often referred to as "the other station.")

One of the problems, according to Witz, was in the call letters themselves. "They're nonphonetic. Just say them to yourself—W-C-F-L. There's nothing to them—no sound, no rhythm, no sex. And our dial position [1000 kHz]—it couldn't be any worse."

But when Witz found the magic phrase "Super CFL," the "sizzle in the steak," as he calls it, his station identification problems were over. People began to remember and repeat the name. If they prove nothing else, the ratings books at least prove that.

When was the last time you heard someone say, "I don't listen to WCFL because they have lousy call letters," or "I like WCFL because they have terrific electronic limiters," or "I heard a dynamite calibrated emotional wave on the radio today"? Pacing, dial position, transmission quality—they're all things that most listeners are unaware of. And yet, Lew Witz and Top 40 programmers like him all over the country apparently know what they're doing. And if the time, money and energy expended on these considerations give any indication, these matters of subconscious appeal are important in determining listener preferences among Top 40 radio stations.

What we have here, it seems, is a classic, clear-cut separation between the *form* and the *content* of Top 40 radio. Under the heading "content" you can place all those things of which you're consciously aware as a listener: the songs, the news stories, the disk jockey banter. Under "form" come all those things that influence your preference without your conscious knowledge: the transitional material, the electronic wizardry, the phonetic sound of the call letters, the flow, the feel, all those calibrated emotional waves.

As it turns out, the form of Top 40 radio shares much in common with rock and roll music itself. It is constant, repetitive, emotional, sensual, ups-and-downs, ins-and-outs—the beat! And that beat—the form—can make all the difference in Top 40, where the content is frequently the same from station to station. The records can be the same old records, the disk jockeys can be the same loud egotists, the news stories can be the same vapid trivia—*yet* one station can pull all the listeners! The one that will do it is the one that's got the beat—not just in the music, but in the whole frapping package.

And the reason why? The reason why is precisely the reason why Lew Witz had to struggle for four years to make the name of his radio station stick in the minds of his listeners. It is precisely the reason why the watchwords of Top 40 are "eliminate the irritants." In many ways, you see, Top 40 radio is not an information medium at all. It is an environment—an emotional bath in which the 18-to-34-year-old children of the electronic age can immerse themselves at the mere flick of a switch.

Consider the places you're most likely to hear Top 40 these days: on the beach, where people are sleeping and playing games; in the kitchen, where people are cooking dinner or cleaning the oven; in the bathroom, where people are shaving or clipping their toenails; in the factory, at the gas station, near the drugstore, in an automobile.

But of course! In an automobile! That 18-year-old fickle bastard! It is on him that this whole thing begins to focus. Here is a child of the rock and roll generation. Here is a man who has lived his life in the midst of the electronic media. He is driving in his Plymouth Roadrunner with the 383 V-8 and the chrome reversed wheels on the back end. He is whomping his 8-ball gearshift knob to keep time with the music. He is on his way, perhaps, to pick up a quart of milk for his mother, or maybe to get together with his cohorts behind the high school gym. He is talking, perhaps, to his girlfriend or his buddy, or thinking about what he's going to do this Friday night. His radio is on, the volume is up, the tools of decision are right there at his fingertips. And what is he getting out of it? The environment! The feel! The beat! His palms sweat, his heart thumps! This is just like rock and roll! You don't have to understand the words! It's the beat that's the important thing!

Remember now, Mr. Radio Programmer, treat this man with kid gloves. He is attack objective Numero Uno. If you dare to jolt him out of his drooling subconscious primal ecstasy, be sure it's a good jolt. Make sure it's a clever joke or a No. 1 tune that does it. Because if it's a bad jolt—a lousy commercial or a dud record—he'll reach for that pushbutton station selector sure as hell. Minimize those moments of decision! Avoid the dread tune-out! Eliminate those irritants! Keep that flow going! The beat! The feel! The calibrated emotional waves! *Gotta find a woman, gotta find a woman!* Keep his sweaty palms on that wheel . . . right there, yes there . . . right where they belong.

1. "Avoid the Dread Tune-Out" is about a big-city radio station. Stations in smaller cities are just as concerned about how many people listen, but they tend to rely more on guesswork to determine what to play. What is your reaction to "psychographic programming" such as that described in the article?

2. The article was about "Top 40" format radio. A station's "format" describes the type of music it plays or the kind of programming it usually broadcasts. A "Top 40" format station programs those records currently in the "top 40" in terms of record sales. Nationally, most teenagers listen to Top 40 format stations. Other common formats include M-O-R (middle-of-the-road), Easy Listening, Rhythm and Blues, Country and Western, Progressive Rock, All News, Educational, Foreign Language, or Classical. Find out what format each station in your area uses.

3. After you have determined the formats of the local stations, try to determine which segment of the audience each station reaches the most. For example, a daytime-only station with "Easy Listening" music and hourly stock market reports probably is most interested in attracting people listening in offices and businessmen and housewives who want "relaxing" music.

The reason for audience segmentation is to allow advertisers to reach specific audiences. A maker of acne cream would not advertise on the station described above; it would advertise on a "Top 40" format station.

4. Make a list of the products advertised during one hour of radio programming on one station. Various students should choose various stations to monitor. Examine the lists and find the relationship between the products advertised, the station's format, and the intended audience.

5. As a class experiment, you can perform a simplified version of the psychographic programming described in the article. A Galvanic Skin Response meter can be attached to volunteers while various records are played. The meter should show the differences in reactions of a number of students to a variety of music. Select records from rock to opera for the experiment.

Your school's psychology, biology, or science department may have a meter that can be used to measure Galvanic Skin Response. If not, relatively crude but workable meters can be purchased for under $20 from Edmund Scientific Corp. (Edscorp Building, Barrington, NJ 08007).

6. The article mentions that the rates advertisers pay for radio time depend on the size of the audience and the time of day. Find out what rates your local stations charge for commercial time. These can be checked at the library in a book produced by *Standard Rate and Data Service*, which lists all the radio stations in the country with detailed information about programming and ad rates. A page from one edition of the book is shown on page 188 with an interpretation of the terms used.

7. According to the statistics given in the article, how much does it cost an advertiser on WCFL to reach one person driving home from work?

8. Find out which radio station is the most popular among students at school. Which is the most popular among their parents? Do you think that when you become a parent your listening tastes will have changed, or will you still listen to the station you do now? Explain the reasoning behind your answer.

THE RATE CARD

KGWA

1950

Subscriber to the NAB Radio Code
Media Code 4 237 2340 2.00
Public Broadcasting Service, Inc., Box 960, Enid, Okla.
73701. Phone 405-234-4230

STATION'S PROGRAMMING DESCRIPTION
KGWA: Programmed for general interest, comtemporary
country blend.
MUSIC: 70% Medium Country 30% General Popular.
11 am-12N phone-in swap programs, NEWS: full-time staff
with mobile facilities. 5 min at :60 every hour except 7 am.
12 N & 5 pm. 1/4 hr expanded news reports. Daily
editorials. Weather forecast & current conditions at :30
with 4 5-min weather summaries daily. SPORTS: 2 5-min
reports daily plus play-by-play during year. Farm & market
programs 3/x daily. Contact Representative for further
details. Rec'd 2/12/73.

1. PERSONNEL
General Manager—Allan Page
Commercial Manager—Chuck Middleton.

2. REPRESENTATIVES
Avery-Knodel, Inc.

3. FACILITIES
1,000 w.: 960 kc.
Directional—same pattern, all hours.
Operating schedule 5:45 am-11:05 pm. CST.

4. AGENCY COMMISSION
15% time only.

5. GENERAL ADVERTISING See coded regulations
General: 1a, 3a, 3d, 4a, 4d, 5, 6a, 8.
Rate Protection: 10b, 11b, 12b, 13b, 14b,
Basic Rates: 22a, 23a, 28a.
Contracts: 40a, 41, 45.
Comb.: Cont. Discounts: 60b, 60i, 61a.
Cancellation: 70b, 70c, 71a, 73a.
Member: Oklahoma Farm Network.

TIME RATES
NATIONAL AND LOCAL RATES SAME
No. 9 Eff 4/1/74—Rec'd 2/28/74.
Prime—Mon thru Sat 6-9 am, 11 am-1 pm & 4:30-6 pm.
ROS—All other times.

6. SPOT ANNOUNCEMENTS
PRIME

	1x	50x	100x	250x	500x	1000	1500x
1 min	6.00	5.7	5.40	5.10	4.80	4.50	4.20
30 sec	4.40	4.20	4.00	3.80	3.60	3.40	3.20

ROS

	1x	50x	100x	250x	500x	1000	1500x
1 min	4.30	4.10	3.90	3.70	3.50	3.30	3.10
30 sec	3.30	3.15	3.00	2.85	2.70	2.55	2.40
15 sec	2.50	2.40	2.30	2.20	2.00	1.90	1.80

*GUARANTEED—52 WK CONTRACT

per wk	3 ti	6 ti	10 ti	20 ti	30+
1 min	4.90	4.60	4.30	4.09	3.70
30 sec	3.75	3.55	3.35	3.15	2.95

(*)May add ROS spots, any quantity not to exceed
1000x ROS rate.

7. PACKAGE PLANS
ROS PACKAGES

7 CONSEC DAYS:	10 ti	20 ti	30 ti	50 ti	70 ti
Rate	1x	50x	100x	250x	500x
30 CONSEC DAYS:	30 ti	60 ti	90 ti	120 ti	150 ti
Rate	50x	100x	250x	500x	1000x

AFTER HOURS 30-SECOND SPOT PLAN
10 ti per wk, minimum 4 wks. 1 per day after 7 pm & 3 ti Sun
daytime per wk 19.50.

8. PROGRAM TIME RATES
*PRIME

	1x	52x	104x	156x	260x	312x
1 hr	50.00	47.50	45.00	42.50	40.00	37.50
1/2 hr	30.00	28.50	27.00	25.50	24.00	22.50
1/4 hr	20.00	19.00	18.00	17.00	16.00	15.00
5 min	10.00	9.50	9.00	8.50	8.00	7.50

*ALL OTHER TIMES

	1x	52x	104x	156x	260x	312x
1 hr	40.00	38.00	36.00	34.00	32.00	30.00
1/2 hr	24.00	22.75	21.50	20.25	19.00	18.75
1/4 hr	16.00	15.00	14.00	13.00	12.00	11.00
5 min	8.00	7.50	7.00	6.50	6.00	5.50

(*) May add ROS spots, any quantity not to exceed
1000x ROS rate.

Annotations (left margin):

Format

Who to contact about adv.

Smallest power is 250 watts—largest is 50,000. 5,000 is typical.

An advertising agency receives a commission from the station equal to 15% of the total cost of the time purchased.

A one minute-spot (ad) will cost $6.00 in prime time if used once. If run 50 times, cost will drop to $5.70 each.

Most stations offer "package plans" that are ways of saying to advertisers—"The more time you buy, the less it will cost per second."

Annotations (right margin):

Some radio towers beam signals in certain directions in order to avoid interfering with each other. These are called directional antennae.

Specific details about advertising policies.

What time the station considers as "prime." This indicates the times of day when the station has its largest listening audience.

This is the cost for sponsoring an entire program or program segment. Note that rates are higher for "prime" times because more people are listening then.

RADIO-TV PROGRAMS FOR TODAY

CHICAGO FREQUENCIES

WGN—720	WJJD—1160
WIND—560	WJOB—1230
WILL—580	WEDC—1240
WMAQ—670	WSBC—1240
WBBM—780	WCRW—1240
WAIT—820	WMOR—1280
WCBD—820	WJOL—1340
WENR—890	WGES—1390
WLS—890	WRMN—1410
WAAF—950	WIMS—1420
WCFL—1000	WHFC—1450
WMBI—1110	WNMP—1590

FM

WGNB—98.7	WEHS—97.9
WBEZ—91.5	WEFM—99.5
WJIZ—92.3	WFMT—100.3
WFJL—93.1	WMAQ—101.3
WAAF—93.9	WMOR—102.7
WRBI—94.3	WRGK—103.1
WENR—94.7	WEAW—105.1
WMBI—95.5	WOAK—105.9
WCHI—95.9	WKRS—106.7
WBKB—96.3	WLEY—107.1
WBBM—97.1	

MORNING

(Central Daylight Saving Time)

6:00A.M.
WGN-Farm hour and news.
WMAQ-Phillip Hayes
WBBM-Paul Gibson
WCFL-Dawnbuster
WIND-News;Morning Watch
WJJD-Breakfast Frolic
WLS-Farm bulletin board
6:15 A.M.
WMAQ-Town and Farm
WLS-Morning Devotion
6:30 A.M.
WGN-Today on Farm
WLS-The Sage Riders
WIND-News,; Purple Sage
6:45 A.M.
WGN-Bob Siegrist
WMAQ-Alex Drier, News
WLS-Bob Lyle, news
WIND-Yawn Patrol
6:55 A.M.
WBBM-News
7:00A.M.
WGN-Bill Evans
WBBM-World News Roundup
WCFL-News
WMAQ-Norman Ross Show
WLS-Buccaneers
WIND-News; Record shop
WJJD-News; Wake Up
WAAF-Breakfast Express
7:15 A.M
WBBM-News reports
WCFL-Morning clock
WJJD-Negro News Front
WLS-Range Riders
7:30 A.M.
WBBM-Bing Sings
WLS-Sage Riders
WJJD-News
WIND-Musical News Review
7:45 A.M.
WCFL-Bill Hamilton, News
WJJD-Wake Up, Chicago
WBBM-Jim Conway show
WLS-Bob Lyle, News
7:55 A.M.
WMAQ-News
8:00 A.M.

*WMAQ - WIEBOLTS, YOUR NEIGHBOR - Musical Variety, with June Marlowe

WGN-Robert F. Hurleigh
WCFL, WLS-Breakfast Club
WIND-News;Top Tunes
WBBM-John Harrington
WJJD-Ernie Simon
WAIT-Record Caravan
WFMF-Morning Melodies
8:15 A.M.
WGN-Two Ton Baker
WBBM-Patrick O' Riley

*Indicates listing paid for by sponsor to give you more information about program

SPECIAL EVENTS

7:25 p. m.—WIND—chicago Bears vs. Cleveand Browns football game.

8:30—WCFL—Chicago Cardinals vs. San Francisco 49ers exhibition football game.

9:00—W-G-N, WMAQ, WBBM, WGN-TV, WNBQ, WBKB—President Truman discusses "The Korean Situation," On WIND at 10:00.

News Broadcasts

MORNING

6:00—WIND	9:00—WIND
6:30—WIND	9:30—WIND
6:45—W-G-N	10:00—WIND
7:15—WBBM	10:00—WCFL
7:30—WJJD	10:30—WIND
8:00—W-G-N	10:45—WLS
8:45—WMAQ	11:30—WIND
9:00—W-G-N	11:45—W-G-N

AFTERNOON

12:00—WMAQ	4:30—WIND
12:00—WAAF	4:40—WBBM
12:30—WBBM	5:00—WIND
12:30—WIND	5:00—WMAQ
1:00—WIND	5:15—WBBM
4:00—WIND	5:45—WMAQ

EVENING

6:00—WIND	10:00—WCFL
6:00—WLS	10:00—WBBM
6:15—WMAQ	10:30—W-G-N
8:00—WCFL	11:00—WMAQ
9:00—WIND	11:00—WIND
9:30—WIND	11:55—WMAQ
10:00—WENR	12:00—WIND

8:30 A.M.
WGN-Tello Test
WMAQ-Music That Sings
WBBM-Gold Coast
WIND-News, Top Tunes
WAAF-Luthern Gospel Hour
8:45 A.M.
WGN-Today's The Day
WBBM-Shopping with Mircus
WMAQ-News, Norman Barry
9:00 A.M.
WGN-Leslie Nichols, News
WMAQ-Welcome Travelers
WIND-News, A. Godfrey
WBBM-This is Bing Crosby
WCFL-Bill Evans Show
WLS-My True Story
9:15 A.M. A.M.
WGN-RECORD Relay. A full hour of recorded tunes with Holland Engle, Pierre Andre, Norm Kraft, and Bill Lansing.

WMAQ-Here's Norman Ross
WLS-Luncheon Club
WIND-News;Music by Martin
WJJD-Swing Lane; Interlude
WCFL-Marriage License Bur.
11:15 A.M.
WGN-VIRGINIA GALE with interesting and helpful suggestions to make the tasks of the homemaker easier

WBBM-Aunt Jenny
WJJD-Guess Tune; Interlude
WCFL-Personalty Time
11:25 A.M.
WLS-Carol Douglas

11:30 A.M.
WGN-The Answer Man
WAIT-Stella White
WBBM-Helen Trent
WJJD-Frankie Lane
WIND-News; Frank Sinatra
WCFL-South American Way
WLS-Martha and Helen
WNMP-Jewels of Music
WGES-Cocktail Time
11:45 A.M.
WGN-Spencer Allen; News
WBBM-Our Gal Sunday
WJJD-Marty Hogan
WCFL-Don Artisite
WIND-Como and Carle

AFTERNOON

12 NOON
WGN-Cedric Foster News
WMAQ-News
WLS-Farm World Today
WCFL-Baukhage Talking
WAAF-News Symphony
WBBM-Big Sister
WIND-News; Benny. Goodman
WJJD-Waltz Time
12:10 P.M.
WMAQ-What's New in Agriculture
12.15 P.M.
WGN-Hostess Hour
WMAQ-Food Magician
WBBM-Ma Perkins
WCFL-Music Mart
WJJD-Noon Time Quiz
WBEZ-Symphony Hour
WFJL-For Listening Pleasure
12:30 P.M.
WGN-Market Reorter
WBBM-Julian Bentley
WMAQ-Phillip Hayes
WJJD-Al Benson
WIND-News, Luncheon Music
WGES-Polish Dinner Bell
WLS-Dinner Bell
WAIT-Radio Gosip Club
12:45 P.M.
WGN-Leslie Nichols; news
WBBM-Guiding Light
2:15 P.M.
WMAQ-Road of Light
WBBM-Hilltop House
WCFL-Fred Waring
2:25 P.M.
WLS-One Man's Opinion
2:30 P.M.
WGN-Meet the Menjous
WBBM-House Party
WMAQ-Pepper Young
WCFL-News
WLS-Quick as a Flash
2:45 P.M.
WGN-Nat'l Consumer's Panel
WMAQ-Right to Happiness
WCFL-Spike Jones
3:00 P.M.
WGN-Radio Quiz
WMAQ-Backstage Wife
WBBM-Strike it Rich
WLS-Nancy Craig
WCFL-Great White Way
WOAK-The Band Stand

3:15 P.M.
WGN-Second Spring
WMAQ-Stella Dallas
WLS-Art Baker
3:30 P.M.
WGN-Linda's First Love
WMAQ-Lorenzo Jones
WIND-Record Shop
WBBM-Julian Bentley
WCFL-Hannibal Cobb
WJJD-Scoreboard
WLS-News
3:45 P.M.
WGN-Lanny Ross
WMAQ-Young Widder Brown
WBBM-Double Quiz
WJJD-Ernie Simon
WLS-Variety Music
WAIT-Footlight Favorite
4:00 P.M.
WGN-Lionel Barrymore
WLS-Bob Atcher
WMAQ-When A Girl Marries
WBBM-Paul Gibson
WCFL-Tommy Dorsey
WIND-News; Spike Jones
WFJL-Discs and Data
WOAK-Musical Matinee
WEFM-Artists Album
4:15 P.M.

WGN-MARSHALL KENT with the popular disc jockey spinning the choice records of the day Sponsored by Colgate Co.

WMAQ-Portia Faces Life
WIND-Harry James
WCFL-Margaret Whiting
4:30 P.M.
WGN-Bakers Spotlight
WMAQ-Just Plain Bill
WIND-News; Tommy Dorsey
WCFL-Merry Go Round
WLS-U.S. Navy Band
4:40 P.M.
WBBM-Harrington News
4:45
WGN-Singing Story
WMAQ-Front Page Farrell
WBBM-Gold Coast
WENR-Beula Karney
WIND-Travel Time
5:00 P.M.
WGN-Cisco Kid
WMAQ-George Stone; news
WBBM-Allen Jackson; news
WENR-Fun House
WIND-News; Musical Scoreboard
WJJD-News; Interlude
WCFL-Variety Time
WFMF-Melody Time
WAAF-Sincerely Yours
5:05 P.M.
WMAQ-Len O' Connor, news
5:15 P.M.
WBBM-J. Harrington, news
WCFL-Benny Goodman
WMAQ-Dave Garroway
WIND-Sports Special
WJJD-Rosemary Wayne
WAAF-From the Keyboards
5:30 P.M.
WGN-Bobby Benson
WMAQ-One Man's Family
WJJD-Race results
WCFL-Music You Like
WIND-Bert Wilson
6:45 P.M.
WGN-Fulton Lewis Jr.
WMAQ-Rich Harkness, news
WCFL-Music for men
WBBM-Edward R. Murrow
WIND-Time to Remember
WJJD-Suppertime Flolic
7:00 P.M.

WGN-RUDY VALLEE SHOW with the "vagabond lover" recalling the early days of show business and reviewing popular records.

3:15 P.M. (cont.)
WMAQ-Stars and Starters
WBBM-Phillip Marlowe
WIND-News; Bob Elson
WLS-The Fat Man
WCFL-Vic Barnes, news
WOAK-Hour of Songs
WEFM-Seranade Music
WNMP-Evening Concert
7:15 P.M.
WCFL-Vaughn Monroe
7:25 P.M.
WIND-Bears vs. Browns
7:30 P.M.
WGN-Xavier Cugat
WBBM-Up for Parole
WMAQ-Cloak and Dagger
WLS-This Is Your FBI
WCFL-Meet the Band
WEFM-Musical Favorites
WFJL-American Jazz Classics
WAAF-Footlight Echoes
WEAW-Concert Favorites
7:45 P.M.
WCFL-Doris Day
7:55 P.M.
WGN, WGNB-Bill Henry
8:00 P.M.
WGN-MGM Theater
WBBM-Songs for Sale
WMAQ-Dimension X
WENR-The Thin Man
WCFL-News; Novena service
WGES-Lithuanian hour
WENR-Stand By
WEFM-Evening Concert
WOAK-For Music Lovers
WRBI-Concert Music
8:30 P.M.
WMAQ-Jack Lait, Confidential
WENR-The Sheriff
WCFL-Cardinals vs. '49ers
WGES-Germanic Broadcast
WFJL-Opera Heirlooms
8:55 P.M.
WENR-Chapion Roll Call
9:00 P.M.
WGN-President Truman
WBBM-President Truman
WMAQ-President Truman
WENR-Music from Pier
WEFM-Musical Memories
WEAW-News; Holiday Paradise
9:30 P.M.
WGN-Theater of Stars
WMAQ-Sports Newsreel
WENR-The Modernaires
WBBM-Capitol Cloak Room
WIND-News; Record Spotlight
WEFM-Composers' Hour
9:45 P.M.
WMAQ-Pro and Con
WENR-Freddie Martin
10:00 P.M.
WGN-Behind the Story
WBBM-Fahey Flynn, news
WMAQ-News
WIND-President Truman
WENR-Paul Harvey
WOAK-Moonbeams
WFJL-Editor's Comment
10:15 P.M.
WGN-Chicago at Night
WMAQ-Rio Rhythms
WBBM-Weather Report
WENR-Barry Wood Show
WFJL-Evening Devotions
10:20 P.M.
WBBM-Tony Wetzel
10:30 P.M.
WGN-News
WENR-Conversation with Casey
WIND-ABC club
WGES-Rhythm Till One
WEFM-Music Guild hour
WMAQ-Big City Seranade
WFJL-Caravan of Dreams
WOAK-Great Music Moments
10:35 P.M.
WBBM-Eddie Howard
10:40 P.M.
WGN-Song Souvenir
10:45 P.M.
WGN-This Is the Story
WENR-Platter Party

9. How does the most popular station in town decide which records to play? To find out for sure, you might call the station or write a letter for the entire class. If possible, invite a speaker from the radio station to talk to the class about radio programming, or visit a radio station and talk to the program director.

10. The article refers to the "form" and the "content" of radio programming. Using the article as a guide to what these terms mean, list or describe the "contents" and the "form" of some local stations.

11. Does the "commandment" of the large market Top 40 station to "eliminate the irritants" have any comparable commandment in network television programming?

12. An old radio directory is reprinted on page 189. It appeared in a daily paper in 1950. Such directories used to be printed in the daily paper just as TV schedules are today. What happened to change radio programming? Radio in 1950 was scheduled in a way similar to the way TV is today. Do you think television in the year 2000 might be as different from TV today as radio today is different from radio in 1950? Do you recognize any of the names or programs on the schedule? Of those you recognize, which have been able to survive in mass media other than radio?

13. Obtain a tape or record of an old radio show and listen to it in class. Will today's radio programming seem "strange " or "old-fashioned" 25 years from today?

14. There are two kinds of commercial radio broadcasting—AM (amplitude modulation) and FM (frequency modulation). The two represent different ways of transmitting radio waves. As recently as 15 years ago, FM was almost unknown. Only the largest cities had FM stations and few people listened to them. But today FM is the fastest-growing kind of broadcasting. In large cities there are more FM than AM stations. More people still listen to AM than to FM but the FM audience grows every day.

Find out what FM stations operate in your area. What is the frequency of each, which are the most popular, what format does each use? Are there any educational FM stations in the area? Educational FM stations are usually found on the lower (or left-hand) part of the FM tuning dial.

15. Have someone in class explain the difference between AM and FM. What are the advantages and disadvantages of each?

16. Spend some time listening to five (if your area permits) radio stations you have never before listened to. Are their formats different from those of your favorite stations? How?

17. At night listen to radio stations in other cities on a car radio or a good table radio. Listeners in the Midwest should have no trouble hearing stations in Boston, Dallas/Fort Worth, Denver, New Orleans, and Pittsburgh. How are these stations just like your hometown stations? How are they different? Listening to stations in distant cities should be done on AM radio, as FM stations have a far shorter reach than AM. FM stations operate on the same region of the frequency spectrum as television stations and have similar reaches. If you could tune your TV set between channels 6 and 7, you could hear FM radio—that is where they transmit.

Featuring the Finest
in Recorded Music

SOLID STA

AMERICANA II

Chapter 9
RECORDS

STEREO

Featuring the Finest
In Recorded Music

WURLITZER

Record Making

Phonograph records are, in a way, like film, because the music heard on a record never existed quite that way in reality. A record is not made by simply recording what musicians play in one sitting any more than a film is made by photographing what actors do on a stage.

The music on today's popular phonograph records usually is recorded first on a master tape in a recording studio. Bits and pieces of tape are spliced together to produce the perfect performance that becomes a 45 rpm single or a record album. Thus both films and records are created by similar processes, called *editing* in the film world and *mixing* in the role of the recording industry.

A popular record album (one LP) might fill 3,000 feet of recording tape (professional tape runs at 15 ips [inches per second]—twice the speed of the fastest home recording units and three times that of a cassette recorder), but that 3,000 feet is assembled from the 30,000 or more feet originally recorded. Most of what is recorded on tape in the studio is thrown away and never reaches the final record, just as in film most of what is shot is thrown away and never appears in the print shown at local movie theaters. A feature film is a skillful blending of hundreds or thousands of pieces of film; a single hit record is usually a skillful blending of 20 or more short pieces of tape.

The person responsible for putting together the record is the producer. In film, the producer is the person who supplies the money for the making of the film. In the record industry, the producer acts in a recording session much like a film director acts at a filming session.

In the early days of film the public knew the names and faces of the "stars" who appeared on the screen. As the public became more sophisticated, the name of the director was often a bigger box office draw than the "star." Records are still best known for the performers—the star system thrives in the record industry today more than in film. But record audiences are slowly beginning to recognize the names of certain producers who have a following and a reputation for a particular kind of "sound."

When Carly Simon first recorded "That's the Way I've Always Heard It Should Be," the song was not an instant hit. A producer suggested the addition of a heavy but short drum passage to act as a bridge between parts of the song. Ms. Simon credits that musical idea with making the song a hit. The producer's idea gave the song a distinctive sound that helped the record stand out from the thousands of others and stick in the listeners' minds. Most records released are commercial flops and barely earn back the money spent to produce them. Those that do succeed are the ones that are recorded by a big name star or group or that demonstrate production genius.

The producer, otherwise known as the A & R (Artist and Repertory) man, works in a glass-enclosed control room filled with recording and sound-altering equipment. He or she communicates by microphone with the performers and at the same time works with a mixing console, directing an "engineer" (who could be compared to the photographer in a film) to give more volume here, soften a tone there, vary the comparative loudness of any one instrument (bring the voice "closer" or mute the drums), overdub (so that one person can be a duet or trio or play a whole orchestra of instruments alone), provide special sound effects, or any one of hundreds of possible variations. If a dozen different record producers were to work with the same song and the same musicians, the final result would be twelve different "sounds" or versions of the song. One record company executive has said, "In the pop field, 70 percent of a record is the creation of the A & R man."

The fact that many performers want to "lip synch" their songs (mouth the words while the recording is played) for TV appearances attests to the importance of the producer. If these groups were to sing and play "live" for the TV camera, the results would not sound at all like the record that viewers play at home or hear on the radio. Because of the work of the producer and the recording studio, many groups are actually unable to play what they've recorded. Live concert performances are different from the sound produced on records, although many groups bring to each concert electronic equipment equivalent to a small recording studio so they can come close to producing the same "sound." Some artists use very little production and so can match their records quite closely in a live performance, while others depend so much on production values that their music can never be performed live.

Once the producer has mixed the master tape to everyone's satisfaction, it is turned into a record. The tape signals are fed to a recording head where the signal is converted to mechanical vibrations of the recording stylus. The vibrating stylus cuts a wavy pattern in a rotating wax-like plate called a master disk. The pattern cut is actually a picture of sound waves that can be seen with proper lighting if the record is placed under a microscope. This master plate is then used as a mold from which the records sold in stores are pressed.

This process of producing and manufacturing records has been used for only about 30 years. Compared with the long-playing record, the inventions of radio, television, and film are old-timers. In spite of the fact that the LP is a recent invention, the story of its creation is not well known.

In 1944 Peter Goldmark of CBS Laboratories visited some friends who played for him a new recording of Brahm's Second Piano Concerto. Being a music lover, Goldmark was disturbed by the frequent interruptions caused by changing and turning over the six records in the album. (At that time, record albums of long pieces of music looked very much like photo albums and contained from three to fifteen separate disks.) Goldmark realized "there was no doubt in my mind that the phonograph . . . was murdering Brahms, and I felt somehow impelled to stop this killer in its shellac tracks."

In 1944 the art of sound reproduction was crude by today's standards. Goldmark resolved to improve the situation even though he admittedly knew nothing about the medium of sound recording. He set out to invent a record that could hold an entire symphony on its two sides. His success led to the multimillion-dollar record industry of today, an industry built on one man's desire to be able to listen to classical music without interruption.

The original records were made to be played at 78 rpm (revolutions per minute), but Goldmark was able to solve the technical problems that prevented slower speeds from being practical. Today's standard 33 1/3rpm speed was not chosen by scientific means but for a very practical reason: at that speed enough music could be put on a single disk to provide background music for one reel of film in a movie theater.

The gradual improvement in the craft of sound reproduction can be clearly heard by listening to a series of records, each made a number of years later than the previous release. The original LP gave way to "high fidelity," which in turn was changed to stereo which today stands ready to give way to quadraphonic (four-channel) sound. No doubt some future invention (perhaps the video disk) will render even "quad" obsolete.

Four-channel sound seems destined to become as standard as stereo (two-channel) is today. Currently no one system of four-channel recording has emerged as obviously the most practical to use. The industry competition in the struggle to capture the market is similar to the battles that took place over what kind of color reproduction to use in color TV, what speed the LP should be, and what format and speed recording tape should be. When four-channel sound does become standard, it will mean that records can go beyond merely an accurate reproduction of real sound. Four-channel systems can create sounds that cannot be heard in live music.

This development in the medium of recording mirrors the history of film, painting, and photography. At first painters and photographers were content to try to imitate reality. They tried to capture in paint or on film what the eye could see, to make images "life-like." But once this had developed, they moved beyond capturing reality and into creating a new reality. Many modern paintings and photographs resemble nothing the eye can see. A comparison of the best paintings and photographs of the first artists in these media with those of modern artists shows very clearly the change that took place. Sound reproduction is also moving into new worlds. The music played on home reproduction systems of the future may be as different from the top tunes of today as the Rolling Stones are from Gregorian chant.

1. Choral director Ray Conniff says, "The simple fact is that people today get a lot better sound on records than they do in live concerts." Do you agree or disagree? Why? Do live concerts have other advantages?

2. Concert pianist Glenn Gould has said that "concerts as they are now known will not outlive the 20th century." Do you agree? Would you distinguish between rock concerts and classical music concerts in debating this statement?

3. Bring to class and play some records that use overdubbing and that illustrate elaborate studio production. Contrast these with some records that are close to "natural," that is, reveal very little studio manipulation of the natural sounds.

4. In what ways are the processes of film editing and record mixing alike? How are they different? For example, in a film a person can open a door and seem to enter a room that is in reality hundreds of miles away. On a record, the drummer and the bass player on the same song may never have met each other.

5. Who are some of the best-known record producers now? Members of the class can bring records that demonstrate various "sounds," such as the Motown sound, the Spector sound, the Philadelphia sound, or others.

6. *Cross-Media Study*: There is a trend in music today toward the more engineered and electronic sound and away from the simple, acoustic (nonelectronic) sound. Even when you attend a live concert, you usually hear electronically amplified sound rather than acoustic sound—sound from the loudspeakers rather than sound directly from the instruments. In your imagination, carry this trend to its extreme and consider the idea of completely electronic music. For example, will the traditional instruments such as drum and guitar be replaced by more sophisticated electronic devices? Can computers be programmed to play electronic music? How will electronics change music in the next 100 years?

7. Play in class some records that illustrate "new" or "avant garde" music that is completely electronic in nature. Do you think this will ever completely replace today's music?

8. Find different versions of the same song and explain how their production is different.

ARLO GUTHRIE: Arlo Guthrie. Arlo Guthrie, vocals and guitar; instrumental accompaniment. *Presidential Rag; Won't Be Long; Deportees; Go Down Moses; Me and My Goose; Last to Leave*; five more. REPRISE MS 2183, $5.98. Tape: • m 82183, $6.97; •• M 52183, $6.97.

High Fidelity Magazine
Oct. 1974

This latest disc by Arlo Guthrie is split between a first side devoted to explicit protest songs and a second side that concerns itself with more universal, less overtly political matters (unless you count "Go down Moses" as a protest song). All the material is by Arlo except for "Deportees," which has words by Woody Guthrie and music by Martin Hoffman, Jimmie Rodgers' "When the Cactus Is in Bloom," and "Go down Moses."

Musically, most of the material is in Arlo's familiar cowboy-country-folk style, although frequently there are added strings (which sound a little syrupy) and chorus (which sounds pretty good). In some ways, he is the sort of performer who works best on-stage, alone and with his guitar and banjo. There his easily winning charm and nice blend of seriousness and wit project very well indeed.

One would like more live albums from him; in a studio context such as this, the result is slightly antiseptic. The protest songs have an element of simpleminded sincerity. The simplemindedness doesn't detract from the sincerity, of course, but it does compromise the songs' artistic effectiveness. For that reason, Side 2 is more successful.

J. R.

10. Are the lyrics to today's songs important or are the "sound" and the "beat" more important? Do today's songs attempt to say important things in their lyrics? Historically, the lyrics to popular songs go through cycles of being mainly nonsense for a period of time and then slowly changing to lyrics that are very meaningful. Which phase are we in today? Bring some songs to class to prove the viewpoint you hold.

THE RECORD INDUSTRY

Radio station programmers play those records that are selling best around the country. But records rarely become best-sellers until they are played on the radio. The more a song is played on radio stations, the more copies it will sell—and the more it sells, the more radio stations will play it more often. Thus a hit is born.

Billboard magazine is a weekly publication for the radio and record industry. Among their services is a weekly listing of the 100 best-selling albums. Their listing looks like this:

Billboard HOT 100®

© 1975 Billboard Publications, Inc. No part of this publication may be reproduced, stored in a retrieval system, or transmitted, in any form or by any means, electronic, mechanical, photocopying, recording, or otherwise, without the written permission of the publisher.

THIS WEEK	LAST WEEK	WKS ON CHART	TITLE—Artist (Producer) Writer, Label & Number (Distributing Label)	
1	2	15	THE HUSTLE—Van McCoy & The Soul City Symphony ● (Hugo & Luigi), V. McCoy, Avco 4653	WBM
2	3	11	I'M NOT IN LOVE—10 cc (10 cc), G. Gouldman, F. Stewart, Mercury 73678 (Phonogram)	HAN
3	1	11	ONE OF THESE NIGHTS—The Eagles (Bill Szymczyk for Pandora Prod.), D. Henley, G. Frey, Asylum 45257	WBM
4	4	11	PLEASE MR. PLEASE—Olivia Newton-John (John Farrar), Welch, Rostill, MCA 40418	HAN
5	5	9	LISTEN TO WHAT THE MAN SAID—Paul McCartney & Wings (Paul McCartney), P. McCartney, Capitol 4091	HAN
6	7	11	SWEARIN' TO GOD—Frankie Valli (Bob Crewe), B. Crewe, D. Randall, Private Stock 45021	SGC
	6	11	JIVE TALKIN'—Bee Gees (Arif Mardin), B. Gibb, R. Gibb, M. Gibb, RSO 510 (Atlantic)	WBM
7	9	4	SOMEONE SAVED MY LIFE TONIGHT—Elton John (Gus Dudgeon), E. John, B. Taupin, MCA 40421	MCA
8	8	15	MIDNIGHT BLUE—Melissa Manchester (Vini Poncia), M. Manchester, C.B. Sager, Arista 0116	HAN
9	11	12	ROCKIN' CHAIR—Gwen McCrae (Steve Alaimo, Willie Clarke, Clarence Reid), C. Reid, W. Clarke, Cat 1996 (TK)	SGC
10	10	11	DYNOMITE—Bazuka (Tony Camillo), T. Camillo, A&M 1666	SGC
11	13	16	THE WAY WE WERE/TRY TO REMEMBER—Gladys Knight & The Pips (Ralph Moss), M. Hamlisch, A. Bergman, M. Bergman/H. Schmidt, T. Jones, Buddah 463	SGC/CHA
12	12	14	LOVE WILL KEEP US TOGETHER—The Captain & Tennille ● (The Captain), N. Sedaka, H. Greenfield, A&M 1672	WBM
13	15	13	WHY CAN'T WE BE FRIENDS?—War (Jerry Goldstein, Lonnie Jordan, Howard Scott), S. Allen, H. Brown, M. Dickerson, L. Jordan, C. Miller, L. Oskar, H. Scott, J. Goldstein, United Artists 629	
14	16	13	ROCKFORD FILES—Mike Post (Mike Post), M. Post, P. Carpenter, MGM 14772	MCA
15	17	11	RHINESTONE COWBOY—Glen Campbell (Dennis Lambert, Brian Potter), L. Weiss, Capitol 4095	SGC
16	19	6	HOW SWEET IT IS (To Be Loved By You)—James Taylor (Lenny Waronker, Russ Titelman), Holland-Dozier-Holland, Warner Bros. 8109	SGC
17	20	6	I'M ON FIRE—Dwight Twilley Band (Oister), D. Twilley, Shelter 40380 (MCA)	SGC
18	18	14	EVERY TIME YOU TOUCH ME (I Get High)—Charlie Rich (Billy Sherrill), B. Sherrill, C. Rich, Epic 8-50103 (Columbia)	SGC
19	22	9	MORNIN' BEAUTIFUL—Tony Orlando & Dawn (Hank Medress, Dave Appell for Medress-Appell Prod.), D. Appell, S. Linzer, Elektra 45260	HAN
20	24	2	WILDFIRE—Michael Murphey (Bob Johnston), M. Murphey, L. Cansler, Epic 8-50084 (Columbia)	WBM
21	21	18	SLIPPERY WHEN WET—Commodores (James Carmichael, Commodores), T. McClary, Commodores, Motown 5338	SGC

THIS WEEK	LAST WEEK	WKS ON CHART	TITLE—Artist (Producer) Writer, Label & Number (Distributing Label)	
34	40	5	COULD IT BE MAGIC—Barry Manilow (Barry Manilow, Ron Dante), B. Manilow, A. Anderson, Arista 0126	SGC
35	41		THAT'S THE WAY OF THE WORLD—Earth, Wind & Fire (Maurice White), M. White, C. Stepney, V. White, Columbia 3-10172	HAN
36	36		SWEET EMOTION—Aerosmith (Jack Douglas), S. Tyler, T. Hamilton, Columbia 3-10155	WBM
37	50	6	BLUEBIRD—Helen Reddy (Joe Wissert), L. Russell, Capitol 4108	SGC
38	46	6	THIRD RATE ROMANCE—Amazing Rhythm Aces (Barry "Byrd" Burton for Southern Rooster), H.R. SMith, ABC 12078	
39	27		I'M NOT LISA—Jessi Colter (Ken Mansfield, Waylon Jennings), J. Colter, Capitol 4009	SGC
40	51	7	SEND IN THE CLOWNS—Judy Collins (Arif Mardin), S. Sondheim, Elektra 45253	
41	49	6	BALLROOM BLITZ—Sweet (Phil Wainman), M. Chapman, N. Chinn, Capitol 4055	
42	45	6	SEXY—MFSB (Kenny Gamble, Leon Huff), K. Gamble, L. Huff, Philadelphia International 8-3567 (Epic/Columbia)	WBM
43	54	4	THAT'S WHEN THE MUSIC TAKES ME—Neil Sedaka (Neil Sedaka, 10C.C.), N. Sedaka, Rocket 40426 (MCA)	SGC
44	56	6	RENDEZVOUS—Hudson Brothers (Bernie Taupin, B. Hudson, M. Hudson, B. Hudson, B. Johnston), Rocket 40417 (MCA)	B-3
45	55	5	FAME—David Bowie (David Bowie, Harry Maslin), D. Bowie, J. Lennon, Alomar, RCA 10320	SGC
46	57	18	LOOK AT ME (I'm In Love)—Moments (Al Goodman, Harry Ray), A. Goodman, H. Ray, W. Morris, Stang 5060 (All Platinum)	BB
47	26		LOVE WON'T LET ME WAIT—Major Harris ● (Bobby Eli), B. Eli, V. Barrett, Atlantic 3248	SGC
48	59	4	OH ME, OH MY (Dreams In My Arms)—Al Green (Willie Mitchell), W. Mitchell, A. Green, M. Hodges, Hi 2288 (London)	
49	60		HOPE THAT WE CAN BE TOGETHER SOON—Sharon Page & Harold Melvin (Kenny Gamble, Leon Huff), K. Gamble, L. Huff, Philadelphia International 8-3569 (Epic/Columbia)	BB
50	61		(Shu-Doo-Pa-Poo-Popp), LOVE BEING YOUR FOOL—Travis Wammack (Rick Hall), J. Williams Jr., C. Whitehead, Capricorn 0239 (Warner Bros.)	
51	80		GET DOWN TONIGHT—K.C. & The Sunshine Band (H.W. Casey, R. Finch), H.W. Casey, R. Finch, TK 1009	MCA
52	63		'TIL THE WORLD ENDS—Three Dog Night (Jimmy Ienner), D. Loggins, ABC 12114	SGC
53	29	11	HEY YOU—Bachman-Turner Overdrive (Randy Bachman), R. Bachman, Mercury 73683 (Phonogram)	ALM
54	73		HELP ME RHONDA—Johnny Rivers (Johnny Rivers), B. Wilson, Epic 8-50121 (Columbia)	
55	39		GET DOWN, GET DOWN (Get On The Floor)—Joe Simon (Raeford Gerald, Joe Simon), R. Gerald, J. Simon, Spring 156 (Polydor)	SGC
56	67		GLASSHOUSE—Temptations (Jeffrey Bowen, Berry Gordy), Charlamagne, Gordy 7144 (Motown)	HAN
57	72		BLACK SUPERMAN/ MUHAMMAD ALI—Johnny Wakelin & The Kinshasa Band (Robin Blanchflower), J. Wakelin, Pye 71012 (ATV)	HAN
58	79		TUSH—ZZ Top (Bill Ham), Gibbons, Hill, Beard, London 220	B-3
			BIGGEST PARAKEETS IN TOWN—Jud Strunk (Don Costa), C. Drew, J. Strunk,	SGC

THIS WEEK	LAST WEEK	WKS ON CHART	TITLE—Artist (Producer) Writer, Label & Number (Distribution)	
	NEW ENTRY		I BELIEVE THERE'S NOTHING STRONGER THAN OUR LOVE—Paul Anka & Odia Coates (Rick Hall), P. Anka, United Artists 685	
69	43	10	EL BIMBO—Bimbo Jet (Laurent Rossi), C. Morgan, Scepter 12406	
70	48	7	TAKE ME TO THE RIVER—Syl Johnson (Willie Mitchell), A. Green, M. Hodges, Hi 2285 (London)	
71	53	19	THANK GOD I'M A COUNTRY BOY (Milton Okun, Kris O'Connor), Sommers, RCA 10239	
72	58	8	SNEAKIN' UP BEHIND YOU—The (Randy Brecker), D. Grolnick, W. Lee, D. Sanborn, M. Brecker, Arista 0122	
73	NEW ENTRY		IT DOESN'T MATTER ANY MORE, BE LOVED—Linda Ronstadt (Peter Asher), P. Anka/P. Everly, Capitol 405	
74	85	3	ACTION SPEAKS LOUDER THAN WORDS—Chocolate Milk (Allen Toussaint, Marshall Sehorn), L. Harris, T. Richards, D. Richards, M. Tio, K. Williams, RCA 10290	
75	NEW ENTRY		THE PROUD ONE—Osmonds (Mike Curb), Gaudio, Crewe, Kolob 14771	
	87	2	CAN'T GIVE YOU ANYTHING (But My Love)—Stylistics (Hugo & Luigi), Hugo & Luigi, G.D. Avco	
76	82	4	DREAM MERCHANT—New Birth (James Baker, Melvin Wilson), L. Weatherspoon, Buddah	
77	82	4	DANCE WITH ME—Orleans (Charles Plotkin), J. Hall, J. Hall, Asylum	
78	89	2	HOW LONG (Betcha' Got A Chick On The Side)—Pointer Sisters (David Rubinson & Friends), A. Pointer, ABC/Blue Thumb 265	
79	90		7-6-5-4-3-2-1 (Blow Your Whistle) (Rick Bleiweiss, Bill Stahl),	
80	84	6	EASE ON DOWN THE ROAD (Not Listed), C. Smalls, Wing &	
81	81		IT ONLY TAKES A MINUTE (Dennis Lambert & Brian Potter),	
82	NEW ENTRY		COME AND GET YOURSELF SOME (Leon Haywood), C.R. Cason,	
83	83	3	WATERFALL—Carly Simon (Richard Perry), C. Simon,	
84	NEW ENTRY		SOONER OR LATER (Ed Townsend), E. Townsend	
85	88	4	PLEASE TELL HIM THAT I SAID HELLO (Andy Di Martino),	
86	86		LET ME BE THE ONE (Kenny Gamble, Leon Huff), Philadelphia 8-3570	
87	NEW ENTRY		ROCK & ROLL RUNAWAY (John Anthony), Anchor 21002	
88	NEW ENTRY		ROCKY (Bob Montgomery)	
89	100	2	LIFE AND DEATH Love Child's Afro Cuban (Jerry Love)	
90	95	2	PHILADELPHIA (Gus Dudgeon)	
91	70	21	SPIRIT OF THE MADNESS (R. Bachman) R.S.	
92	62	17	SU—	
93	97	2		
94	NEW ENTRY			

1. Obtain a current issue of *Billboard* (from a large newsstand or by ordering one copy from *Billboard*, 1515 Broadway, N.Y., N.Y. 10036, $1.25) and determine if any of the records on the chart on the previous page are still listed. Why do the most popular records change so fast? The big hits of five years ago are hardly heard at all today—why not?

2. Using the most current *Billboard* list you have, go through your own record collection and check off the records you own. Would it be fair to say that if the class as a whole owns quite a few of those on the list, then its taste in music is "typical" and conforms to that of teens across the country?

3. Have each person in class go through his or her own record collection and write down the name of the record company who made the record (for example—Warner Brothers, Motown, Bell, etc.). Note how many records are owned by students and how many are from the most often listed companies. The ten largest companies account for over 75 percent of all records sold. The largest record companies are Warner Communications (labels include Asylum, ATCO, Atlantic, Cotillion, Elektra, Nonesuch, Reprise, Capricorn, Bearsville & Chrysalis), Columbia, RCA, A & M, Capitol, MCA, Motown, ABC/Dunhill, Bell, and London Records.

4. Does the pattern of class ownership of record albums resemble the national pattern? If not, what special circumstances might explain the difference?

5. If you have a favorite record next year, it will very probably be one that has been selected and approved by the handful of people who make the final decisions at the five largest record companies. If you have a favorite television program next year, it will probably be one that has been selected and approved by the handful of people who make the final decisions at the three networks. Most of the money you will spend to go to the movies next year will go to a few of the largest film companies. Do you see any problems in this arrangement? Why does this concentration exist in the media industries? Does it exist in other industries?

6.

Rock Hysteria

As a direct result of the death of one fan and injuries to many others at the David Cassidy concert recently, the British tour of the Jackson Five has been postponed.

The group's manager and the group were extremely disturbed by the 1,000 casualties at the open-air David Cassidy concert. Despite heavy crowd control precautions, hysterical fans among the audience of 30,000 crashed barriers and massed dangerously in front of the stage, leading to the death later of a 14-year-old fan.

It has now become clear that the disaster poses serious questions for the future of open-air concerts that are likely to attract hysterical teeny-boppers.

a. Why do recording stars attract such fanatical and huge followings?

b. What are the main attractions of "live" concerts?

c. What causes hysteria at a rock concert?

d. Many auditoriums and arenas in large cities forbid rock acts because of the problems with crowd control and damage to the building. Why do rock concert crowds have such a bad reputation?

e. What values do popular music "heroes" embody and preach by their songs and lifestyles?

Rock, Riches and the Record Industry

In the 1950s and earlier the dream of many teenagers was to become either a big time ball player or a movie star. In the 1970s a new dream began to occur more often. Every neighborhood has at least one group of a few high school students who play music together and call themselves a "group" or a band. The dream of many of these groups is to land a record contract, to become famous and tour the world living as only multimillionaire rock stars can.

No doubt some of the neighborhood groups who now play at garden parties for $50 will become tomorrow's superstars. But their dreams of success in the future should be tempered with knowledge of how the record industry operates and what it takes to survive. In the following article, Allan Parachini gives a behind-the-scenes look at the world of the struggling musician versus the harsh demands of the record industry.

Lincoln Perry

Rock & Riches

Those kids are all making a bundle, right?

By Allan Parachini

The houselights dim; the clamor of the crowd falls to a low buzz—low enough that the anticipatory coughing can be heard amid the hum of the PA system. In a moment the show will begin. It makes no difference what band is about to play, and it doesn't matter where. What is about to be unleashed, like a genie out of a bottle, is an IMAGE—magical, mysterious, and glamorous—one of many raised up by that energetic cultural force known as Rock, swathed in clouds of sumptuous glory, lauded in hymns of hyperbolic praise, and flattered by the proliferation of those smaller-scale imitations known as Lifestyle. This pantheon of heros and heroines has no parallel in contemporary culture, and we must go back to the early days of the silver screen—of Valentino, Pickford, and Garbo—to find anything like it. What it is is *myth*, a highly selective metaphor about life, of which both performers and their audiences, romanticized and romanticizing, are at once creators and consumers.

But myths are like Chinese boxes, one nestling inside the other on into infinity. The myth immediately inside the myth of the Rock Star is that of Untold Riches, and there is just enough truth (though not much) to it to make it an effective magnet, drawing young people to New York, Los Angeles, Nashville, or wherever else music is made and recorded to declare themselves in on a piece of the action, a slice of the fabulous take.

205

They arrive in Los Angeles, for instance, by battered car or bus, check into the YMCA, and hit the street. They walk up to Yucca Street, or Vine near Hollywood Boulevard, look in the Yellow Pages under "Records," and start feeding change into a payphone. Then they wait, lounging on the sidewalk outside a liquor store, having given the payphone as "a number where I can be reached," for the return call that never comes. They have a common desire—a career in the music business—and a host of very uncommon, often highly original, misconceptions about just what that business is. They are, in short, as much prisoners or victims of their myth as any Forty-niner ever was, feeding

their hopes on the good news of occasional rich strikes and ignoring the multitudinous evidence of failure all around them.

The J. Geils Band, they will tell you, slaved away, first as two separate groups and then together under the Geils name, for five years in Boston barrooms before managing to land a record contract; they now average $10,000 to $15,000 a night. Black Oak Arkansas played insignificant dates throughout the South for four years waiting for what they finally got—a luscious contract with Atlantic Records. Dr. John was an obscure New Orleans studio musician for ten years before a chance hit single miraculously transformed his career in 1973. Rod Stewart, who once slept on a Spanish beach because he couldn't afford a hotel room, who used to play professional soccer to support his music habit, now earns, by reliable estimate, between $750,000 and $1,000,000 annually. At the top, the money piles up like winter snow in Donner Pass, and the bulldog tenacity that keeps so many musicians struggling up the lower slopes is fueled by the expectation that they too will eventually, if only they hang on, get to frolic in it. What are their chances?

Record companies sold 1,436,000,000 (that's one and one-half *billion*) seven- and 12-inch discs in the United States in 1973. There were 196 releases certified "gold" (meaning they sold 500,000 copies for an album, 1,000,000 copies for a single). Such figures translate very readily into Big Money, of course, and the myth has it that the musician is first in line to collect. And myth it is, for there are very few performers indeed in the most favored position.

The performer derives revenue primarily from two sources: live performances and record royalties. He may also earn something from song-publishing royalties (if he writes his own material), since there will then be royalty income from others who perform his songs and from radio stations that play them on the air as well. But before the musician realizes any income whatsoever, he must normally commit a percentage of all his earnings "up front" to a manager, unless he is clever enough to handle his own business affairs—including negotiating complicated contracts with record companies and booking agents; insuring that the provisions of those contracts are fulfilled; securing the most favorable possible terms for such seemingly incidental arrangements as production, promotion, and marketing of records, travel provisions for performance tours, and even the reservation of recording-studio time.

A few musicians are just adept enough at business to have come to the unwise conclusion that self-management is a realizable goal. Few reach it, and many budding careers are ruined each year because some overconfident youngster insisted he knew enough about the music business to fend for himself in the jungle of accountants, lawyers, and systems analysts who run modern record companies. Creedence Clearwater Revival was probably the most successful group in recent history that was actually self-managed, but John Fogerty, Creedence's leading light, had the benefit of powerful good advice from Saul Zaentz, president of Fantasy Records, the small Oakland, California, label on which Creedence appeared for the duration of its professional life and for which some of its individual members, including Fogerty, still record.

Poco's manager, John Hartman, put management in this capsule: "Management is not a person, it's a force that exists in the artist's consciousness. If the guy's manager tells him one thing and his old lady tells him another—and he listens to his old lady—then the old lady is that force." For most musicians, a professional personal manager is an absolute necessity. Managers normally retain between 10 and 15 per cent of the musician's entire gross income and can in some cases get as much as 20 or even 50 per cent. Accountants (more and more indispensable the higher the sales figures get) are another accoutrement, and they get $200 to $500 a month. Such people are necessary not only to help the performer retain a reasonable part of his initial gross, but also to interpret the complex financial systems that appear to be peculiar to record companies; they are needed to make certain the musician does not, plainly and simply, get ripped off.

Managers are usually blamed for the failures, but they are seldom credited for the successes of the musicians they handle; they generally find themselves in the position of gamblers at a high stakes game—lose once and you're out. Peter Casperson, who owns Castle Music Productions, a small management firm in Boston, employs ten people to minister to the needs of four active acts, in which Casperson estimates he has about $50,000 invested. One of the acts is Jonathan Edwards, whose top-selling single *Sunshine* failed to reach first position in the *Billboard* sales charts two years ago only because *American Pie* got there first. The Edwards windfall from that single alone was sufficient re-ward for Casperson, who has stayed with Edwards (who frequently falls victim to a strong desire to move to the country and who dislikes the grueling pace of live performing anyway) since *Sunshine* was a hit. But Casperson's operation is small potatoes in every respect when measured against such management "giants" as Los Angeles' David Geffen, whose stable includes more than twenty performers, from the Eagles to Linda Ronstadt.

Managers are not a race of white knights, of course. Their ranks are heavily populated by the shady and by the inept, either of whom can leave a client musician, in the manner of one of those bilked innocents in an old prize-fight movie, with no return whatever for his efforts, gold record sales or no. Selection of a good (honest, capable) manager is therefore one of the music business' biggest risks.

207

But to return to the question of income. Record royalties, unlike the fees paid for live performances, are established contractually between record companies and musicians for periods of between one and five years. Gross royalties are computed on a base of 90 per cent of the wholesale (just over $2.00 for albums) for the retail ($5.98 average) prices of each record actually sold. Retail discount prices do not bear on royalties. The performer gets between 5 and 18 per cent of 90 per cent of retail, say (depending on the terms of his contract), and though there are several ways to compute the amount, they generally work out to about 42 cents per album. The record producer gets a 2 or 3 per cent royalty, which may in some cases be deducted from the musician's share, and the a-&-r (for "artists and repertoire") man who signed the artist to a record contract in the first place frequently gets 2 or 3 per cent, normally from the record company's gross.

Under the royalty system, the *potential* for income from a record that sells well is actually not bad (more than $200,000 for a gold album, for example), and if a musician has written his own songs, he receives an additional gross of 1½ cents per song, per record, in song-publishing royalties. Normally, the manager has unobtrusively procured for himself some of the publishing proceeds; if he is honest, he has also done as much for his client. Otherwise, the naive musician may likely find that he has unknowingly signed away some or even all of the potential publishing income as part of a cash "advance" in an innocent-looking contract with a music-publishing firm or even his own record company.

Record companies have established what seems to be a unique sort of company-store relationship with their artists, one that tends to cut handsomely into the income potential of royalties. First, the record companies normally try to charge back to the artist as much of the actual cost of recording and marketing a record as possible. Such costs can amount to $15,000 or $20,000 (for the most modestly produced album) to as much as $100,000 (for an overproduced spectacular). They include studio time, union pay for extra musicians, and other expenses too numerous and too unimaginable to mention—even the cost of the recording tape is levied against royalties. The record companies also charge their artists for some of the expenses of promoting and publicizing the resulting recording, including, for example, press parties and the cost (from $750 to $1,500 per month) of retaining a private publicist. A modest tour may also be under-

written by the record company—and charged against the royalty gross; even a short introductory series of engagements in small clubs can run to as much as $50,000.

What results is in many cases an arrangement that would be bitterly familiar to any old-time Appalachian coal miner. Some recording acts owe so much of their soul to the company store that they never overcome their indebtedness; they can only watch helplessly as the royalties of their successful later records are eaten up in mid-career by early advances. Then too, determining the number of copies of a record actually sold is a task of no little difficulty. Records are distributed on consignment, meaning that unsold goods may be returned—for full credit—by individual record stores to small distributors, by small distributors to large, and large distributors to the original record company. The consignment arrangement is a necessary one, since without it distributors and their clients would probably never gamble on a first release by an artist they had never heard of, or even on a great second release by someone who had bombed with his first. The problem with this system is that it can take at least several months, and at times as much as several years, to determine accurately the exact number of copies of a recording sold. Record companies manage this situation to their advantage, often withholding a portion of royalties against the possibility of such returns.

Most record contracts stipulate that sales records may be audited, but the auditing process itself is one comprehensible only to an accountant with extensive experience in the business. "I always audit," says Casperson. "It's just part of the game with big record companies." Poco's Hartman agrees. "You find that if you audit, you turn up discrepancies. I don't think it's so much the result of blatant, intentional stealing as it is that the bookkeeping system is so complicated and the price structure so complex."

Royalties are usually paid out only once every six months. For a group as battle-scarred and successfully established as Poco, whose albums regularly sell between 200,000 and 250,000 copies, the royalty hassle is little more than that, and one that will ultimately be amicably resolved. But for a struggling new act whose first album sold only 50,000 copies (or even 1,000 copies) the shock of meager royalty return (or none at all)—with the inevitable appropriate deductions—can be devastating, even mortal.

Special arrangements are frequently negotiated under which a manager or record company pays a weekly salary or underwrites the rent of musicians. But what the performers usually seem to forget is that there must ultimately come a day of reckoning. Scrupulous managers try to avoid the certain shock of the bottom line by establishing trust savings accounts for client musicians. One semi-prominent English blues band's management, seeking to avoid the budgetary trauma that comes with the eventual end of the short earning life of his clients (it is, after all, somewhat shorter than that of professional athletes), has put $10,000 in a bank account for each of the four members of the group without their knowledge. Other managers, however, are content simply to break the news that there is no money, that advances have eaten up every cent.

To be successful, a group or solo performer must, of necessity, be caught up in a vicious circle formed and controlled by the whims of the fickle popular music market. Live performances are most profitable when they are booked simultaneously with the appearance (and the promotion) of a relatively new piece of recorded product. Conversely, it is difficult to develop an ongoing, steady market for the purchase of records without spending a great deal of time On The Road (thus capitalized because of its rigors). The road's merciless, cold reality is of such awesome proportions that few performers who have been moving around the circuit for any length of time can resist writing a song or two about it, thus adding to its lore. (In this it is not unlike the musical theater, which is simply filled with works telling us there's no lifestyle like show business.) Janis Joplin, of course, died on the road; so did Jimi Hendrix and Cass Elliot. The road killed Jim Croce—and Buddy Holly, Patsy Cline, and many others. Poco's Tim Schmit has been saving his motel-room keys from the last two of his five years on the road, and they now half fill an enormous carton he keeps in a closet at home.

Live performances are usually arranged by a professional booking agent or by someone in the musician's management who fills the function of a booking agent. Agency work is dominated by about a dozen big firms with offices around the country. Agents retain between 10 and 20 per cent of the gross proceeds of live performances they arrange. The fees paid for such performances is an area in which there simply are no norms. Rates are set either on a flat basis (so many dollars per performance, regardless of eventual audience size), or they are based on a combination of a cash guarantee and a percentage of the gross proceeds. Under the system, a group such as New Riders of the Purple

Sage probably averages about $7,000 a night; the Nitty Gritty Dirt Band, which plays a murderous schedule of more than 200 one-nighters a year—most of them before college audiences—between $5,000 and $10,000 a night. Only a tiny number of groups consistently earns more—and it is hard not to know just who *they* are.

Such sums may look rather impressive to the average struggling wage-earner, but gross figures are misleading—they do not take into account the expenses, the short earning lives of the musicians, or the years of near-starvation they put in before anyone paid attention to them. Poco, for instance, has been a working, self-supporting, comparatively well-to-do group for only five years, the Nitty Gritty Dirt Band for seven. That makes both of them fairly *senior* in a business in which five to ten years is often required just to get established. The Dirt Band was playing high schools in the San Fernando Valley for $300 a night as late as 1966—and one must remember that that is not $300 *every* night. The reasonably good money lasts, in most cases, only two or three years. Groups as big as Creedence can, in those two or three years, amass a fortune. But members of a group of the stature of Blue Cheer, for example, which enjoyed a brief fling at the height of the San Francisco acid-rock movement, have long since faded into obscurity and (perhaps) poverty.

Even assuming a respectable pay scale, the tricks of survival on the road are learned only after bitter experience and (usually) the squandering of a great deal of money. For instance, a band must, of necessity, invest heavily in electronic equipment. The Dirt Band, which could not be said to carry an extraordinary amplification system, travels with 8,000 pounds of equipment valued at more than $50,000. Even the least elaborate array of equipment sufficient to produce a respectable stage sound these days requires an initial investment of more than $20,000. Sometimes this money comes from the record company or management—another advance against royalties.

But the biggest hazard of the road (except for the constant problem of awakening in a strange Holiday Inn with no idea of the name of the city in which it is located) is that inexperience, incompetence, or both will result in most of the proceeds being spent even before the tour has been concluded. Managers and booking agents have varied theories about how much it should cost to live and travel on the road. Poco's Hartman, for instance, figures costs of transportation, lodging, equipment shipping, insurance, and the like at about 25 per cent of the gross from the tour. In the case of one Poco expedition a couple of years ago to a relatively "tight" cluster of 39 cities in 45 days, the 25 per cent amounted to between $50,000 and $60,000.

Steve Miller, an established, almost universally respected musician who waited about ten years for the public to become aware of his prowess, frugally manages and books himself, holding costs to a barebones minimum in the five months a year he's on the road. He figures the percentage at less than 10—with costs amounting to only about $21,000 for a recent tour that grossed $300,000. Miller travels modestly with a small party of eight, two of whom are equipment managers who normally drive trucks (which must be bought, gassed, repaired, and insured, by the way) laden with equipment while the rest of the entourage flies from city to city. Many groups, frustrated by the loneliness of the road, take friends and/or wives along on tour with them—a comforting touch of home, but it eats very quickly into the gross.

Bruce Nichols, a booking agent with Agency for the Performing Arts (APA) in New York City, sees Hartman's 25 per cent figure as realistic and desirable as a norm, but he believes that, for many groups, expenses run as high as 50 per cent and even higher. The differences are owing to a variety of reasons. "New" groups all too frequently fall prey to the temptation to spend unreasonably large amounts of money on expensive hotel rooms or even suites. Some rent limousines to drive from airports to hotels and from hotels to auditoriums. These indulgences may add a touch of glamour to relieve the strenuous life of the road, but they also absorb much of the money that should remain as earnings at the end of the tour.

Croesus

A groups first couple of years at the threshold of the Big Time are the most critical simply because they are most often fatal. The figures below represent an attempt to estimate, by the most liberal and optimistic of standards, what a "new" group might earn that first or second year out. It should be noted, however, that this optimistic reckoning, which is based on a realistic assessment of potential, does not necessarily bear any relation to the experiences of an actual group—averages seldom do. It should be noted too that the hypothetical group Croesus, for whom these figures were run up, would be—if it existed—a lot better off than some real groups. Croesus' income, meager though it is, is substantially higher, for instance, than what the Kinks earned in their first twelve months as an entity in the United States.

● **Income**

One album, selling 75,000 copies; royalties established at a rate to yield 42 cents per copy $31,500

One tour of forty-five engagements, at an average fee of $1,000 per performance $45,000
_____
Total $76,500

● **Outgo**

Advance on royalties from record company at signing of contracts (spent to purchase amplifying equipment, pay union dues, settle old debts, etc.) .... $ 5,000

Cost of recording first album 19,000

Manager's 15 per cent of record royalties.......... 4,725

Manager's 15 per cent of booking proceeds........ 6,750

Road expenses (15 per cent of gross) 11,250

Booking agent's share of live-performance revenues at 20 per cent 9,000

Publicity agent for six months 6,000

Additional equipment expenses, normal wear and tear 5,000
_____
Total $66,725
Net income $9,775

Croesus is a four-man band, sharing equally in all income. The net result for each member, under this very optimistic accounting........... $2,443.25

Such considerations aside, the most important single factor in successful live booking is routing, the plotting of the course of the tour from day to day—or week to week. Ideally, a tour should be booked with no city farther than 250 or 300 miles from the one preceding it, and there should be only one day off per week. That way one avoids paying $200 a night for motel rooms unnecessarily. Routing is a tricky thing to manage, even for a skilled professional booker. More than one group has met the fate of Taos, a small-time West Coast act which may have lost its chance at the big time after an agent arranged dates in two nearly contiguous California cities—separated by a one-nighter in Dallas!

The internal financial structure of groups also has an effect on income. Some, like the Dirt Band, are legally incorporated, with members sharing the profits. Others, like the old Jeff Beck group, have one or two prominent members enjoying a share of the gross (in that case, Beck himself and vocalist Rod Stewart) and remaining members drawing merely a salary. There are shadings in these arrangements *ad infinitum* between.

An essential ingredient of life on the road is the road manager, or "roadie," as he is known. He is the one who keeps the group together, sees that they arrive on time, finds out why hotel reservations have been confused, flights canceled. Some groups absorb the functions of the roadie themselves. The Dirt Band's John McEuen, for instance, carries a banjo case in one hand and an airline schedule book in the other on tour, shifting roles according to demand. But, most often, the roadie (and his assistants, who move the equipment) is another separate employee who draws a salary right off the top.

Though it is true that there is a comfortable living to be made in music (from $50,000 to $100,000 a year) for a small number of anonymous, unglamorous studio musicians (usually older, always highly skilled), the performing musician whose name appears on records and concert billings is usually not nearly so well off. Groups in the middle area of prominence, like the Dirt Band and Poco, can, if management is competent, enjoy an upper-middle-class income. Poco's Schmit, for instance, like many other musicians, is buying his own modest home. The individual members of the Dirt Band have earned as much as $40,000 in one year—but as little as $3,000 in many others. They cannot, therefore, compute an "average" because their musical and financial fortunes have simply been too widely spread.

More frequently, the rule of the game is that of performers like Sherman Hayes. Hayes, who is thirty years old, has been playing professionally since 1964. He comes from a family of musicians, so he was prepared for the lean times, especially those preceding the release last fall of his first Capitol album. Sherman is married, with a three-and-a-half year old son. He owns a 1958 Chevrolet panel truck and rents a small house in Hollywood. It costs him between $600 and $800 a month to live—probably more now. He is $8,000 in debt from earlier group efforts, but Hayes, his booking agent, and his record company have faith.

He went on the road for three months last winter, playing club dates for between $150 and $500 a week. His first album, as first albums will, did not sell spectacularly. Anyway, Capitol is figuring the recording costs and their sponsorship of the tour against royalties. Hayes paid two sidemen $175 a week each on the road. He crammed his equipment (the act is acoustic and requires only one amplifier) into two trunks. There was no money for a roadie, so Hayes and his sidemen horsed the trunks all along the route. "I'm losing my ___ on this tour," he commented over coffee in New York one afternoon. "I don't see how anyone can be in music and not be thinking about the fact that it is a *business*," Hayes said. "I'm just happy to be still on the label! For people like Sherman Hayes, the lure of money is still rather farfetched, but the music is there, and for now it has to be a good part of the reward.

Musicians are, in general, people of fragile egos and are often afflicted with a profound naivete. Those who can learn to adapt to the *business* of music survive—sometimes—and a few, very few, can move beyond that to the Big Money. But, for the most part, what the uninitiated see when they look up from the orchestra or down from the balcony is an illusion. Those are not dollar signs, but just the beam of a Super Trouper spotlight reflecting off a guitar purchased through an advance against royalties.

Allan Parachini, *formerly a staff writer for the Los Angeles* Herald Examiner, *is now a resident fellow and visiting scholar at the Columbia University Graduate School of Journalism.*

Mediolab

Rock, Riches, and the Record Industry

1. What media help to spread the image of the rock star as glamorous and rich, with a wild lifestyle? Why aren't the thousands of others who make records written about as much?

2. Why is the image of the rock group presented in the mass media so glamorized and missing so much of the truth?

3. What do you think is the motivation that drives rock performers most—the desire to make good music or the desire to make big money?

4. Have someone make a class presentation on the realities of the record industry. The presentation can be based on library research, but someone with some real-life experience could probably make a more interesting presentation.

5. Do people in other media (television, film, writing, art, etc.) need managers?

6. After reading the article, draw up a class list of "qualities needed to become a rock star." What qualities on this list are different from those needed to become a successful business leader?

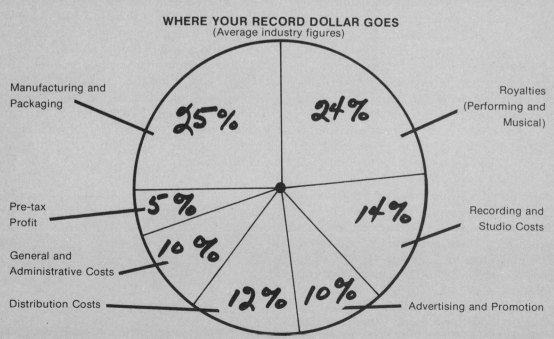

WHERE YOUR RECORD DOLLAR GOES
(Average industry figures)

Manufacturing and Packaging — 25%

Royalties (Performing and Musical) — 24%

Pre-tax Profit — 5%

Recording and Studio Costs — 14%

General and Administrative Costs — 10%

Distribution Costs — 12%

Advertising and Promotion — 10%

Chapter 10
MEDIA CONTROL

The Government and Freedom of the Press

In one sentence of the Bill of Rights, you will find the most significant statement about government and the media. The First Amendment to the U.S. Constitution says: "Congress shall make no law. . .abridging the freedom of speech, or of the press; or the right of the people peaceably to assemble. . . ."

The First Amendment does *not* say that anyone can say anything. It says simply that Congress shall make no *law* that prevents (abridges) a person's freedom to speak. One reason for the First Amendment's existence is that a democracy needs an informed electorate who can vote and make decisions. Freedom of speech and freedom of the press exist not only for the speaker or the owner of the press but also for the audience. In other words, part of freedom of speech is the right of the people to have access to a variety of viewpoints and opinions.

Freedom of speech, like any freedom, is not absolute. No society has ever existed that did not propose some kind of restrictions on the press, on free speech, and on the right of the public to have information. If a newspaper owner writes and publishes a scathing attack on someone, calling him "a crook without morals and a danger to our society," that person could take legal action against the publisher. An attack on another person in print (or pictures or speech) that damages his or her character or reputation and is without truth is called *libel*. A person so attacked can sue the source of the libel for damages.

TO

Freedom of speech and the press exist to promote a free exchange of information and opinions. According to Thomas Jefferson, one of the framers of the Constitution, the public interest could be best served by a society in which there were numerous newspapers free to express themselves without fear of government censorship. The citizens would have to make up their own minds and would be able to do so because they were able to consider the various viewpoints on important public issues. Citizens could also use these newspapers and pamphlets to make known their own views.

But in 1787 Thomas Jefferson and the others at the Constitutional Convention could not foresee the invention of electronic media and mass broadcasting. They could not see into the future and realize that by 1980 major cities would have a free press controlled financially by only a handful of individuals. They could not foresee that printing a newspaper would become a multimillion dollar industry or that there would be a device like television which gives citizens very little opportunity to "talk back."

Newspaper Freedom

Freedom of the press is a long-established tradition for newspapers in the United States and remains today a carefully guarded right. In recent years one of the "new" questions raised concerning newspaper freedom is the right of reporters to conceal their sources of information. In several cases in the late 1960s and early 1970s, reporters went to jail rather than reveal who their sources were. The reporters contended that if they were forced to reveal their sources, they would be hampered in their ability to report the news in the future. People who might talk to reporters if they could remain unknown would probably keep quiet if courts could force reporters to tell who they were. Such a law would hamper the flow of news to the people and would, in effect, be a restriction on the public's right to know. On the other hand, such a privilege might place the reporter above the law and interfere with the judicial process. Some groups advocate a "shield law" that would protect reporters from court orders to reveal their sources, and such laws do exist in some places. Although public interest in this issue has died down in recent years, the problem is still unresolved and open to debate.

A newer issue in the question of newspaper freedom concerns school papers. Students at some colleges and high schools claimed they were being denied the right to freedom of speech and a free press. School officials argued that the school newspaper was an extension of the school and could be controlled by administrators just as could course selection, rules of discipline, and other school requirements.

The Supreme Court has made it clear that the Bill of Rights is not for adults only. In 1969 the Court clarified the First Amendment rights of students in the ruling in *Tinker* vs. *Des Moines Independent School District*. The case involved three Iowa high school students, aged 13 to 16, who wore black armbands to school to protest the war in Vietnam. They

SERVE

were asked by school authorities to remove the armbands but refused and were suspended from school.

The Supreme Court sided with the students and observed that wearing an armband is "symbolic speech" and is thereby protected by the First Amendment. More importantly, the Court held that students are indeed "persons" under the Constitution and have fundamental rights that school authorities must respect. *The Harvard Law Review* summarized the deeper meaning of the court decision as "the process of education in a democracy must be democratic." Schools that censor, control, and otherwise restrict the student press are, in effect, teaching the values of a system of governing that is not democratic.

A series of court cases in the early 1970s expanded the concept of freedom of the press for school papers. The general direction of these opinions is that the school must prove that such freedom of expression will lead to substantial disorder in the school or to a violation of the rights of others. Courts have never upheld the absolute right of students to publish whatever they wish in a school paper, but neither have they upheld the right of the school administration to allow students to publish only what the administration considers acceptable.

Broadcasting Freedom

Electronic broadcasting is still in its infancy. Many people alive today remember the very first radios, and the early days of television are still part of the memories of most adults. Because of their newness, radio and television have no tradition of First Amendment rights. The subject of broadcasting freedom is still very complicated and controversial.

The complications exist because the airwaves, unlike printing presses, are a limited resource. There can be only a few television channels in each city (although the technology now exists to expand this number considerably), and even the number of radio frequencies is severely limited. In any city, the people who control the radio and TV stations could

assemble easily in an average classroom. Since both TV and radio are basically one-way communication devices, great care must be taken to assure the "free exchange of information and opinions" that so concerned Thomas Jefferson. But how can the government act to ensure this free exchange without setting itself up as dictator of what people may hear and see? This is the problem that is still unsolved.

In many countries, the government owns and completely controls all radio and TV stations. In the United States, these outlets are privately owned; anyone with a few hundred thousand dollars can own a small radio station; TV stations cost more, often in the millions. If there were no central control over broadcasting, the result would be chaos. So many broadcasters would fight for the limited amount of airspace (a handful of TV channels, 97 AM frequencies, and about 120 FM channels) that stations would interfere with each other, and few people would get clear reception from any station. In the early days of radio this is precisely what did happen, as many amateurs and basement scientists set up their own radio stations. Finally, confusion grew so great that in 1934 the Federal Communications Commission was established to regulate broadcasting.

According to U.S. law, the airwaves are "owned" by the people. They are a natural resource like air and water and cannot be bought or sold by individuals or corporations. The FCC grants licenses to qualified groups or individuals to use the airwaves for the purpose of *serving the public good.* Licenses are granted for a limited number of years

and are renewed if the station can prove it has indeed served the public interest. Radio and TV stations are required to ask the people in their broadcast areas for criticisms and suggestions for improvement of their programming.

The FCC controls broadcasting by deciding which of the many applicants for a radio frequency or a TV channel will be granted a license. Once the license is granted, the FCC does little to control program content.

The FCC does, however, require each radio and TV station to program time (how much time is not specified) in each of the following categories:
1. Opportunity for local expression (time for people in the local areas to express themselves on the air).
2. Development and use of local talent.
3. Programs for children.
4. Religious programs.
5. Educational programs.
6. Public affairs programs.
7. Editorials (expressions of opinion) by the license holder.
8. Political broadcasts.
9. Agriculture programs.
10. News.
11. Weather and stock market reports.
12. Sports.
13. Programs for minority groups.
14. Entertainment.

Another way in which the FCC has some control over programming is through what is commonly called the "fairness doctrine." This "doctrine" (it is not a law) requires radio and TV stations to present issues of local importance and to air all the various viewpoints surrounding a controversial issue.

The "fairness doctrine" is designed to ensure that citizens are told the facts about issues of public controversy and to prevent radio and TV stations from presenting slanted news. Those opposed to the doctrine claim that it is impossible to present all viewpoints and that broadcasting stations should be allowed, as part of their own freedom of speech, to present what they consider the "correct" viewpoint. The opponents claim the doctrine allows the FCC to control programming, thus setting a dangerous precedent for government control of mass media.

Another less controversial, government rule is called the "equal time" rule. This means that if one candidate in a political campaign receives or buys time, the station must offer other candidates the same amount of time.

Part of the idea of "fairness" includes protection against personal attack. If a station airs a discussion or a comment that attacks the honesty, integrity, or character of a person or group, the station *must* send to the person or group attacked, first, a notice of the attack along with an exact description of what was said and, second, an offer of time to respond to that attack without charge for broadcast time. For instance, if your local TV station airs a Sunday morning discussion about education in which a participant specifically attacks the students of your school as a "bunch of lazy, sloppy kids with nothing better to do, than hang around street corners," then your principal or student government should be able to obtain free TV time to refute that attack.

PUBLIC

Government Control of Advertising

Advertising in the United States is not as strictly controlled by the government as it is in other countries. In Germany the "Unfair Competition" law prohibits advertisers from making "water is wet" claims. German law also forbids an ad that might lead to a wrong conclusion. Even "so what" claims like "Margarine packed by hand" are forbidden under German law, since packing margarine by hand gives it no extra advantage.

In Sweden the "truth-and-nothing-but-the-truth Marketing Practices Act" gives the government strict control to ensure that ads are scrupulously honest.

In the United States the federal agency charged with some degree of advertising regulation is the Federal Trade Commission (FTC). The FTC has a small staff and very little power, but can take court action and order advertisers to "cease and desist" from what it considers deceptive advertising. The company simply agrees to "sin no more" and usually escapes with no other punishment. In recent years the FTC has become more strict with advertisers; it has levied fines and has even required a few advertisers to run corrective ads to make up for misleading claims made in their past advertising.

The kind of order issued by the FTC is illustrated by the following order as printed in the government's *Federal Register*:

GOOD.

Other than broadcasting and advertising, the federal government exercises little control over the mass media. Newspaper, magazine, and book publishers are subject to U.S. laws, but there are few specific regulations or controls on what they can print.

In re Bristol Myers Co., et al., CCH ₱19,765, F.T.C. File No. 712 3035 (August, 1971); BNA ATRR. No. 527 (August 24, 1971, A-7. [D.C.]

The Federal Trade Commission has announced its intention to issue a complaint against Bristol Myers and its advertising agency, Ogilvy & Mather, for using false commercials for Dry Ban spray anti-perspirant.

In one commercial a "leading spray" and Dry Ban are sprayed on a dark surface. The other spray appears white and thick but Dry Ban appears clear and dry. At the conclusion of the demonstration a voice asks, "Which do you prefer?" In another commercial Dry Ban and a "leading spray" are sprayed on separate eyeglass lenses. The leading anti-perspirant spray appears white and thick while Dry Ban appears completely clear and dry.

The proposed complaint alleges that actual proof of the product's superiority over competing brands is not presented because, contrary to the demonstrations, Dry Ban is not a dry spray. It is wet when applied to the body, and after application dries out, it leaves a visible residue.

The proposed order would prohibit deceptive product feature or product superiority demonstrations (1) by Bristol-Myers for any of its products, and (2) by Ogilvy & Mather for Dry Ban or any other anti-perspirant or deodorant.

Control by Sources

All mass media are controlled in some way by their sources. Newspapers can print only the news that is delivered to them or that their reporters uncover. Television programs and films are controlled by their producers and directors; magazine articles are subject to the complete control of editors, writers, and publishers. As media content passes through these hands, it is influenced by the normal human biases and perceptions.

Each medium has within it people who act as censors, although the word "censor" is rarely used. No magazine or book publisher has an official censor as an employee, yet all those who must pass judgment on the suitability of articles and photos (the "gatekeepers") act in a way as censors.

Motion picture production is subject to several levels of censorship. The scriptwriter, the director, and the producer of a film control its contents so as not to produce a film that too many people will find revolting or disgusting. Their consideration in censorship is not so much to protect the public morals as it is to maintain a good box office.

In the 1960s the motion picture industry found that parents were afraid to allow their children to go to movies because they had no way of knowing whether the film was suitable for youngsters. A voluntary rating system was established to rate films: G—acceptable to general audiences; GP—parental guidance suggested; R—restricted to those over a certain age (varies locally but usually about 16-18) unless accompanied by a parent or adult; and X—for adults only. Many theaters interpret these ratings very strictly and will demand proof of age for admission to R-or X-rated films. The rating system is voluntary and does not, in itself, carry the force of law.

Some cities and counties have local censor boards which screen all films about to play in the city or county. They have the power to demand that certain scenes be eliminated or that a film be banned altogether. The power of these censor boards has decreased in recent years, especially in large cities.

Each of the three major television networks has a censor who watches commercials and programs for parts that might offend viewers. Feature films are often "edited for television" to remove some of the violence, sex, or language in the original version. Local television stations also have the right to refuse network programs, although they rarely do so.

The reason for television's self-censorship is that the medium is public, open to anyone who turns on a TV set, including young children. Motion pictures, books, and magazines can be less restrictive since to gain access to them one has to pay admission or purchase a copy.

Radio stations often refuse to play songs the station director feels have double meanings, encourage drug use, are unpatriotic, or are in some way in bad taste. During listener call-in shows, many radio stations use a seven-second delay system. Each caller in such a system actually speaks to a tape recorder which plays his call over the air several seconds later. This delay is introduced so the program director can "bleep" out offensive words or cut off possible libelous remarks.

Economic Control

Magazines, newspapers, television, and radio stations, book publishers—all, with a few rare exceptions—share one common goal; to make money. This fact controls to some extent the content of what these media produce.

With the exception of book publishing, all these media receive most of their income from advertising. The question thus arises: Does advertising in any way influence the content of mass media?

One illustration of economic influence is the true case of the Car-Puter Company's attempt to buy ads in major newspapers and magazines. Car-Puter is a company that supplies customers with a computer read-out of dealer costs on any new car they may want to buy, including options. The company also supplies the name of a local automobile dealer who, through a special arrangement, will sell the customer the car for about $150 over dealer cost. The company charges the consumer $5 for this service, which is legitimate and helpful to consumers. However, when Car-Puter attempted to run a small ad, they were refused by most newspapers as well as by some magazines.

The ads were refused without a detailed explanation. The newspapers claimed they had a right to turn down any advertising—and they do. But the reason for the refusal most certainly is related to the fact that automotive ads are an important source of income for newspapers and magazines. Car-Puter Company would not be approved of by other auto advertisers.

As another example, sponsors of television programs are not likely to buy time for programs that attack business. Sponsors carefully monitor network TV shows. A group called "Stop Immorality on Television" asked major TV sponsors about their "moral stance" on the programs they sponsored. Gillette replied that "we try to see that our advertising runs in programs which are suitable for general family viewing. Under this policy we have declined to participate as sponsors in programs such as *The Smothers Brothers* and *Laugh-In*." Eastman Kodak commented that they preview all scripts before the airing of a program: "If we find a script is offensive, we will withdraw our commercials from the program."

Although advertisers have no formal censorship power, they can exert great influence on the kinds of programs that networks will offer the viewers. A TV network would think twice before showing a documentary exposing the faults of the over-the-counter-drug industry, because so much of its advertising revenue comes from painkillers and headache remedies.

A question often asked at networks is "Will the show gain sponsors?" The importance of this question can easily limit consideration of another question: "What is in the best interests of the public?"

Newspapers and magazines vary widely in the amount of control they allow advertisers to exert. Some keep "news" and ads completely separate and will report the problems and failings of local food chains or auto dealers even though these provide the paper with thousands of dollars yearly in advertising revenue. Some newspapers, however, still have a policy of not "biting the hand that feeds them." If the health department closes or issues a warning to a local food store or restaurant, such papers will ignore the story for fear of "hurting" the advertiser's reputation. A story about a shady car dealer or home builder might go unreported if that company is a large advertiser in the newspaper.

Such control is less frequent now than it used to be, but it still exists, especially among smaller newspapers struggling to stay in business.

Record companies put pressure on radio stations to play their records. Every time a radio station plays a record, the "exposure" is as good as or better than an ad for the record. The more radio stations play any given song or record, the more it sells. Record companies can give away free records but are not supposed to give money to stations as an inducement to play the records. There have been many instances, though, of record companies slipping a little extra money ("payola") to disk jockeys to gain air time for a song. As with newspapers, this practice is less common among the largest stations and offers a greater temptation to small stations.

Control by the Audience

The most common kind of control over mass media is the one most often overlooked—control by the audience. If few people watch a TV show, it dies. If only a few hundred people subscribe to a city newspaper, it stops publishing. If a film is a box-office flop, similar films will be less likely to receive backing.

A complicating factor in audience control or censorship of the mass media is the fact that no two people in the same mass audience experience a program or news story in exactly the same way. Each member of the audience brings along prejudices, biases, and a lifetime of experiences that shape his or her feelings and reactions to the content presented in the media.

An interesting experiment suggests exactly how important this factor is in control-by-the-audience. A special slide viewer was constructed with one hole for each eye; a person looked into it as into a pair of binoculars. In the slide viewer were two pictures, one for each eye. One slide pictured a baseball player and the other a bullfighter. First, a group of American teachers looked into the viewer and were asked what they saw. Next a group of Mexican citizens looked and reported what they saw. The results? More Americans reported "seeing" the baseball player, while more Mexicans reported "seeing" the bullfighter. The experiment points out that people "see" what they have been taught to see.

Every time we look at a picture, an inkblot, a cloudy sky, a painting, a film, or a newspaper, we see those things that are most comfortable to see. We see only those things that fit in with our view of the way the world should be and filter out those things that don't seem to fit. This process of selective seeing is called *perceptual filtering.*

Each time a newscast shows a policeman struggling with a young person, the viewing audience gives the event a variety of interpretations. Some see the event as yet another example of police brutality, while others see "young punks" getting what they deserve; some see law and order at work while others see society falling apart.

No matter how much the government or advertisers attempt to control mass media, there is no way to insure that the audience will agree with what is presented or even "see" the same thing as the people next door.

In addition to the process of perceptual filtering, the media consumer controls the content of the media by selecting which program to watch, which magazines to subscribe to, which books to buy, which newspapers to read, or which radio stations to listen to. Each decision to use a mass medium can be thought of as a sort of vote approving that medium's content.

The owners of any media outlet keep a constant record of the size and type of audience they attract. The number of units sold is the main measurement for magazines, books, newspapers, and films. Television and radio must rely on estimates of audience numbers called "ratings."

A number of companies offer rating services to television and radio. The largest and best-known is the A.C. Nielsen company—so much so that ratings are sometimes called "Nielsens." The Nielsen ratings have been accused of reflecting only the habits of those who watch a lot of television. But the networks have found the system the best available, and so the Nielsen ratings are usually the ones that determine a program's future—or lack of it.

The ratings list below, from *Variety,* reflects the popularity of certain shows in early 1975. The rating number 32.1 for *All in the Family,* the top show, means that 32.1% of all TV households had the show on. There are about 60 million "TV households" in the nation. So a Nielsen rating of 32.1, applied to the country as a whole, means that *All in the Family* was being watched in about 19 million homes. Networks estimate that each household represents about 2.3 viewers, and so they conclude that All in the Family was seen by an average of over 44 million people— one out of every five people in the country.

A rating of at least 17 is needed to keep a show alive. It would represent about 10.2 million households, or 21 million people. In other words, even a network TV show with more "consumers" than any national magazine is still in danger of being cancelled for lack of interest.

A.C. Nielsen compiles its ratings by installing devices called "audimeters" in the households of 1,200 volunteers. For their services, the volunteers receive small gifts, 50 cents a week payment, and assistance in paying for TV repairs. Inside the audimeter is a slow-moving 16mm. film that records which channels are turned on during the day (though it does not show whether anyone is actually watching). These 1,200 families mail each week's film to Nielsen headquarters near Chicago, where the films are processed and fed into a computer that compiles the ratings. In addition to the audimeters, about 2,200 TV diaries are kept by volunteers and also sent each week to Nielsen.

The ratings give the audience some control over the survival of programs but none in their creation.

Wednesday, February 26, 1975

Second Season Rating Leaders

The top 30 series, per national Nielsen SIA rating numbers, for the "second season" first five weeks (Jan. 13 through Feb. 16) are listed below with comparative averages for the first half of the 1974-75 season (as of Jan. 12), plus the gains or losses logged since the Jan. 12 date.

Rank	Series	2d Season	As of 1/12	Change
1.	All In the Family (CBS)	32.1	30.0	+2.1
2.	Sanford & Son (NBC)	31.5	30.0	+1.5
3.	Chico & the Man (NBC)	30.9	29.0	+1.9
4.	The Jeffersons (CBS)	28.4	-	
5.	The Waltons (CBS)	28.2	26.3	+1.9
6.	Mash (CBS)	27.7	26.7	+1.0
7.	Police Woman (NBC)	27.0	21.1	+5.9
8.	Good Times CBS)	26.6	24.6	+2.0
9.	Rhoda (CBS)	25.9	26.8	−0.9
	Rockford Files (NBC)	25.9	22.5	+3.4
11.	Maude (CBS)	25.3	25.4	−0.1
12.	Mary Tyler Moore (CBS)	25.1	23.7	+1.4
13.	Little House/Prarie (NBC)	25.0	23.7	+1.3
14.	Hawaii Five-O (CBS)	24.8	24.1	+0.7
15.	Cannon (CBS)	24.7	20.0	+4.7
16.	Kojak (CBS)	24.4	22.7	+1.7
17.	Mannix (CBS)	23.4	20.4	+3.0
18.	Cher CBS)	23.0	-	
19.	Bob Newhart (CBS)	22.7	22.8	−0.1
	Sts. of San Francisco (ABC)	22.7	20.9	+1.8
21.	ABC Sun. Movie	22.5	17.7	+4.8
22.	NBC World Prem Movie	22.0	18.0	+4.0
23.	Police Story (NBC)	21.7	18.5	+3.2
24.	NBC Sun. Mystery	21.6	22.4	−0.8
25.	The Rookies (ABC)	21.1	21.1	-
	Smothers Brothers (NBC)	21.1	-	
	Tony Orlando & Dawn (CBS)	21.1	18.0	+3.1
28.	Medical Center (CBS)	20.8	21.6	−0.8
29.	Gunsmoke (CBS)	20.8	20.8	-
30.	Emergency (NBC)	20.3	20.9	−0.6

Medialab

1. Do you think the current film rating system (G, GP, R, X) is fair and just? What problems would arise if films were not rated? Is it fair to restrict admission to certain films to those over 17 years of age?

2. The class is to act as a group of network censors meeting to draw up a list of examples of things not to be allowed on commercials and programs. What is on that list?

3. Write a short paper explaining your position on the "fairness doctrine." Before writing the paper, do some library research on the topic in books or magazines. Once the papers are completed, have a class debate between those who favor the "fairness doctrine" and those who find parts of it objectionable.

4. Prepare a brief report on mass media (or one of the media) in some country other than the United States. Compare the operation and control of the media in that country with the situation in the United States.

5. Have a number of students go to the offices of local radio and television stations and ask to see the "public file" concerning license renewal. Report to the class on some of the file's more interesting contents.

6. *You Be the Jury:* The following are brief descriptions of several court cases concerned with media

Medialab

control. Discuss and debate each case and reach a decision of your own before looking at the court's decision at the end of the section. Each case is presented here with few details, but the basic facts come from real court cases.

Scoville vs. *Board of Education of Joliet Township High School*

Two students were expelled for distributing a "literary journal" on school grounds. The magazine contained an editorial critical of the school administration and urged students to disregard school rules. There is no direct evidence that the publication actually caused any disruption in the school process. The students wrote the magazine and sold 60 copies at a price of 15 cents each.

The lower court ruled that the language took the "form of immediate incitement to disregard legitimate administrative regulations necessary to the orderly maintenance of a public high school system." In other words, the magazine was a "clear and present danger" to the orderly operation of the school and so was not entitled to First Amendment protection. The students could reasonably be punished for their conduct.

The case was then taken to a court of appeals. Discuss the case and reach your own decision before looking up the appeals court decision.

ACT vs. TIO

The *Television Information Office* (TIO) is an organization that acts as a public relations arm for the television industry. It prepares TV spots, printed reports, and other services designed to enhance the image of television. One of its TV spots (made by TIO and offered free to TV stations to use as public service announcements) pointed out the benefits of TV programming for children. Many stations around the country used the spot.

Action For Children's Television (ACT), a group concerned with improving children's programming and often critical of the television industry, requested that the FCC, under the fairness doctrine, order stations that carried the TIO ads also to carry a counter-ad pointing out that children's television is "unimaginative, inartistic, commercial-ridden, and harmful to children." The FCC, rather than a court, made the ruling on this case. What do you think?

Decisions: In *Scoville* vs. *Joliet Board of Education*, the Court of Appeals found that the expulsion of the students was unjustified and constituted an invasion of their First and Fourteenth Amendment rights.

In *ACT* vs. *TIO*, the FCC denied the argument of *Action for Children's Television* and emphasized that the fairness doctrine required an overall balance on issues and that ACT had not proved the spots created an imbalance.

7. Here are typical comments from a network censor about an old NBC series called *High Chaparral*: "Victims of homicide are to be shown with their eyes closed and not positioned grotesquely." "In the montage of the warring Indians being hunted down and shot, take care that this is not overdone so that it becomes a brutal thing; nor should we see Buck (one of the characters) grinning fiercely just before the killing. This would give him the aspect of a sadist." "As the kid is shot and he starts to fall, please avoid sensationalizing the fall as he goes tumbling down the rocks. It will be unacceptable to see the kid bouncing from rock to rock in his fall." "As Maria cradles the dying Ramon in her arms, avoid showing the knife protruding from Ramon's chest."

Do you think these observations are valid? Do the observations tend to make the violence that does appear more unreal and therefore more harmful than if it were presented in a realistic way?

Chapter 11

MEDIA AND OUR IMAGE OF THE WORLD

STEREOTYPE

Each person has a mental picture of what the "world out there" is like. For centuries, this picture was shaped by personal experience and education. These two factors are still present in shaping mental pictures, but there is a third force that assumes an ever increasing importance. Today, the mass media play a major role in teaching people what the world is like.

By pushing aside the limitations of experience and schooling, mass media have created a nation of people who have opinions on just about every subject and mental pictures of places never visited, people never encountered, and events experienced only as tiny images on a television screen. News and entertainment media distribute so much information about the world that many educators claim schools are no longer the main source of learning for most people. Mass media have taken over the role of forming our mental image of the world.

Our mental "map" or picture of the world is in some areas quite detailed and well-developed. But sometimes our picture of the world "out there" is only a rough sketch with few details. Human psychology seems to demand that the sketch be filled in with details. Once the outline is formed, we use what we are taught by our parents, schools, and mass media to fill in the details. Often what we are taught, though, is stereotype.

A stereotype is an oversimplified idea of something, based on limited experience. For example, for four years, between the ages of 6 and 10, Henry lived in a neighborhood where there was one French family on the block. This particular family was unable to keep a neat house or yard, and people in the neighborhood talked about those "sloppy Frenchies." From this limited experience, Henry generalized that people from France were generally sloppier and dirtier than Americans. Henry never went to France, never met many other Frenchmen, and did little reading. When he married and had

children he still made occasional remarks about "sloppy Frenchies." Henry's children also grew up believing that people from France were dirty and sloppy.

The application to an entire group of the qualities of a limited sample of that group is a stereotype. In themselves, stereotypes are a convenient mental device. They help us deal with the vast amount of reality that can never be known in detail. The problem is that most stereotypes contain only a kernel of truth and so are dangerous if taken to be the whole truth.

Stereotypes give people a feeling of security, a feeling that something complex is understood. They provide the illusion that we know our way around in what otherwise would be unknown territory. When the stereotypes we hold (and everyone believes *some* stereotypes) are attacked or challenged, we view this as a personal attack and often actively defend our stereotypes.

Clearly, stereotypes are not limited to the prejudiced or bigoted, to racial categories, or to the unschooled. Many stereotypes are strengthened by the mass media, although at other times it is the same media that replace a commonly held stereotype with a fuller picture. Because of the power of mass media, some stereotypes are rather commonly accepted as the full truth.

Television, for example, often shows "cardboard characters"—people whose personalities are not developed in the plot. These cardboard characters— such as the jolly fat man, the dumb secretary, or the hard-boiled cop—are easily recognized by viewers and car. be used for laughs or instant plot development. The constant repetition of such characters tends to condition viewers to expect fat people to be jolly and secretaries dumb or cops hard-boiled. People who belong to often-stereotyped groups find it difficult to overcome media-created expectations.

Even criminals are stereotyped by television and other media. A professor of communications at Queen's College in New York and seven assistants monitored one week of prime-time TV and found that criminals on TV were 85 percent male, 78 percent between the ages of 20 and 50, and 90 percent white. The picture of the criminal presented by television is that of a white-collar, middle class person. On TV much crime is committed to cover up for other crimes. In reality, however, 35 percent of those arrested are under 20, and 30 percent are nonwhite.

On television, murder, assault, and armed robbery are the most common crimes. In reality, quiet burglaries, clever larcenies, unspectacular auto thefts, and drunkenness are the most common. Video detectives solved 90 percent of their cases. In reality, the figure is considerably lower. On TV only 7 percent of violence occurs between relatives. In reality this accounts for 25 to 30 percent of interpersonal violence.

Films have also contributed to the national store of stereotypes. In Donald Bogle's study of blacks in films, five stereotypes emerge. Perhaps you can recall seeing some of these, especially in older films:

Toms: These blacks are socially acceptable and "good." They never turn against whites, are submissive, generous, and often chased, enslaved, harassed, and hounded. James B. Lowe in the old film of *Uncle Tom's Cabin* is the prime example; the nickname "Tom" came from this character.

Coons: These are the black buffoons. They are presented as unreliable, crazy, lazy, and good-for-nothing but eating watermelon and stealing chickens. Stepin Fetchit is an example of a Coontype.

Mulattoes: They could and often did pass as whites. But, typically, in the end, "bad blood" makes this type a victim of his or her divided racial inheritance.

Mammies: These were the big, fat, bossy but warmhearted servant women and washerwomen. They were substitute mothers for whites; they took no nonsense and often endured much suffering with strength and humiliation.

Bucks: Big, bad males. Oversexed, savage, and violent.

Films and TV shows with "real people" blacks who didn't fall into these categories have been very rare.

Other groups that are often stereotyped include the following:

Scandinavians	People over 65
Poles	Housewives
Women	Intellectuals
Texans	Construction workers
Italians	Professional athletes
French	Straight-A students
Spanish	"Jocks"
Mexicans	Wealthy persons
Artists	Librarians
"Freaks"	Radicals/Conservatives/
"Straights"	Liberals
People on welfare	Professors
Jews	Scientists
Teenagers	Overweight people

1. Are stereotypes always bad? Are they always partially wrong? What use do stereotypes have?

2. Why do stereotypes exist?

3. Find examples of some of the stereotyped qualities of as many of the groups on the list as you (as a class) can. Add to the list other stereotyped groups. A good way to fill in the details about a stereotyped group is to brainstorm each group, starting with the statement, "Most (*name of stereotyped group*) are . . . ."

4. Find examples of stereotypes in any mass medium and bring them to class.

5. As a research project select one group you believe has been unfairly stereotyped. Describe the stereotype and bring evidence of its falseness. For example, you might believe that the stereotype of people on welfare being lazy loafers is unfair. As proof you could bring reliable statistics showing that only 1 percent of those on welfare are able-bodied men—most are disabled, or elderly, or women with dependent children.

6. Find someone in the class who can tell of a stereotype that he or she has recently learned is not true.

7. Find examples of "cardboard characters" on TV.

8. How do cartoons use stereotypes for humorous effect?

9. Assume you are the "National Minister of Stereotypes" in a country where all mass media are government-controlled. You have access to whatever media you desire. Devise a media campaign to create a stereotype of a certain group you want discredited. For your campaign to be most effective, the citizens of your country should remain unaware of it, yet become completely convinced of the truth of the stereotype you are creating.

10. Find some group of which you are a member that is the target of occasional stereotyped comments. Refute those stereotypes.

11. Pick some group that is frequently stereotyped on TV (e.g., women, teenagers, fathers, criminals). Conduct a study similar to the one described in the chapter dealing with criminals on television. Watch as much prime-time TV as you can for a week or longer and note each time a member of the group appears in any way on a show or ad. Take notes on how the person is presented. Combine your notes and present your own report titled "How Television Stereotypes *(name of group).*" Your report should be specific.

12. The study of the television image of criminals mentioned in this chapter pointed out some unrealities. Do you think these could have an effect on people's attitudes towards crime or law enforcement?

RUMOR AND DISTORTION

Rumors are stories that grow as they go. Rumors are somewhere between gossip and news. Rumors and stereotypes are distant cousins. Both contain some truth combined with a large and often dangerous amount of nontruth. Both can lead people to irrational action, both are often accepted as truth, and both can be created, intensified, and lessened by the mass media.

Rumors often start out as truth. A psychologist once "planted" a rumor in the cafeteria of an Air Force base by asking, "Is it true they are building a tunnel big enough to move B-52's to town?" A half day later the planted question came back to him as a statement: "They are building a tunnel to move B-52's to town." Notice the differences: The original question came back as a statement, without the "Is-

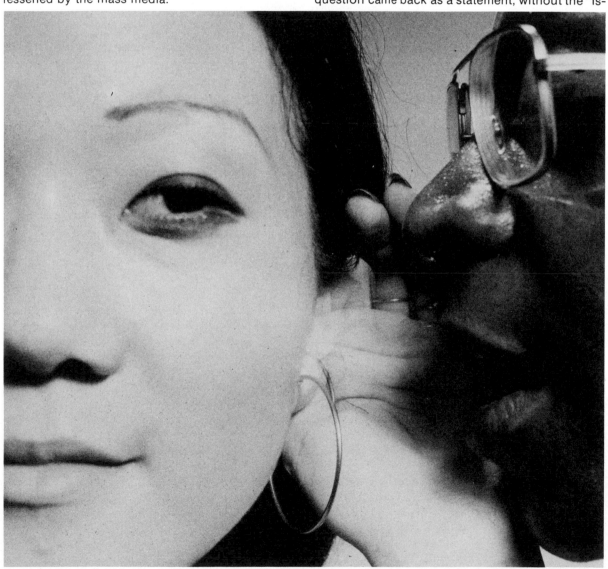

it-true?" at the beginning. Added to the statement was the "fact" that a tunnel was being built to move B-52's, whereas the original question merely referred to a tunnel "big enough" to move B-52's. The distortions introduced are typical of those that convert fact to rumor.

True stories are distorted in three main ways in becoming rumors—sharpening, leveling, and assimilation. *Sharpening* refers to the tendency for items in the original story to become more dramatic. A "weapon" becomes a "loaded gun." A "large octopus" becomes a "sea monster."

Leveling refers to the fact that as the story is repeated, details drop out rapidly at first and then level off to a simple, easily repeatable version.

Assimilation refers to the tendency for stories to be repeated in terms familiar to the person telling the story. A rumor that starts about an event in a European cafe might end up being told in the U.S. as happening in a drive-in restaurant.

Rumors usually serve some kind of emotional need. One researcher has coded rumors into three basic varieties: (a) pipe dreams, expressing wishful thinking; (b) bogie rumors, arising from fears and worries; and (c) wedge-driving, dividing groups and destroying loyalties.

Pipe-dream rumors seem the least frequent. A common example of a bogie rumor is the sighting of a flying saucer—a report often verified by numerous people. The wedge-driving rumor is particularly popular in politics. During the 1972 presidential campaign, a New Hampshire newspaper attacked Sen. Edmund Muskie for supposedly making an insulting remark about the French-Canadians in the state, calling them "Canucks." The only evidence the paper had was a letter from someone who said he had heard the remark. Though this letter was later discovered to be a fake planted by the opposition, the incident harmed Muskie's standing with French-Canadian voters in the primary election.

Writer Norman Mailer has coined the phrase "factoid" to describe rumors that have no existence except that they appear in print or in another medium. In spite of their lack of truth, people repeat them as if they were facts. "Pseudo-facts" might be another appropriate term.

A pseudo-fact can cause harm. In 1883, the Brooklyn Bridge had been open only six days when tragedy struck. Even though thousands of people had walked safely across the bridge, rumor had spread that it was unsafe and would collapse. Someone screamed while walking across the bridge, and panic followed as the cry spread, "The bridge is falling." Forty people were injured and 12 were trampled to death as a result of panic caused by rumor.

Mass media have the ability to cause a rumor to sweep the nation. In 1938 a famous radio broadcast of the drama *War of the Worlds* set off a nationwide rumor that invaders from outer space had landed in New Jersey, causing a small panic.

Since mass media can spread facts quickly, they usually tend to control rather than inflame rumors. For instance, during urban rioting, TV and radio have both provided "rumor control centers," reassuring viewers and listeners that disturbances were only in certain areas, that fires were under control, that the trouble was not spreading, and so on.

One exception to this tendency serves to illustrate the power of the media and people's belief in television. At 11:35 p.m. on the night of December 19, 1973, Johnny Carson said on national television, "You know what else is disappearing from the supermarket shelves? Toilet paper. There's an acute shortage of toilet paper in the United States."

By noon the next day supermarkets all over the country were faced with a stampede of people buying from 5 to 25 extra rolls. The kind of toilet paper that was in short supply was not the kind sold in stores, but government issue toilet paper bought only in large lots by bids. Carson had made the point clear that his comment was not a news report, but only a humorous speculation. But because of leveling, sharpening, and assimilation, within four days there was a real shortage of the better quality supermarket paper because people were hoarding.

Officials of the Scott Paper Company assured the public to "stay calm. There just isn't any shortage." By the middle of January supermarket shelves were full again, thus assuring shoppers there was no shortage. One TV star watched by millions can start a national spree of toilet-paper buying. One wonders in what other ways the remarks of widely watched TV personalities influence what people do.

Medialab

1. As a class experiment, conduct a study in the process of rumor creation. One person looks at a picture and describes it to another. The second person, who does *not* see the picture, repeats the description he has heard to a third person. The third person repeats the description to a fourth and so on, until a sixth person has received the verbal picture description. The first and last picture descriptions should be tape-recorded for study. Compare the first description with the final to see what differences there are. Are any of the differences explainable as leveling, sharpening, or assimilation? The best kind of picture to use is one from a newspaper or magazine that shows several people doing something. (A drawing designed for precisely this experiment can be found in *The Psychology of Rumor* by G.W. Allport and L. Postman, published in 1947 by Holt.)

2. What are some interesting rumors you've heard recently? Note: gossip is more personal (about someone in the school, for example) than rumor.

3. Plant a rumor in the school (make sure it is a harmless one) and see if it grows.

4. Find out if your city has a "rumor control" center. If so, find out what it does and perhaps invite someone from the center to talk to the class.

5. If there were no mass media do you think there would be more rumors or fewer? Why?

Chapter 12
NEW MEDIA & FUTURECASTING

Videotape Revolution

Most revolutionary changes in media are not totally new inventions that sweep the world. Instead, they are changes in already existing media. The recording of visual images began with the use of film and remains that way today, although many improvements have been made over the first crude films. The medium of film had no challengers to its supremacy until the recent invention of videotape. Videotape raises the possibility that film will go the way of horse-drawn buggies, the stagecoach, and high-button shoes. Perhaps going to theaters to see a film will be replaced by watching the same "film" (made either with film or videotape) on a wall-sized home TV screen.

Currently both film and VT are used extensively on television, but feature-length movies are still made with film rather than VT. More and more TV commercials use VT rather than film as do some new TV series. In order to understand the advantages and differences of VT and film, a comparison is necessary.

A Comparison of

Film

Images can be seen when film is held up to the light (film is transparent).

Needs to be developed by a long, complicated, and expensive process that takes days or weeks.

Inexpensive super-8 cameras, projectors, and screens make it possible for anyone to purchase and make films. All necessary equipment can be purchased for $150 or less.

Film can be used once and only once and is not erasable.

One hour of 16mm sound film is $200, one hour of sound super-8 is about $85.

Sound is an expensive and complicated option.

Can be shown easily to a large audience on a huge screen.

Copies of films can be made at film laboratories at low cost.

Easy to cut and edit. A viewer and editing equipment for super-8 film costs under $50.

Does not have a practical fast-forward or fast-reverse speed in the projector.

There is no "standard" film size. 8mm, super-8, and 35mm all require different projectors. But a film made in any one format anywhere in the world can be shown on any projector of the same format.

Clear, sharp image.

Many special effects require complicated and expensive laboratory work.

Film and Videotape

Videotape

Videotape all looks alike, whether blank or filled with images (tape is opaque).

Can be seen immediately after shooting on a TV monitor.

Videotape cameras, monitors, and connecting hardware are still expensive. Even a beginning set-up for VT should have a $1,500 budget. Prices are moving somewhat lower.

Videotape can be reused hundreds of times but also can be accidentally erased.

One hour of reusable videotape is about $30.

Sound is automatically part of every videotape.

Screen size limited to the size of TV receiver. The ability to project a large picture exists but is very expensive.

Videotapes can be copied with two recorders, just like audio tapes.

Since the images cannot be seen with the eye, VT is difficult to edit. Good equipment for editing tape easily could run into thousands of dollars.

Tape can be fast-forwarded or reversed quickly and easily.

Various sizes of VT (1/4", 1/2", 1") are not compatible, and all require different recorders and playback units to use. International compatibility is weak.
Clear, sharp image. A greater sense of "presence" than with film.

Special effects require special equipment (e.g., a special effects generator or multiple cameras and a switching board) but can be observed as they are being done and can be played back instantly and redone if desired.

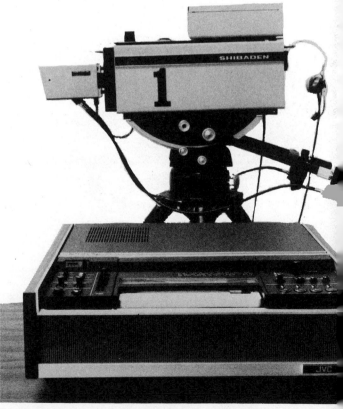

Medialab

1. Judging from the chart, what are the advantages of film over VT? What are the advantages of VT over film?

2. While watching commercial television, you should be able to tell the difference between material that is filmed and material that is on videotape. How would you describe that difference? However, you will not be able to tell VT from a "live" broadcast.

3. Are most commercials on VT or film? Most weekly programs? Do you have any idea why this is true?

4. Make an educated speculation on the future of film and VT. Will film become obsolete? Will film improve so it is superior to VT in some way? In what different areas will each method be used?

5. What impact on film will the lowering of prices of VT equipment have?

6. Try an experiment in class: film and tape the same scene or bit of action. Watch both the VT and film version together and discuss the differences.

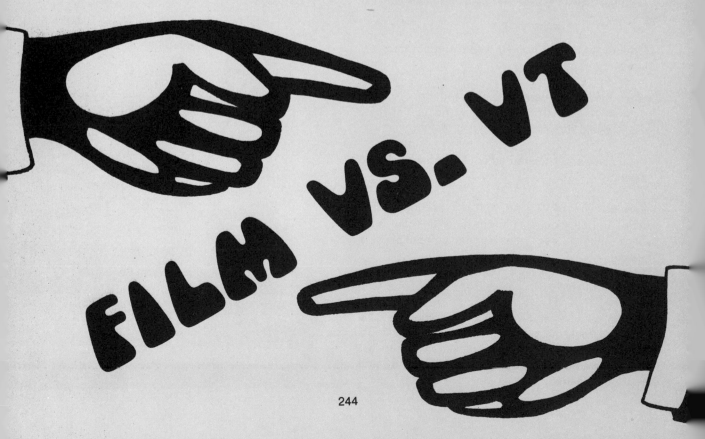

FILM VS. VT

Cable Television

Of all the communication devices studied in this book, cable television might turn out to be the most important and the one that most changes your life.

Cable TV began about 25 years ago as a simple solution to a problem in rural areas. In mountainous areas far from TV stations, an enterprising businessman would construct a huge master antenna on a mountaintop to capture TV signals from stations a hundred or more miles away. People in the area paid a fee to have their own set wired by a cable to the master antenna. People thus had good TV reception without the expense of an elaborate rooftop antenna. Any signal fed into the antenna could be relayed easily through the cables to the system's subscribers.

The next step in the development of cable TV was the realization that since everyone was hooked up by wire, it would be relatively easy and inexpensive to set up a small TV studio and feed original programs into the antenna. Some stations set up an automatic revolving camera that scanned a clock and a weather forecast and sent this service to subscribers on an otherwise unused channel.

245

From isolated rural areas, cable TV moved to the large cities. There, the problem of TV reception becomes difficult because signals ricochet off tall buildings and airplanes, causing "ghosts" on home TV receivers. With TV sets connected directly to a tall master antenna, such problems were eliminated; so cable TV moved to some cities. A few cable systems offered subscribers additional channels brought in from nearby cities as an added service.

The cables used to connect the TV antenna to the set can transmit hundreds, some say thousands, of channels of information. Cable TV opens up the possibility of more TV channels than are now possible with broadcast television. The combination of this multichannel potential, plus the perfect picture fed into every set could lead to cable television replacing broadcast television. If this does happen, cable TV, like the telephone and water lines, would become a service provided for a monthly fee.

The greatest potential of cable television is that it offers a great number of channels to everyone. With current television programming, millions of viewers are needed to make a program a lasting success. If "only" a few hundred thousand people are interested enough to watch, the program dies. This leaves many large minority interests unsatisfied. With cable TV, a local chess tournament that might attract only 2,000 viewers could easily be shown, as could the city council meeting, the stock market ticker, a wire service video teletype machine, and similar programs for other specific interest groups. In addition, the Federal Communications Commission has required each cable operator to provide a channel for ordinary citizens to express their viewpoints—a public access channel. The cable operator is also charged with providing assistance with VT equipment to interested parties who wish to make a tape to be used on the public access channel.

The most revolutionary aspect of cable television is that it can easily function as a two-way communication system. Since each house is connected by a cable, messages can be sent back to the central sending station. Just like telephone wires, the video cable can carry video or audio messages in both directions. Two-way cable TV is technically possible now; no new inventions need be perfected in order for the "wired city" to exist.

Robert Galvin, board chairman of Motorola, has claimed that the acceptance of two-way cable will do away with the need for standard broadcasting and that a date should be set for closing down all ordinary TV stations. Two-way cable TV could easily become as common and essential as a telephone in the not-too-distant future.

With two-way cable and the necessary coding and message-sending "boxes," subscribers could gain access to their savings and checking accounts to pay bills via TV; they could take part in school or special education classes from home; they could shop, vote, or express opinions on important public issues, or even call up research information from the local library computer.

Most of the 3,000 cable systems now in existence in the United States (with more than 15 million subscribers) are still one-way systems. But new FCC regulations require two-way capacity in all newly constructed systems.

Medialab

1. Find out what sort of cable systems exist in your area. If none exist currently, do some research to find out what applications for cable "franchises" exist. Who has made the applications and what have they promised?

2. If a cable TV system with 50 channels started operation tomorrow, what sort of programs would you like to see carried? Remember that the ideas would have to be inexpensive to produce (to put a camera in a city council room is easy, but to produce a weekly filmed TV show is much too expensive for such an operation.)

3. If cable TV were offered tomorrow, would you subscribe? If cable TV already does exist in your area, find out what factors influence people's decision about whether or not to subscribe.

4. Do you think first-run movies on TV would bring about the end of movie theaters? Would the public acceptance of cable TV change your opinion?

Comparison of Over-The-Air

Over-The-Air

Quality of signal varies with location of set and with weather.

Number of channels available is limited. Even a large city like Chicago has only eight channels.

Currently reaches 65 million households—about 95% of all families.

Requires a TV set and sometimes a rooftop antenna.

Free. No monthly bills.

One-way system.

Needs many viewers to interest advertisers.

Few individuals can obtain TV time to state their opinions.

Cable

Consistent high quality for everyone.

Up to 48 channels available including commercial networks.

Currently reaches about six million homes.

Requires that the house be wired to the cable operator. The hook-up charge ranges from nothing to $100.

Those wired to the system pay an average monthly fee of $6.

Has the potential of two-way communication.

Needs far fewer viewers to be economically workable.

Each cable franchise will be required to have at least one channel for citizen access.

248

Cable TV with Transmission

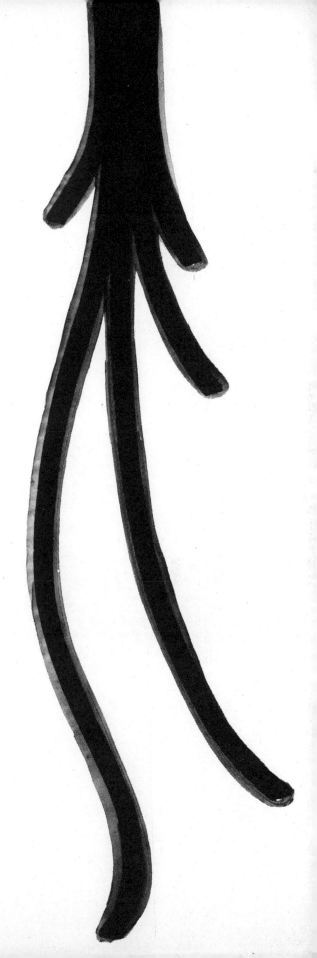

One possible far-reaching effect of cable television is to make movie theaters a thing of the past. Attendance at films declined enormously with the invention of television. More people went to films more often in 1940 than they do today. To attend a movie requires an auto or bus trip somewhere, a $2.00—$5.00 admission fee, maybe parking or baby-sitting costs, perhaps standing in line and putting up with a noisy crowd, and tolerating overcooled or overheated movie houses and overpriced popcorn and candy, not to mention finding a seat only to have a 6 foot 8 inch basketball player sit in the next row.

All these problems vanish when first-run feature films are offered through cable television systems. A few systems have already experimented with offering subscribers first-run films for an additional fee. In Sarasota, Florida, a cable company called Theater-Vision offered first-run films at $2 per movie. Three different films were shown on even days, three on odd days—each played several times during the day on one of the three channels. A subscriber paid only once for each movie by inserting a coded ticket in a box connected to the TV set.

OTHER NEW MEDIA INNOVATIONS

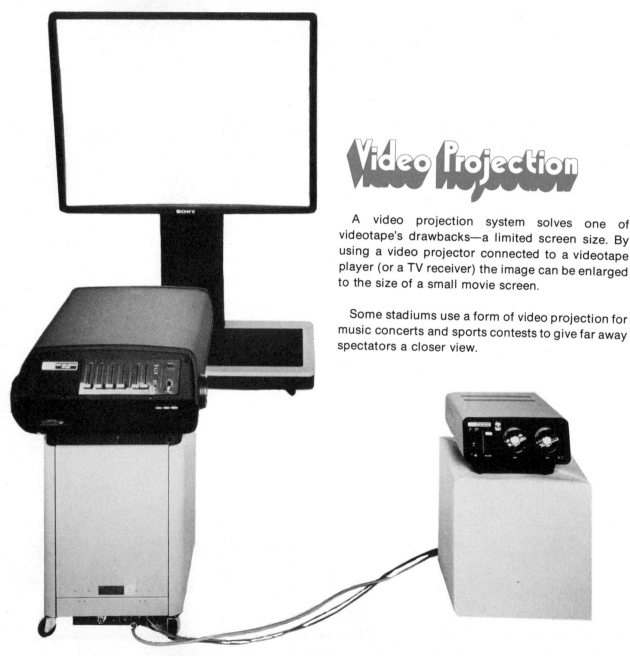

Video Projection

A video projection system solves one of videotape's drawbacks—a limited screen size. By using a video projector connected to a videotape player (or a TV receiver) the image can be enlarged to the size of a small movie screen.

Some stadiums use a form of video projection for music concerts and sports contests to give far away spectators a closer view.

Variable Speech Control

The human ear is a mechanism far superior to the rather clumsy tongue and mouth. If only people could talk as fast as others can listen. You can easily listen to speech at 500 words per minute, but no one can talk at that speed with the possible exception of a few talented auctioneers. If people could talk twice as fast then we could do our listening in half the time.

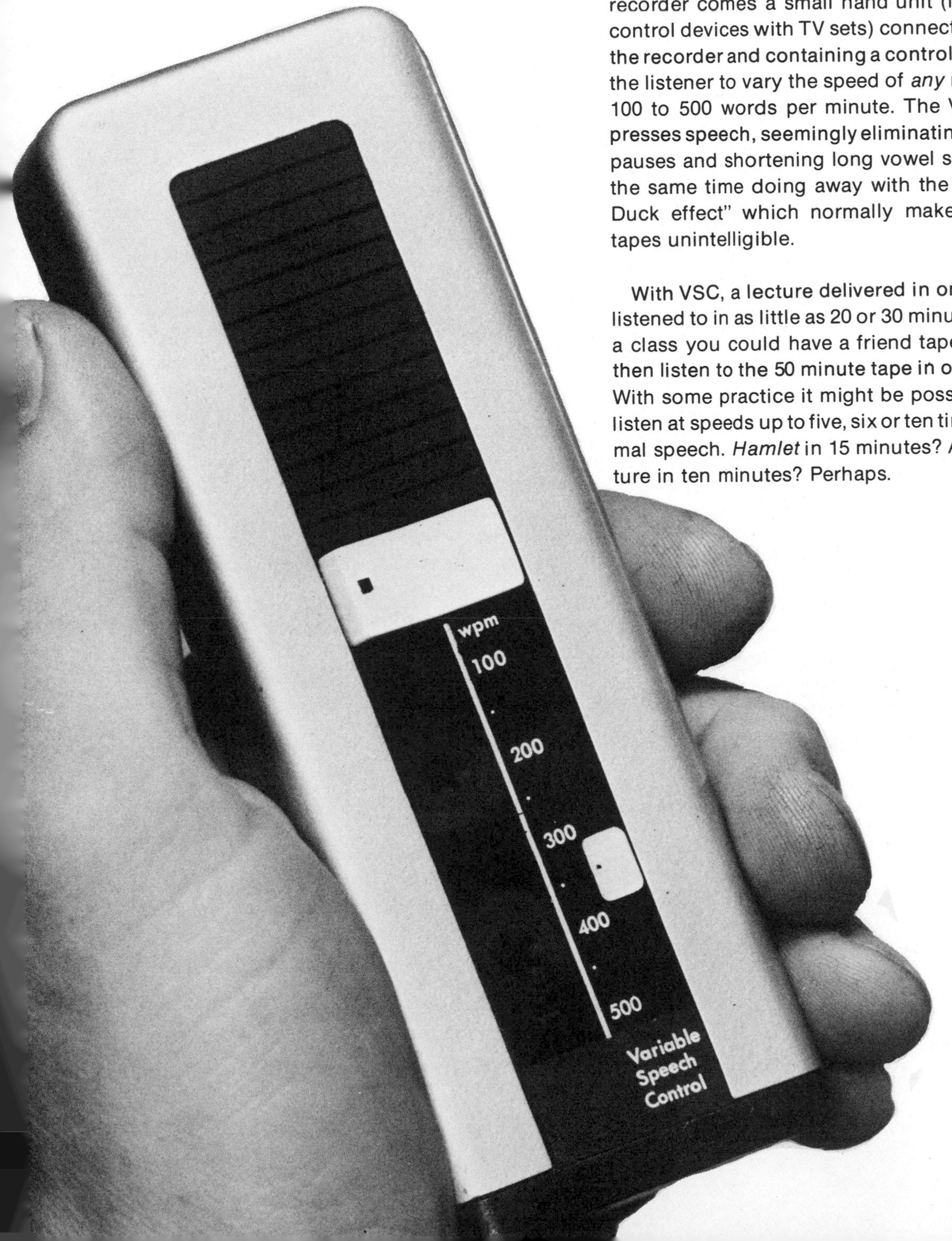

Variable Speech Control is an invention that will allow a tape recording to be played back two or three times faster and still be easily intelligible. VSC already exists and might even be on the market as part of some tape recorders by the time you read this. The VSC unit is smaller than a sugar cube and is wired into a tape recorder. With the VSC-equipped recorder comes a small hand unit (like the remote control devices with TV sets) connected by a wire to the recorder and containing a control which enables the listener to vary the speed of *any* recording from 100 to 500 words per minute. The VSC unit compresses speech, seemingly eliminating unnecessary pauses and shortening long vowel sounds while at the same time doing away with the usual "Donald Duck effect" which normally makes speeded up tapes unintelligible.

With VSC, a lecture delivered in one hour can be listened to in as little as 20 or 30 minutes. If you miss a class you could have a friend tape the class and then listen to the 50 minute tape in only 20 minutes. With some practice it might be possible to learn to listen at speeds up to five, six or ten times that of normal speech. *Hamlet* in 15 minutes? A one hour lecture in ten minutes? Perhaps.

wpm
100
200
300
400
500

Variable
Speech
Control

HOLOGRAPHY

Holographic film looks like a piece of clear plastic about the size of this page. But if that piece of plastic is held up so that a laser beam can pass through it after first going through a special lens, the plastic reveals an amazing sight.

Appearing on the plastic is an utterly realistic three-dimensional picture—say, for example, of a child's alphabet block. Looking down into the picture, you can see the top "A" of the block. As you move your head around you can see the other sides of the block, even the back and bottom. Holography may well be the most important addition to photography and film since color. Holography (the word translates roughly from the Greek meaning "the whole picture") is not a dream of the future; it exlsts now.

To add to the aura of magic, that piece of plastic could be removed from the ruby-red laser light and cut into one-inch squares. When each and every tiny square is put into the light, the entire picture remains intact.

Holographs can be made so real that a viewer can walk around an image and be convinced it is real. If a holograph is made of a scene that includes a magnifying glass, viewers will see a magnifying glass that actually works. As the viewer moves his head, whatever appears behind the magnifying glass will be enlarged.

Making holographs is still an expensive and highly specialized process. But if holography can be made practical for film and television, movies in the future might be projected all around the audience instead of on a two-dimensional screen.

PICTUREPHONE

A picturephone is a combination of two familiar communication devices—the telephone and television. When combined, the two make person-to-person communication possible visually as well as audially. The picturephone service already exists in some large cities but its cost currently limits its value to businesses.

253

VIDEO DISC PLAYBACK SYSTEMS

At least three companies are currently planning to market a device that is easily connected to any ordinary television set. The device (called Discovision or Mavicard) enables the user to play video records.

The Sony Mavica System pictured on this page allows both recording and playback on thin, plastic cards resembling audio recordings sometimes bound into magazines. Sony claims that the "mavicards" can be reproduced by a printing process at low cost. A six-by eight-inch card allows up to ten minutes of color recording and playback. Sony's system is not yet scheduled for production. But other disc-video systems that allow only playback (owners cannot make their own discs) should be available for the home very soon.

The problem with television is that the people must sit and keep their eyes glued on a screen; the average American family hasn't time for it. Therefore, the showmen are convinced that for this reason, if for no other, television will never be a serious competitor of broadcasting.

—New York Times
March 19, 1939

FUTURECASTING
FUTURECASTING
FUTURECASTING
FUTURECASTING
FUTURECASTING
FUTURECASTING
FUTURECASTING
FUTURECASTING
FUTURECASTING
FUTURECASTING

In attempting to predict what the communication media of the future will be like, there are few certainties. Perhaps the only sure thing is that tomorrow's media will be as different from today's as today's are from those of the nineteenth century. High school students who read this book will one day tell stories to their grandchildren of the old days of broadcast television, of the days when computers were giant machines costing at least tens of thousands of dollars, and of the time when pictures were projected in only two dimensions. The grandparent of the year 2020 might well recall the quaint custom of going to something called movie theaters, the old-time stereo FM radio, the plastic disk phonograph records, and the days when even large cities had no more than a half a dozen television channels.

Predicting or speculating about the future is more than a mere exercise of imagination. To the unprepared the future arrives as a shock; to the prepared the future arrives as a logical extension of the present. To speculate about how the communications media will develop, is to take some part in that development. To have considered what is desirable in human communication, is to be able to make a value judgment about what the future of media should be.

(AP)—New York. Speed Viewing, Inc., announced today that it is expanding its services to 50 major population areas. Speed Viewing claims that schools have not properly taught students how to watch cinema. Their course helps young and old alike to increase their viewing speed. Special projectors with adjustable speeds are used as practice aids. Some students, the institute claims, are able to view such classics as *War and Peace* and *Woodstock* in twelve minutes with full retention.

(AP)—Washington. The U.S. Office of Education announced today that 8% of the population is still unable to make films. In fact many of these ill-cinemates cannot distinguish between a zoom and a cut. It also announced that funds are being made available so that adults can take remedial filmmaking at night school. The office reminded Americans that such a basic skill as filmmaking is utterly essential for survival in contemporary society.

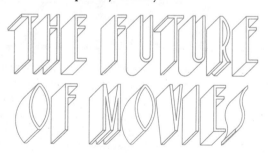

THE FUTURE OF MOVIES

An 1877 prediction of global radio was considerably easier to make than a 1924 prediction of what the young invention of film would be like in the year 2024. But in 1924 the man most qualified to make such a prediction was David Wark Griffith, an early American film director often considered the "father of American cinema." Back in 1924 D.W. Griffith looked into his educated crystal ball marked 2024 (100 years later), and this is what he saw.

David Wark Griffith

the movies 100 years from now

. . . In the year 2024 the most important single thing which the cinema will have helped in a large way to accomplish will be that of eliminating from the face of the civilized world all armed conflict. Pictures will be the most powerful factor in bringing about this condition. With the use of the universal language of moving pictures the true meaning of the brotherhood of man will have been established throughout the earth. For example, the Englishman will have learned that the soul of the Japanese is, essentially, the same as his own. The Frenchman will realize that the American's ideals are his ideals. All men are created equal.

. . . You will walk into your favorite film theatre and see your actors appearing in twice the size you see them now, because the screens will be twice as large, and the film itself twice as large also. With these enlargements, "close-ups" will be almost eliminated, since it will be relatively easy to picture facial expression along with the full figure of the performer. It will always be necessary to picture the face in pictures. It is the face which reflects the soul of a man.

Our "close-ups," or "inserts," as I call them, are sometimes cumbersome and disconcerting. I invented them, but I have tried not to overuse them, as many have done. It is a mechanical trick, and is of little credit to anyone.

We shall say there are now five elaborate first-run picture theatres on one New York street, Broadway. In 2024 there will be at least forty. Cities of 1,000 will average at least six. Cities of 20,000 and thereabout will have over a hundred. By virtue of its great advantage in scope, the motion picture will be fitted to tell certain stories as no other medium can. But I must add that the glory of the spoken or written word in the intimate and poetic drama can never be excelled by any form of expression.

In the year 2024 our directors of the better order will be men graduated from schools, academies, and colleges carrying in their curriculum courses in motion-picture direction. Our actors and actresses will be artists graduated from schools and colleges either devoted exclusively to the teaching and study of motion-picture acting or carrying highly specialized courses in acting before the camera. This is inevitable.

It really seems to me a little bit humorous now to realize how narrow a place in our everyday life the film is playing, despite the great rise in attendance in the last few years. One hundred years hence, I believe, the airplane passenger lines will operate motion-picture shows on regular schedule between New York and Chicago and between New York and London. Trains, which will be traveling twice or three times as fast as they do now, will have film theatres on board. Almost every home of good taste will have its private projection room where miniatures, perhaps, of the greater films will be shown to the family, and, of course, families will make their albums in motion pictures instead of in tintypes and "stills." Steamships will boast of first runs, which will be brought to them in mid-ocean by the airplanes, and I may add that almost all subjects in our schools will be taught largely with the use of picture play and the educational animated picture.

By the time these things come to pass, there will be no such thing as a flicker in your film. Your characters and objects in pictures will come upon the screen (which by then may not even be white, and certainly may not be square, or look anything like what it does now), and they will appear to the onlookers precisely as these persons and objects appear in real life. That much-discussed "depth" in pictures, which no one as yet has been able to employ successfully, will long since have been discovered and adopted. The moving canvas will not appear flat, but if a character moves before a fireplace you will recognize the distance as between the character and the fireplace. Likewise, in landscapes, you will feel the proper sense of distance. Your mountain peaks will not appear to rise one on top of the other, but will appear exactly as if you stood and looked at them. Of course these are merely details that will require long and intense study and experiment, but they will come. In other words, from the standpoint of naturalness, motion pictures one hundred years from now will be so nearly like the living person or the existing object pictured that you will be unable, sitting in your orchestra seat, to determine whether they are pictures of the real thing.

By a perfection of the studio lighting system, film will be smooth before the eye as if it were a stationary lighted picture. By that time the studios will have changed greatly, and instead of actors being forced to work before great blinding lights, which now at times register 117 degrees of heat, we shall have "cold" lights. We are experimenting in these already. Our studios will be great spreading institutions, as large as many of the cities surrounding New York. I think that one hundred years from now there will be no concentrated motion-picture production such as our Hollywood of today. Films will be made in various cities, most of which will be located near to New York.

Now let us prepare for a small-sized shock. One hundred years from today it will cost perhaps twice as much as it costs today to see the really first-class cinema. It is perfectly proper that it should. Time, effort, energy, and preparation put into pictures at that time will have advanced greatly. I am just honest enough to say that I do not at the moment understand how more time, effort, energy, and preparation could have been put into my own pictures; but, then, for the average large picture play this will hold true. The average supposedly high-class film play in 2024 will be on view at not less than $5 a seat.

In looking into the crystal I have seen many things which I have not touched upon here. Perhaps they would be too tedious to bring out and discuss. But of one thing I may place myself on record plainly and without qualification. The motion picture is a child that has been given life in our generation. As it grows older it will develop marvelously. We poor souls can scarcely visualize or dream of its possibilities. We ought to be kind with it in its youth, so that in its maturity it may look back upon its childhood without regrets.

Colliers May 3 1924

Medialab

Predicting the Future

1. Griffith predicted that film will contribute to international understanding. Has it done so, or has it increased misunderstanding between peoples?

2. What predictions did Griffith make that turned out correct? Which were incorrect?

3. Look into your own crystal ball and write a brief essay in which you predict any one of the following:

   "The Movies 100 Years From Now"
   "Television 100 Years From Now"
   "The Electronic Home of the Future"
   "Radio and Records in 100 Years"
   "The Newspaper in 100 Years"

4. Do you think either of the two fictional "news items of the future" might come true? Why or why not?

The Magnavox Reproducer and
the Magnavox Power Amplifier

"*These two devices have revolutionized Radio*"

MAGNAVOX Radio equipment takes the feeble sound vibrations produced by your receiving set and builds them up into full, round tones in exact accordance with the original broadcasted speech or music.

The development of the Magnavox is one of Radio's spectacular achievements.

Magnavox R3 Reproducer and 2 stage Power Amplifier, as illustrated . . . $90.00

R2 Magnavox Reproducer with 18-inch curved horn: the utmost in amplifying power; requires only .6 of an ampere for field . $60.00

R3 Magnavox Reproducer with 14-inch curved horn: ideal for homes, etc. $35.00

Model C Magnavox Power Amplifier insures getting the largest possible power input for your Magnavox Reproducer . . 2 stage $55.00 3 stage 75.00

Magnavox Products can be had from good dealers everywhere. Write for new booklet.

THE MAGNAVOX CO.
Oakland, Cal.
New York: 370 Seventh Ave.

MAGNAVOX
Radio
The Reproducer Supreme

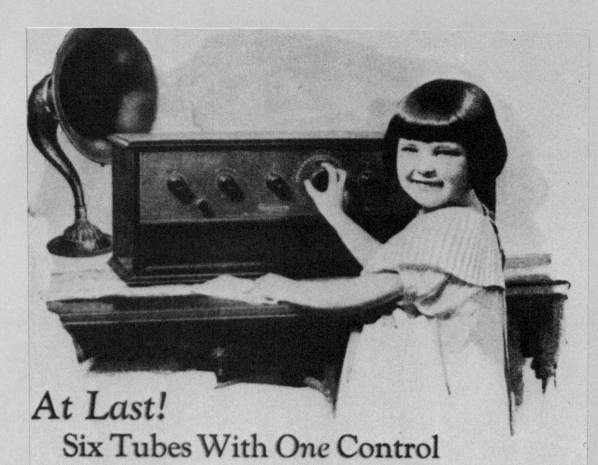

At Last!
Six Tubes With One Control

NOTHING like it has been seen or heard before. Thermiodyne embodies an entirely new principle of radio reception—so simplified and so certain that a child can tune in six to ten stations a minute. If it's in the air Thermiodyne will get it.

Calibrations are in wave lengths, just as listed in the daily press. There is nothing to remember, no figuring to do, no fuss or bother. Select the station wanted, turn arrow to position—the station clicks in at once.

It comes in at the same point *always*, no matter where the set may be—all

other stations are shut out completely —and each signal is loud, clear and wholly free from distortion. Local stations and distant stations cannot interfere.

Tubes, batteries or loud speaker of any kind may be used. Mounted on Bakelite panel and enclosed in handsome mahogany cabinet. Unconditionally guaranteed.

Write for descriptive folder containing the whole wonderful story of Thermiodyne. Ask your dealer to demonstrate Thermiodyne against any set he has, regardless of cost.

Price **$140**

Without Accessories

DEALERS and JOBBERS

Write for full particulars regarding franchise for selling the most remarkable receiving set on the market. A few territories are still available, but act quickly.

THERMIODYNE RADIO CORPORATION   PLATTSBURGH, N. Y.

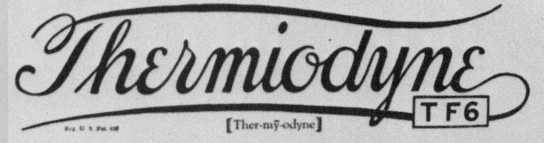

Reg. U.S. Pat. Off.   [Ther-mў-odyne]

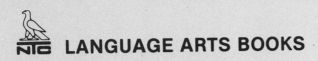

NTC LANGUAGE ARTS BOOKS

Speech

Person-to-Person, Galvin and Book	5202-8
Person-to-Person Workbook, Galvin and Book	5202-7
Speaking by Doing, Buys	5025-2
Adventures in the Looking-Glass, Ratliffe and Herman	5208-5
Oral Interpretation, Gamble and Gamble	5107-0
Contemporary Speech, HopKins and Whitaker	5204-2

Media

Understanding Mass Media, Schrank	5226-3
Understanding the Film, Johnson and Bone	5037-6
Photography in Focus, Jacobs and Kokrda	5414-2
Televising Your Message, Mitchell	5011-2

Theatre

Play Production in the High School, Beck et al.	5101-1
The Dynamics of Acting, Snyder	5106-2
Acting and Directing, Grandstaff	5115-1
Stagecraft, Beck	5104-6
An Introduction to Theatre and Drama, Cassady and Cassady	5102-8

Mystery and Science Fiction Literature

The Detective Story, Schwartz	5608-0
You and Science Fiction, Hollister	5555-6

Business Communication

Successful Business Writing, Sitzmann	5230-8
Successful Interviewing, Sitzmann and Garcia	5229-8
Working in Groups, Stech and Ratliffe	5145-3

Grammar

The Great American Grammar Machine Vol. 1, Pratt	5500-2
The Great American Grammar Machine Vol. 2, Pratt	5500-4

Writing and Composition

Snap, Crackle & Write, Schrank	5235-2
Journalism Today!, Ferguson and Patten	5208-4
An Anthology for Young Writers, Meredith	5604-8
Writing in Action, Meredith	5605-6

Tandem: Language in Action Series

Point/Counterpoint, Dufour and Strauss	5248-4
Action/Interaction, Dufour and Strauss	5249-2

Teacher's Editions, Workbooks, Testing and Evaluation Spirit Masters, and Student Record Profiles available.

NTC *NATIONAL TEXTBOOK COMPANY* • *Skokie, Illinois 60077*